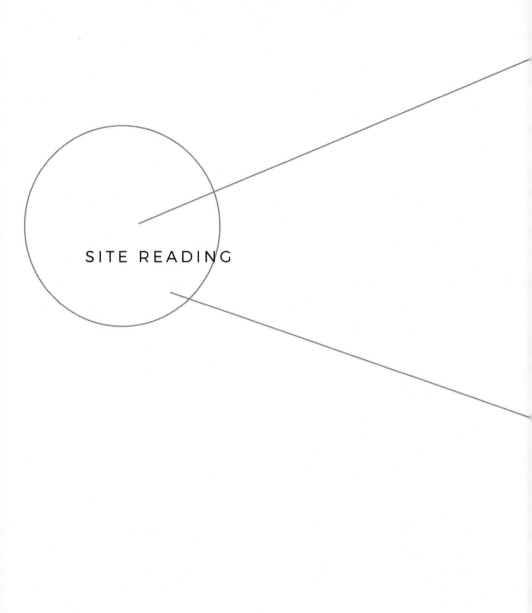

SITE READING

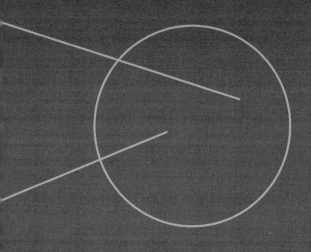

Site Reading

FICTION, ART, SOCIAL FORM

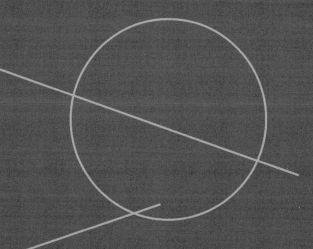

DAVID J. ALWORTH

PRINCETON UNIVERSITY PRESS
PRINCETON AND OXFORD

Published by Princeton University Press,
41 William Street, Princeton, New Jersey 08540

In the United Kingdom: Princeton University Press,
6 Oxford Street, Woodstock, Oxfordshire OX20 1TW

press.princeton.edu

Jacket Art or Photograph: (1) In the grocery with our little helpers © Jaro Larnos / Flickr;
(2) Scrapyard / © CG Textures; (3) Roads, © Jacobo Cortés Ferreira / CG Textures;
(4) DebrisStone, © Jonas De Ro / CG Textures; (5) Restrain, © Rikke68 / Thinkstock

ISBN 978-0-691-16449-6

Library of Congress Control Number: 2014959229

British Library Cataloging-in-Publication Data is available

This book has been composed in Montserrat, Bulmer MT Std
and Sabon Next LT Pro

Printed on acid-free paper. ∞

Printed in the United States of America

10 9 8 7 6 5 4 3 2 1

For the little collective

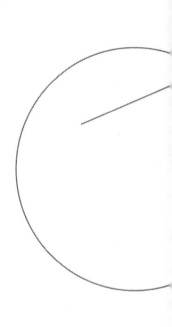

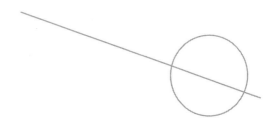

There is a question implicit in the foregoing analyses and interpretations. It is this: what is the mode of existence of social relations? No sooner had the social sciences established themselves than they gave up any interest in the description of "substances" inherited from philosophy: "subject" and "object," society "in itself," or the individual or group considered in isolation. Instead, like the other sciences, they took *relationships* as their object of study. The question is, though, where does a relationship reside when it is not being actualized in a highly determined situation?

—HENRI LEFEBVRE, *The Production of Space*

CONTENTS

ILLUSTRATIONS

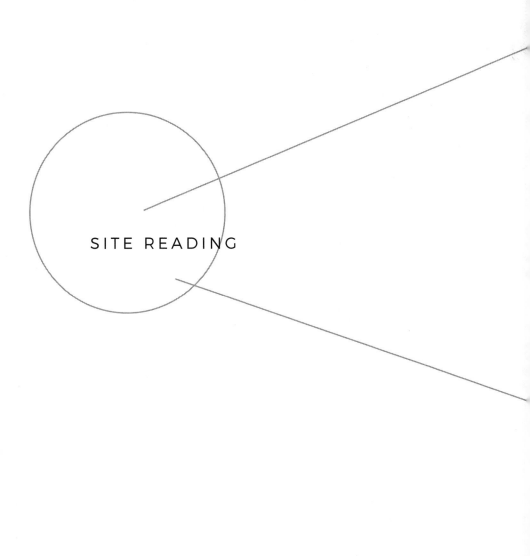

SITE READING

INTRODUCTION

The Site of the Social

With the close of the door, the room gets quiet. The scene is familiar enough: a college English class, where the topic of the hour is narrative setting. The assigned reading might be Wendell Berry or William Faulkner, but it also could be Jane Austen or James Joyce, Geoffrey Chaucer or Cormac McCarthy. After all, what literary narrative (aside from the most experimental) omits setting? When the instructor starts to speak, the mode of sociality here, what Erving Goffman would call the "interaction order" at this site, begins to shift: the students peer up from their iPhones, turning away (hopefully for the hour) from Twitter, Facebook, and Instagram, to begin addressing the complex questions raised by literary form.[1] What are these questions? The answer itself is site specific, or at least context dependent. If, for instance, this course resides in the environmental humanities, then the conversation might analyze setting in order to confront the many urgent concerns of the climate crisis, from the calamity of "slow violence" in the Global South to "[t]he challenge that deterritorialization poses for the environmental imagination."[2] If, alternatively, this course has taken its cues from the recent material turn in literary criticism, from the new scholarship associated with "thing theory" and "object-oriented philosophy," then the discussion might be, as Walter Benjamin said of the surrealists, "on the track of things," pursuing the way that literature resists the commodifying force of capitalist modernity to disclose what Martin Heidegger called "the thingness of things" or what Georg Lukács termed "the immediate—qualitative and material—character of things as things."[3]

And yet, however influential these modes of inquiry have become, however rigorously they have examined the link between literature and what Lawrence Buell calls "the palpable world," a traditional understanding of setting still predominates within literary studies.[4] "Setting is practically terra incognita," lamented Seymour Chatman in 1978, a lament that continues to resonate these days, not only because our interpretive procedures tend to privilege other aspects of narrative prose fiction (plot, character, theme) but also because setting is generally regarded as a static background for narrative action, a "framework," as the *Oxford English Dictionary* explains, for the unfolding of plot, the development of character, and the situating of theme.[5] *Site Reading* aims to challenge this view. Against the notion that setting is a fixed container for the characters that are presumed to define the social world of a given novel, I argue that sites figure in novels as determinants of sociality—as dynamic networks of *actants* in Bruno Latour's sense, exercising a kind of agency with and through their human and nonhuman constituents.[6] To elaborate this argument, I employ an interpretive method—site reading—that lies at the intersection of environmental criticism and textual materialism. If environmental criticism has taught us that setting is so much more than the "mere backdrop for the human drama that really count[s] in a literary text," and if textual-materialist approaches have revealed literary things (a golden bowl, mahogany furniture, a kaleidoscope) to be lively and dense with "fugitive meanings," then site reading takes lessons from both discourses, yet seeks to explore a question that neither has formulated in quite the same way.[7] How does literary fiction theorize social experience? One answer, the answer that I want to propose, is by transposing real sites into narrative settings and thereby rendering them operative, as figures in and of collective life.

To ask how literature theorizes sociality would seem to be a rather familiar way of doing business. Even Franco Moretti, surely among our most forward-thinking critics, has argued that "society, rhetoric, and their interaction" is, finally, "the only real issue of literary history."[8] Still, to perform a site reading is not to undertake a conventional "sociology of literature," insofar as the latter designates the project of locating the deep roots and meanings of literary form in the social forces that underlie it. Such a project, as James F. English has observed, relies on the "long-dominant paradigm of critique" that has come to seem less dominant in recent years, with critics such as Moretti, Rita Felski, Heather Love, Ross Posnock, Leah Price, Stephen Best, and Sharon Marcus pioneering various alternatives to "symptomatic reading" and "the hermeneutics of suspicion."[9] One happy consequence of this methodological flux is that, as English speculates, we seem "to be arriving at a point of especially rich potential" for a newly productive encounter between sociology and literary studies, two disciplines that are acknowledging the limits of critique while developing "more rigorously 'descriptive' or 'pragmatic' approaches" to their objects of study.[10] *Site Reading* strives to enact such an encounter primarily but not exclusively through an engagement with Latour's recent work, his sociology in particular. Latour is a rather peculiar sociologist—one might even call him an antisociologist—because he contends that there is no such thing as society or the social, traditionally understood: no such thing as a special domain of reality (distinct from, say, the material or the natural) governed by abstract laws, structures, and functions.[11] Rather, for him, and for the other thinkers associated with Actor-Network-Theory (ANT), the social "just is the act and the fact of association," as Felski puts it, "the coming together of phenomena to create multiple assemblages, affinities, and networks."[12] In this analytical model, in other words, the social is not a preconstituted setting or container where anything can be situated, but "a process of assembling" whereby persons, things, texts, ideas, images, and other entities (all of which are considered actors or actants) form contingent and volatile networks of association.[13]

This conception of the social prompts a new mode of literary interpretation. One of Latour's main intellectual adversaries is Émile Durkheim, the foundational sociologist whose understanding of society has been widely (if often implicitly) accepted within literary studies. In *The Elementary Forms of Religious Life*, for example, Durkheim writes:

> Since the universe exists only insofar as it is thought, and since it can be thought totally only by society itself, it takes its place within society, becomes an element of its inner life, and society may thus be seen as that total genus beyond which nothing else exists. The very concept of totality is but the abstract form of the concept of society: that whole which includes all things, that supreme class under which all other classes must be subsumed.[14]

While this passage encapsulates precisely what Latour rejects, the notion of society as a sui generis totality that "includes all things," it also forms part of the second epigraph to one of the most influential works of literary criticism, Fredric Jameson's *The Political Unconscious: Narrative as a Socially Symbolic Act* (1981). The latter, as Best and Marcus explain, "popularized symptomatic reading among U.S. literary critics," establishing the protocols for a certain method of historicism that remains important to this day.[15] While the critical value of this method has been hotly debated in recent years, I want simply to recall how it conceptualizes the link between literature and society. For Jameson, the literary text expresses—often through gaps, elisions, repressions, all that "remain[s] unrealized in the surface of the text"—the history, politics, and ideology of the society from which it has emerged: this is finally what it means to think of narrative as a "socially symbolic act."[16] But what if there is no such thing as society? What if, in other words, the very definition of society that Jameson imports from Durkheim, and that we all invoke spontaneously whenever we speak of "placing a text in social context," must be modified because it has come to seem unconvincing? Surely such modification would precipitate a somewhat different practice of literary criticism, not merely an attempt to move beyond the paradigm of critique, an attempt that has already taken Latour as a kind of patron saint, but a new sociology of literature that would seek to apprehend the sociology *in* literature: the way that literary texts assemble an impression of social form.[17]

Pursuing this project in the following pages, I strive to demonstrate that the novel is an acute instrument of sociological thought, or, more specifically, that the "terra incognita" of setting contains vivid and valuable insights about the experience of collectivity. This does not mean overlooking the formal qualities of narrative prose fiction but looking at them in a certain way: with an eye toward how they effect something like a radically literary sociology. If the novel's delineation of consciousness has long instructed us (however unevenly and unsystematically) about both individual personhood and the human mind, and if its treatment of physical things has prompted us more recently to pose fresh questions about matter and materiality, then perhaps its figuration of sites, vibrant assemblages of persons and things, might occasion a new inquiry into the nature of sociality. This is the premise of *Site Reading* as well as the hope.

*

Back in the classroom, the discussion proceeds apace. The students are raising their hands and taking notes, underlining the text and responding to questions, occasionally even engaging one another. The assigned reading for the hour turns out to be Emma Donoghue's 2010 novel *Room*, which includes one of the more intriguing experiments with narrative setting in recent literary history. This class appears to be an ordinary social unit, composed of people and their internalized protocols of behavior, and this unit appears to be acting out *its own* protocols in this setting (the setting of the classroom) through a discussion of narrative setting. But then, much to the chagrin of a certain student, something happens. As the instructor is introducing the novel, a loud ringtone interrupts her remarks, and suddenly everybody looks away from the PowerPoint. The familiar rustling and fumbling ensues, but after a few exasperated grunts, class is back on track. This moment is not merely a reminder that the classroom constitutes an assemblage of humans and nonhumans—a social site where a whole range of nonhuman entities (books and other cultural artifacts, laptops and tablets and projection equipment, a fully operational heating and cooling unit) are central to the pedagogical enterprise—but also a rift in the interaction order that discloses the people and things at this seminar table as actants in vast social, material, and informational networks. Now it makes no sense to distinguish the class (as a social unit) from the material environment. Now sociality seems so much more promiscuous. When class is going well, though, this promiscuity, this sharing of sociality among humans and non-humans, does not register as a distraction. On those serendipitous afternoons, when the discussion of literary art assumes a kind of urgency and tacks in a surprising and challenging direction, the social network can feel quite immediate and intimate: just the teacher and the students thinking together with the text.

These are the days when the text itself attains full potency as a nonhuman actant or as what Latour would call a "matter of concern," something that solicits attention, care, interest, and desire from human agents and that, consequently, forms the center of a collective project, however ephemeral.[18] The dice are loaded in the case of novels, of course, for novels have that incredibly powerful means of solicitation that we call the narrator. "Today I'm five," begins Donoghue's *Room*, her young narrator addressing us directly.[19] Up to this point, Jack has spent his entire life in a cramped room, a site that is only eleven feet long by eleven feet wide, yet nevertheless constitutes his entire world. Donoghue's novel, for this reason, compels us to study its setting in a sustained way; as a matter of concern, it solicits the kind of critical attention that I call site reading. "We have thousands of things to do every morning," Jack tells us early on, "like give Plant a cup of water in Sink for no spilling, then put her back on her saucer on Dresser." The gendered pronoun ("her") and capitalized nouns ("Plant," "Sink") signify the status that Jack accords to the nonhuman environment, whose particular constituents—Wardrobe, Stove, Bed, Lamp, Desk, TV, Blanket—are his only companions, aside from his mother. She gave birth to him five years before the start of the narrative, after being raped by Old Nick, the villain in the novel, who holds her and Jack in captivity. Despite this appalling scenario, however, *Room* is not a horror story but a compressed and spatialized bildungsroman. The climax of the plot is a nail-biting escape scene where Jack first encounters the realm that he calls Outside Space. "Looks like a TV person," he thinks when he sees a human being who is neither Ma nor Old Nick, "but nearer and wider and with smells, a bit like Dish Soap and mint and curry all together" (*R*, 143).

Evident here and throughout the novel, Jack's ebullient, searching intelligence is especially striking as he starts to fathom a world beyond his site of internment. "How can TV be pictures of real things?" he wonders (*R*, 62). This question sends him into a frenzy:

> I think about them all floating around in Outside Space outside the walls, the couch and the necklaces and the bread and the killers and

the airplanes and all the shes and hes, the boxers and the man with one leg and the puffy-hair woman, they're floating past Skylight. I wave to them, but there's skyscrapers as well as cows and ships and trucks, it's crammed out there, I count all the stuff that might crash into Room. I can't breathe right. I have to count my teeth instead, left to right on the top then left to right on the bottom, then backwards, twenty every time but I still think maybe I'm counting wrong. (*R*, 62)

Feeling suddenly overwhelmed—"I can't breathe right"—as he wrestles for the first time with the difference between reality and representation, Jack displays his desire for assemblage, his longing to gather "all the stuff" of reality into a mental economy that might impose some order on his tumultuous experience of coming to grips with the mystery of existence. Donoghue combines the trope of confinement with a strong narrative constraint, telling the entire story from Jack's perspective and through his distinctive voice, in order to explore the nonhuman world from a unique vantage point. To see Room through his eyes is not only to glimpse a tiny yet vibrant environment—"We have a pretty busy morning. First we undo Pirate Ship that we made last week and turn it into Tank. Balloon is the driver, she used to be as big as Ma's head and pink and fat, now she's small like my fist only red and wrinkly" (*R*, 39)—but also to register nonhuman entities, both physical things and televisual images, as *friends*: intimate others who constitute a social network.

Indeed, as Jack tries to grasp the nature of TV, his sense of sociality is thrown into crisis: "Dora is a drawing in TV but she's my real friend, that's confusing. Jeep is actually real, I can feel him with my fingers. Superman is just TV. Trees are TV but Plant is real, oh, I forgot to water her. I carry her from Dresser to Sink and do that right away" (*R*, 63). Jack has to water Plant himself on this day because "Ma is Gone," so depressed that she fails to emerge from a catatonic stupor (*R*, 60). At these times and others, he relies heavily on his nonhuman companions for succor and support, partly by interacting with them as Ma interacts with him. "When I'm having some," he says, referring to the breast milk that he still drinks, "Ma won't let me bring Jeep and Remote into Bed even though they're my friends" (*R*, 46). Moments later, just before Nick arrives, as he does most nights, Jack curls up with his buddies in Bed: "Can't you sleep, little switches?" he whispers; "'It's OK, have some? I put them at my nipples, they take turns. I'm sort of asleep but only nearly" (*R*, 47). In addition to "animat[ing]" the novel's physical space," as Aimee Bender suggests, such rituals help Donoghue's narrator stay sane.[20] If, despite the circumstances, Jack's jovial narration suggests something like a healthy mental state, then this state depends on both his doting attention from Ma and his experience of nonhuman entities as *actual* friends: social beings who solicit his care and motivate his action, rather than compensatory trinkets meant to distract him from the trauma of isolation. Donoghue amplifies this suggestion in the second half of the novel as Jack acclimates to Outside Space. Stressed by the pressures of a foreign lifeworld—"I try to rock," he rues, "but it's not Rocker. Everything's wrong" (R, 160)—Jack longs to be comforted by his old buddies: "Ma and me keep knocking into each other in the night. The third time I wake up I'm wanting Jeep and Remote but they're not here" (R, 190).

How to make sense of Jack's mode of sociality? It is easy enough to say that this utterly traumatized subject looks to objects, the only objects he has ever known, for stability amid stress and chaos, but there is more to Donoghue's project. While the imperatives of psychological realism—representing the consciousness of a child narrator, this *particular* child narrator, in a manner that simultaneously recalls and revamps key precedents set by Mark Twain, Henry James, and William Faulkner—have Donoghue depicting playthings as pals, *Room* is also an exercise in defamiliarizing the palpable world: "Houses are like lots of Rooms stuck together, TV persons stay in them mostly but sometimes they go in their outsides and weather happens to them" (R, 41). This exercise works by exploiting the complex relation between character and setting. "I'm not in Room," Jack speculates during his frenzied escape, "Am I still me?" (R, 138). Yes and no. Jack's first five years have been marked by an extreme form of environmental determinism, so extreme that his conscious self is all but entirely shaped by the small architectural enclosure that constitutes his phenomenal and social realm. With the massive expansion of that realm, a kind of Big Bang at the climax of the plot, Jack begins a difficult journey through contemporary America—through the institutions of mass media, the health care system, his own suburban family—yet the site of his birth nonetheless retains a certain power over him. Moments after his escape, snuggling with Ma in a police cruiser, he longs to return to Room: "I've seen the world and I'm tired now," he says, and upon being rebuffed, begins "crying so much [he] can't stop" (R, 155).

Jack's tears register his sensory overload as he tries to process the deluge of new perceptual data. Yet it is not simply that his point of view (the point of view through which the entire narration is focalized) has been formed by the severely confined setting of his birth and early childhood, but that his mind becomes a zone of conflict between two social sites, Room and Outside Space, as he struggles to acclimate to a world like ours. Indeed, the degree to which he is successful in that struggle, the degree to which he becomes a well-adjusted social actor, can be measured precisely by the degree to which the novel achieves the *effect* of what Gérard Genette calls "variable focalization" without ever varying the focal character.[21] By the end of the novel, it is clear that Jack sees the world differently than he did when he first emerged, that nothing less than an encounter with the world itself has changed his point of view. "I look back one more time," he says in the final scene that brings him and Ma back to Room. "It's like a crater, a hole where something happened" (R, 321). The trajectory of this bildungsroman is anything but smooth, however, and the turbulence of Jack's journey results from the profound mismatch between him and his new lifeworld. Through this mismatch, Jack's alterity in Outside Space, Donoghue generates much of the novel's humor and satirical bite. "I'm learning lots more manners," he tells us after some time in an inpatient ward. "When something tastes yucky we say it's interesting, like wild rice that bites like it hasn't been cooked" (R, 204). He has to acquire manners and other social graces, to be sure, including the habits through which people inhabit social space: "We have our breakfast in the dining room that's for eating just, persons in the world like to go in different rooms for each thing" (R, 192). As Jack familiarizes himself with Outside Space, then, he defamiliarizes our world for us, spotlighting its conventionality and artificiality through participant observation and wide-eyed social commentary. "The woman with the puffy hair puts on a special voice"—he says of the crass talk-show host who interviews Ma a mere six days after their escape—"she has her hands together for praying" (R, 231).

If Jack transforms from a strange social being (a kid with no friends other than nonhumans) to a keen social analyst (a student of contemporary America) over the course of the novel, then this transformation depends on a friction at what Chatman calls the "critical boundary" between character and setting.[22] Jack's relative happiness in Room is no less startling than his alienation in Outside Space, because Room is a site of massive trauma, and "we expect," as Goffman asserts with a nod to Kenneth Burke, "some coherence among setting, appearance, and manner."[23] Yet Donoghue consistently violates this expectation in order to run a two-part sociological experiment: first, to imagine a site where it would be scandalous *not* to extend sociality to nonhumans; and second, to satirize the social conventions of contemporary America by viewing them through the eyes of a brilliant young misfit. The eponymous site, Room, facilitates this experiment in a novel that finally registers less as a true-crime story and less as a revision of a classic child-narrator tale (*What Maisie Knew* or *Huckleberry Finn*) than as a reworking of *Robinson Crusoe*. "They're a lost tribe of two," Donoghue said of Jack and Ma soon after the novel had been published. "They've got things in their heads like Kylie Minogue songs, which Ma has brought from the old civilization, but what they've come up with is a strange kind of island culture, island religion, and a pidgin form of English."[24] In fact, Donoghue's "main concern," as she explained to the *Economist*, "was to avoid the True Crime genre," partly by modeling *Room* on Defoe's canonical story and other "wonderful 18th-century novels with wide-eyed traveller narrators."[25] Her allusion to *Crusoe* is obviously imperfect—a room is not an island; our narrator is never alone; our narrator is five—but the intertextual affiliation nonetheless underscores how the novel, as both a form and a genre, so often imbricates the figuration of sites with an exploration of sociality.

Recall the moment when Crusoe lands on the shore of his island, the key site in the novel. Soon after "making a thousand gestures and motions" to celebrate his survival, he realizes that all his shipmates have perished in the wreck, leaving him "entirely destitute of all comfort and company."[26] His solitary condition—what he deems, at his lowest moments, a "dreadful deliverance" into "a scene of silent life" (*RC*, 39, 52)—precipitates what will become a familiar lament: "Why were not they sav'd and you lost? Why were you singled out?" (*RC*, 51). These questions, which he poses both to himself and to God, preoccupy him as he undertakes the day-to-day labor of trying to survive on the island—salvaging tools and materials from the ship; fabricating shelters and fortifications; learning to hunt and gather, bake bread, make pots, baskets, furniture, and clothes; to plant crops; to domesticate animals—all told, to master his new habitation and finally to become "like a King" (*RC*, 118). By the end of the novel, long after he has discovered the cannibals and enslaved Friday, Crusoe certainly envisions himself as an emperor surrounded by subjects and treasures, a fantasy that Susan Stewart calls "the most inimically social of all illusions," yet his arduous journey to that point occasions one of literary history's most searching meditations on social ontology.[27] Defoe uses Crusoe's site-specific predicament—his being "banish'd from human society" on a remote island (*RC*, 124)—to ask the question of who or what society includes, to wonder whether a talking parrot, for instance, counts as a "sociable creature" or whether the beings that Crusoe finds most abhorrent, the "savage wretches" who enjoy "inhuman feastings upon the bodies of their fellow-creatures," might form a legitimate society that he has no right to decimate (*RC*, 114, 131). This is really just to recall a key claim of Ian Watt's, from *The Rise of the Novel*, that Defoe "annihilated the relationships of the traditional social order" in his ambitious effort to construct "a network of personal relationships on a new and conscious pattern," casting his protagonist in a setting where interactions with human others, nonhuman animals, and even material things would stretch the definition of society.[28]

Donoghue alludes most forcefully to Defoe, then, when she imagines a protagonist that copes with being "banish'd from human society" by turning to the nonhuman, for just as Crusoe mitigates the misery of his solitude by fabricating "things" (tools, weapons, the famous earthenware pot) that will "supply [his] wants" (*RC*, 54), so too Jack inhabits a society of nonhuman "friends" (Bed, Desk, Meltedy Spoon) that provide for his developmental needs, however inadequately. Regardless of the way he experiences it, though, Jack's Room constitutes a social dystopia that nonetheless registers as a structuralist utopia—a narrative setting that includes none of the "superfluous" details or notations that Roland Barthes, in his well-known essay on the reality effect, considers "scandalous (from the point of view of structure)."[29] For Barthes, of course, many details of setting in realist narrative, such as the barometer in Gustave Flaubert's "A Simple Heart," are included only to signify the "category of 'the real'" and not "its contingent contents," or as Elaine Freedgood puts it, "to signify a generic real rather than to suggest something particular about it."[30] But there is nothing superfluous in Jack's Room, nothing that could be understood as a mere device to produce the reality effect, for everything in that site plays a particular (and particularly meaningful) role in his social milieu: "I jump on Bed and teach Jeep and Remote to shake their booties. It's Rihanna and T.I. and Lady Gaga and Kanye West" (R, 45). The really difficult ethical question that Donoghue raises—the question that preoccupies the mass public of Outside Space, as well as many in the novel's actual reading public—of whether Jack would be better off banished from human society in Room, arises only because Jack has such rich and nuanced relationships with the things that make up his material setting there, things that, as Lukács said of "the tools rescued from the shipwreck in *Robinson Crusoe*," produce a "profound poetic effect" as our protagonist interacts with them.[31]

To draw the line from Defoe to Donoghue in this way is to see a literary tradition that extends from the emergence of novelistic realism in the eighteenth century to the vicissitudes of the contemporary period as a tradition in which the question of setting (how to represent the palpable world) is imbricated with the question of social form (how to represent society and its constituents). And it is, more specifically, to apprehend Defoe's effort to ask what counts as a social being (a parrot, a cannibal, a slave, a material thing) and his effort to portray what Watt calls the "solidity of setting" as two parts of a single project, a project that Donoghue inherits and cleverly reorients.[32] There may be a good historical explanation for this unity, at least in Defoe's case, since he was imagining a setting populated by animals and cannibals at the exact moment when the term "social" was undergoing a major etymological shift, coming to designate a key attribute of "human nature," but it also could be that the novel form is especially suited to rendering sociality in situ.[33] Lukács makes this point, a point echoed by Allen Tate, in his influential reading of Flaubert: "the minute description of setting"—the agricultural fair where Rodolphe woos Emma in *Madame Bovary*—"is absolutely essential to Flaubert's purpose, that is, to the comprehensive exposition of the social milieu."[34] Indeed, what Lukács considers Flaubert's sociological objective, to convey "the public and private banality of the petty bourgeoisie," relies on both ironic juxtaposition (Rodolphe confesses his desire for Emma at the precise instant when the prize is awarded "For manures!") and what I think of as *site specification*, the process whereby imaginative literature defines and delimits a locale, which in this case means rendering a "display of pomp" at a public venue that ironically expresses what Rodolphe calls the "provincial mediocrity" of Yonville.[35] If, in other words, Flaubert can be read as a quasi-sociologist, which is how Pierre Bourdieu tended to read him, or as a novelist who "undoubtedly regarded his work as a finer kind of social science," which is how Wolf Lepenies defines him, then some of his best insights about society and social relations are, as Lukács suggests, built into his specification of sites.[36]

Can we generalize Lukács's suggestion? Might the ground for a new sociology of literature, one that would seek to discover the sociology in literature, be found in the way that literature itself grounds social experience, the way that it imagines sociality in situ? One method of answering these questions, the method that I adopt here, begins by revisiting the tradition of the novel in English and selecting a cluster of case studies from the American canon—test sites—with the topic of social form in mind.[37] My framing of this topic, as I discuss in detail below, is animated by Latour's broad provocations, yet narrative theory (Barthes, Burke, Lukács, Genette, Chatman) also provides inspiration, not least because Latour's sociology employs narratology and semiotics. If I do end up providing an account of narrative setting that manages to unlock its sociological force, then this account should be understood partly as an elaboration of something we already know—a certain sense of how setting works that is both intuitive and implicit in many of our reigning theories. What is a "chronotope," after all, if not a spatiotemporal figure in novelistic discourse that mediates the "multiplicity of social voices," which Mikhail Bakhtin called "heteroglossia"?[38] And what do we recall whenever we encounter, say, Dickens's London or Faulkner's Mississippi if not how imaginatively novelists have worked to disclose Henri Lefebvre's basic lesson that "[s]ocial relations, which are concrete abstractions, have no real existence save in and through space"?[39] If Bakhtin and Lefebvre have taught us, in different ways, that sites mediate sociality, then Latour helps us to recognize such mediation as *active participation*. "Mediators," Latour writes, "transform, translate, distort, and modify the meaning or the elements they are supposed to carry."[40]

*

Now suppose, returning to the classroom, that this is not a course on contemporary fiction but a standard introduction to theories and practices of literary interpretation, for which *Room* provides a case study. The instructor has led the students through various formalisms and historicisms, introduced them to major works in French, Russian, German, English, and American intellectual history, and helped them navigate the trade winds of the current critical climate. What happened during the week devoted to the sociology of literature? Does the syllabus even include such a week? In previous years, at the height of what Tony Bennett calls "the sociology of literature 'moment',"[41] the readings likely would have come from Raymond Williams, Lucien Goldmann, and Bourdieu, among others, but these days, as English has argued, there is less need to flag the "sociology of literature" as a specific critical subfield "because so many literary scholars [are] now, in this very basic sense of the term, sociologists of literature," which is to say, variously committed to "the shared disciplinary mission of coordinat[ing] the literary with the social." By covering queer theory or new historicism or postcolonial studies, for instance, it is possible to indicate "just how wide a swath of the discipline has undergone some form of sociological reorientation" since the 1980s.[42]

So where does Latour fit into this swath? He has already spurred some literary critics to rethink critique while inducing others to address the paradox of nonhuman agency in newly productive ways. Two other aspects of Latour's thought, however, are more directly related to the emergence of a new sociology of literature. The first is his claim, evident in his rejection of Durkheim in favor of Gabriel Tarde as his sociological forefather, that society cannot be presupposed.[43] "It is no longer clear," he writes at the outset of *Reassembling the Social: An Introduction to Actor-Network-Theory*, "whether there exists [*sic*] relations that are specific enough to be called 'social' and that could be grouped together in making up a special domain that could function as a society. The social seems to be diluted everywhere and yet nowhere in particular."[44] This claim challenges both common sense, the notion that society is a big container that holds us all, and specialized knowledge, the notion that society is what Mary Poovey calls an "objectified abstraction," an autonomous, sui generis, and exclusively human domain whose laws and forces have "become thinkable as part of the long history of reification that we call modernity."[45] What Latour attacks, in other words, is the definition of society that Williams provides in his keyword entry for the term: "the body of institutions and relationships within which a relatively large group of people live," as well as "the condition in which such institutions and relationships are formed."[46] As its title implies, therefore, the main objective of *Reassembling the Social* is to articulate an "alternative social theory," one that concentrates on associative processes: the coming together of actors (variously defined) into networks that must be traced in order to be understood.[47] Society is not presupposed as a cause, then, but understood as the effect of how actors assemble, disassemble, and reassemble anew.

The second aspect of Latour's thinking that informs the sociology of literature is his contention that literary texts, from the poetry of Francis Ponge to the novels of Richard Powers, are crucial "resources," both for apprehending social reality and for producing social theory.[48] As part of their storytelling mandate, Latour intimates, novelists in particular assemble an impression of the social (however realistic or fantastic) that can be instructive for analysts of the real social world, not because novels transmit the ideology of a given social context but because "the worlds of fiction invented on paper" pose questions and invite speculation. This is why "some continuous familiarity with literature" has been important to Latour for many years, and why he holds the conviction that "sociologists have a lot to learn from artists."[49] Such a conviction aligns him with other unconventional sociologists, perhaps Goffman above all, who have looked to literature as a conceptual resource.[50] While Goffman and Latour engage the literary in different ways—Goffman tends to cite literary texts as illustrations of social phenomena, whereas Latour tends to see them as thought experiments that can stimulate fresh inquiry—both thinkers consider literary authors to be fellow travelers on the journey to discover and explain the intricacies of sociality. Could we receive their work, across the disciplinary divide, as both a gift and a challenge? To do so would be to glimpse, in their rather undisciplined approaches to literature, a salutary reorientation of our discipline, an invitation to treat literary authors as allies in the immensely difficult task of comprehending something as perplexing as *society*. "Like all sciences," Latour declaims, "sociology begins in wonder," in a "passionate attempt" to fathom "the paradoxical presence of something at once invisible yet tangible, taken for granted yet surprising, mundane but of baffling subtlety."[51] No less passionately than sociologists, though, novelists seek "to tame the wild beast of the social" when they spend hours upon hours dreaming up the scenarios of social interaction that we call plot and dialogue and situating them in the framework that we call setting.[52] This is a way of reaffirming the conviction, first voiced by eminent sociologist C. Wright Mills and more recently echoed by Avery Gordon, that "literary work" constitutes a major contribution of the "sociological imagination."[53]

While there are many ways to explore this imagination in literature, I follow Latour (and, to some extent, Goffman as well) in pursuing an analysis of sites, for his radical sociology first appeared as a site-specific project. When he asserts at the beginning of his introduction to ANT that "the study of scientific practice has provided the main impetus for this alternative definition of the social," he is referring to his earlier scholarship in the field of science studies, specifically *Laboratory Life*, his still-controversial collaboration with Steve Woolgar.[54] A bête noire in what would come to be known as the culture wars of the 1980s, *Laboratory Life* provides an ethnographic account of Roger Guillemin's laboratory at the Jonas Salk Institute in La Jolla, California.[55] Striving to make "a detailed study of the daily activities of scientists in their natural habitat," Latour conducted nearly two years of fieldwork (beginning in 1975), observing "the routinely occurring minutiae of scientific activity."[56] In the end, he and Woolgar concluded that the scientific laboratory is best understood as "a system of literary inscription, an outcome of which is the occasional conviction of others that something is a fact," but this conclusion is finally less significant than the way

Laboratory Life begins to depict social action and interaction.[57] By scrutinizing the humdrum business of laboratory research, "focus[ing] on the work done by a scientist located firmly at his laboratory bench," Latour and Woolgar started to recognize the importance of the physical setting to the scientific endeavor. "Without the material environment of the laboratory," they argue, none of the scientifically observed phenomena "could be said to exist," for so much of the "apparatus" at this site—the gamma counter, the X-ray machine, even the workbench—had been "invented specifically to assist in the construction of laboratory objects."[58] Thus, as Latour and Woolgar develop a certain epistemological claim, that knowledge is produced rather than simply discovered by laboratory science, they also project a sociological vision, revealing this site as a vibrant assemblage of human and nonhuman actors that forms a complex social unit.

Reassembling the Social refines this image of sociality by attending to a different site, the supermarket, and by adapting the narratological conceptions of actor and actant for sociological inquiry. It is for this reason that, even though Latour has not said much about any given literary work, I want to propose that his understanding of sites (whether science labs or supermarkets) might prove useful for the analysis of narrative prose fiction, including fiction that seems more concerned with psychological than with social phenomena. Suppose that *Room*, for instance, has been dislodged from a course on literary interpretation and repositioned in one on narrative setting. Consider the syllabus for a moment. Such a course might reasonably start with Defoe and end with Donoghue, perhaps analyzing works by Radcliffe, Scott, Austen, Dickens, Melville, and Faulkner before pausing for a while to consider how setting—or what Eudora Welty called the "lowlier angel" of "place in fiction"—was reworked by the modernist novel, with James, Woolf, Proust, or Joyce providing exemplary cases.[59] *Ulysses*, in particular, would seem to reward close reading in this context, for even as Joyce was eager "to reveal the flickerings of that innermost flame which flashes its messages through the brain," as Woolf famously wrote, he was equally captivated by what he himself called "Dublin street furniture."[60] Much of the novel's audacity lies in the way that it shuttles (smoothly or jarringly) between these two poles, between the workings of what Woolf called "an ordinary mind" and the flux of phenomena that is Dublin on "an ordinary day."[61] As Joyce depicts it, such flux can be opaque and elusive, to be sure, yet also stunningly precise: "By Brady's cottages a boy for the skins lolled, his bucket of offal linked, smoking a chewed fagbutt. A smaller girl with scars of eczema on her forehead eyed him, listlessly holding her battered caskhoop."[62] Indeed, it was Joyce's august procedure of site specification, his exacting treatment of the Irish capital, that led Hugh Kenner to see the novel as a bid for cartographic posterity, whose "pages, indicating which street intersects with which, might afford the clues to an excavator's map."[63]

But while Joyce maps Dublin through what Kenner called Bloom's "circuitous wandering," he also uses the site in a subtle exploration of sociality.[64] Take the "Lotus Eaters" episode, for example, when Leopold Bloom "walk[s] soberly" around the city in the hour before Paddy Dignam's funeral (*U*, 58). In this episode, which provides the first extended treatment of Bloom's mental life, our protagonist emerges as both a social actor and a sort of sociologist, an inquisitive (if also crude) guide to modern Dublin. As he makes his way from the post office, having just retrieved a letter from his would-be mistress, Martha Clifford, he recognizes someone: "M'Coy. Get rid of him quickly," he thinks (*U*, 60). The ensuing social interaction would be rather dull were it not for Bloom's antisocial behavior. While the two characters chat, mostly about Dignam's funeral, our protagonist's eyes start to wander—"Clearly I can see today"—ultimately fixing their covetous gaze on an "outsider" across the road. "Careless stand of her with her hands in those patch pockets," he thinks, "[l]ike that haughty creature at the polo match. Women all for caste until you touch the spot" (ibid.). His lust builds as the outsider reveals her silk stockings, so he "move[s] a little to the side of M'Coy's talking head," but at the exact moment when he is about to catch a glance of something really thrilling—"Watch! Watch! Silk flash rich stockings white. Watch!"—a "heavy tramcar slew[s] between" him and his object of desire. "Lost it. Curse your noisy pugnose," he thinks, just before responding blandly to M'Coy: "Yes, yes, Mr Bloom said after a dull sigh" (*U*, 61). He is pretty pleased with himself as the two characters part ways: "Didn't catch me napping that wheeze" (*U*, 62).

This scene is fairly typical of *Ulysses*, not only in its toggling between thought and action but also in its rendering of Dublin as an assemblage of human and nonhuman actors. Bloom is the central player in a site-specific social drama that includes his interlocutor, as well as an unsuspecting stranger and a nonhuman entity. In fact, as the scene unfolds, that interlocutor recedes into the background, for Bloom's primary object of address is the anthropomorphized tramcar, whose "pugnose" he "curses" inaudibly but decisively, just as his primary object of attention is the woman in white stockings. Our protagonist, in this sense, appears enmeshed in what Latour would call a "thick imbroglio" of action and interaction, only a portion of which is visible from M'Coy's perspective, but all of which appears to us through Joyce's storytelling technique.[65] Meanwhile, in the midst of his dialogue with M'Coy, Bloom performs another social role, or participates in another social charade, the one that casts him as "Henry Flower," the pseudonym that he uses to begin the correspondence with Martha that sends him to the post office at the outset of the chapter. Epistolarity, of course, establishes an old-fashioned social network between two characters and two sites, between Martha's scene of writing and Bloom's reception of her letter, which, incidentally, gets interrupted by the appearance of M'Coy.

There are thus two overlapping social networks here: one composed of Bloom, M'Coy, the tramcar, and various other constituents, both human and nonhuman, of Dublin at midmorning on June 16, 1904; the other composed of Bloom, Martha, and the letter that facilitates their interaction. If the first is synchronic and site specific, contained in a discrete time and place, then the second is diachronic and multisited, extending from one time and place to another through the infrastructure of the postal system.

And yet, *Ulysses* upsets any neat division between synchronic and diachronic sociality as Bloom continues his stroll, "wishing he hadn't met that M'Coy fellow," a thought that registers the ongoing psychological aftereffects of a completed social exchange (*U*, 63). By this point in "The Lotus Eaters," it has become clear that our protagonist is not just a social actor but also a social thinker whose perambulations spark reflection on the experience of collective life. "He passed the cabman's shelter. Curious the life of drifting cabbies. All weathers, all places, time or setdown, no will of their own. *Voglio e non.* Like to give them an odd cigarette. Sociable. Shout a few flying syllables as they pass" (ibid.). What begins as a casual effort to ponder a social formation (a group of laborers and their labor conditions) becomes a desire to commiserate by enlisting an object, an odd cigarette, to facilitate an intersubjective bond. A similar desire takes hold moments later, as the Jewish Bloom sits for the Catholic mass at All Hallows. When "[t]he cold smell of sacred stone call[s] him," he enters the "swingdoor" of the church to discover "[s]omething going on: some sodality" (*U*, 66). Both the physical site and its collective rituals are captivating. "Something like those mazzoth," he thinks, watching the transubstantiation; "it's that sort of bread: unleavened shrewbread" (ibid.). Soon enough, such observations precipitate speculation on the great mystery of this scene, which ultimately is not the transubstantiation itself but the question of why these people are here at all: "Now I bet it makes them feel happy. Lollipop. It does. Yes, bread of angels it's called. There's a big idea behind it, kind of a kingdom of God is within you feel. First communicants. Hokypoky penny a lump. They feel all like one family party, same in the theatre, all in the same swim" (ibid.). For a moment, then, Bloom identifies something like the social function of religion, playfully acknowledging the intimate link between Holy Communion and community, or what Bloom calls "confraternity" (ibid.).

Eventually he exits the church (in a ploy to avoid the collection basket) and ends his stroll around Dublin, but not before this period of flânerie discloses the significance of the city to Joyce's sociological imagination. By the time we have finished following Bloom around—as he curses the "honking" tramcar, admires the "multicolored hoardings" at the shops, listens to the "[f]lat Dublin voices," passes the "ruins and tenements," as well as the "hopscotch court with its forgotten pickeystone," smells "the dank air" in the streets, and finally makes his way from the church to the chemist to the gate of Trinity College (*U*, 61–71)—it is easy to agree with Joseph Frank's classic argument that "Joyce's most obvious intention in *Ulysses* is to give the reader a picture of Dublin seen as a whole," but one that consists of many moving parts, a varied and volatile composite of humans and nonhumans. As Frank elaborates, in a remark that echoes Lukács, Joyce sought "to re-create the sights and sounds, the people and places, of a typical Dublin day, much as Flaubert had re-created his provincial country fair."[66] That re-creation is so complex, alternately baffling and fascinating to so many readers, precisely because of how Joyce constructs setting as a *relation* between the metropolis and mental life, between the commotion of midmorning Dublin and Bloom's processes of cogitation, as in the moment when the "train clank[ing] heavily above" him transforms a mental image of porter into "barrels bump[ing] in his head" (*U*, 65). The setting of "The Lotus Eaters," as in other episodes of *Ulysses*, is not a fixed framework for narrative action but a dynamic interplay between mind and matter, which is why the novel's figuration of sociality (as in Bloom's interaction with M'Coy) often emerges through a vertiginous oscillation between thought and action.

Another way to put this point would be to say that the figure of the social in "The Lotus Eaters" depends on how Joyce exploits the unstable boundary between character and setting. Chatman has explained just how difficult it can be to define that boundary; it is inadequate, he suggests, to say that "setting 'sets the character off' in the usual figurative sense of the expression," that it constitutes "the place and collection of objects 'against' which' his actions and passions appropriately emerge."[67] Such a definition runs into trouble not only because nonhuman objects can assume the role of characters (as in *Room*) and because setting can span both human interiority and the external object world (as in *Ulysses*) but also because human figures (walk-ons, extras, crowds, masses) can be elements of setting—too minor, relative to the plot and its protagonist, even to warrant the designation *minor character*.[68] So how do we distinguish character from setting? Chatman offers one compelling answer, arguing that "a human being who is named, present and important is *more likely* to be a character" than any other figure in the story world, but Edgar Allan Poe offers a different and equally compelling answer in "The Man of the Crowd," his classic tale from 1840.[69] As Poe's unnamed narrator sits in a London coffeehouse, he peers through the window at a "throng" that moves along "one of the principal thoroughfares of the city."[70] While "scrutinizing the mob," producing a capacious taxonomy of social types, he is suddenly transfixed by "a countenance which at once arrest[s] and absorb[s] [his] whole attention" (*PT*, 392). At this instant, the narrator's casual attempt to label all the different figures in the crowd transforms into an obsessive quest "to know more" about one particular man—to glimpse something of his interior life (his "vast mental power," perhaps, or his "blood-thirstiness") and to uncover his "wild history"—by following him through London, studying his appearance, noting his actions, and speculating about his motives (ibid.). The pursuit leads all over the city and ends, grimly enough, with the narrator deciding that this man is "the type and the genius of deep crime," yet nevertheless still inscrutable. "It will be in vain to follow," he concludes. "I shall learn no more of him" (*PT*, 396).

Poe's tale was important to Walter Benjamin, who called it "an X-ray of the detective story" that "does away with all the drapery that a crime represents" so that "only the armature remains: the pursuer, the crowd, and an unknown man."[71] But surely Poe provides a more comprehensive scan of narrative structure than this—not only a detective story in skeletal form but also a metanarrative about how character gets distinguished from setting through the sustained attention of a narrator. From "a tumultuous sea of human heads," Poe's narrator selects only one, lifting him from the substratum of setting to the perch of character by tracking his movements and wondering about the hidden contours of his subjectivity (*PT*, 389). This process produces an antagonist (the man) for our protagonist (the narrator) and distinguishes them both from the urban mass, which forms a portion of the setting as the chase unfolds through bazaars and shops and various London neighborhoods. Poe's tale in this sense reveals a familiar and potent force of narrative prose fiction: how a narrator simultaneously directs our attention and affection toward character while instructing us to consider setting significant only insofar as it influences what Lukács calls "the mesh of human destinies" in the story.[72] And yet, there is also a counterforce at work in narrative—readily discernible in *Room*, *Ulysses*, and even *Robinson Crusoe*—that blurs the line between character and setting to disclose the Lukácsian mesh as an assemblage of humans and nonhumans. The critical gambit of *Site Reading* is to take this assemblage as a primary unit of analysis and to examine how it manifests in and through a site that is especially important to a given story.

Examining literary sites, as in the case of Joyce's Dublin or of Donoghue's Room, becomes a kind of sociological project, because sites (both imagined and real) mediate sociality. This is why ethnographers such as Latour and Woolgar undertake site-specific fieldwork: an analytical procedure that not only designates a given locale for immersive analysis but also renders social relations, which are what Lefebvre calls "concrete abstractions," graspable as empirical objects. The English term *site* comes from the Latin *situs*, which is the perfect passive participle of *sino*, a multipurpose verb that means to place, to situate, to grant, or to allow. *Situs* is almost always used in Latin literature for somewhere that is inhabited, and the most common usage is to describe a physical location where it is good to build a city.[73] We retain these meanings in contemporary English, since we use *site* to designate "a piece of ground or an area which has been appropriated for some purpose" and to identify "the scene of a specified activity" (as in phrases such as *test site*, *work site*, or *launch site*). For archaeologists, moreover, the premise of any excavation is that a given site preserves "the remains of former human habitation," the material evidence for apprehending a lost civilization.[74] Whether in ordinary language or in more technical idioms, therefore, *site* implies both human activity and sociality. For this reason, I privilege it over other terms, such as *place*, *space*, and *environment*, that enjoy wider currency in literary studies. Although I do not entirely avoid the latter, my emphasis on *site* is meant to underscore the sociological ambition of this book, while acknowledging that many important and related topics, from the space/place dialectic to the global environmental crisis, reside beyond its purview.[75] Nevertheless, *Site Reading* shares with critical works on these topics the conviction that analyzing literary form entails asking questions about society and collective life.

*

So how do these questions emerge? By what method of literary interpretation does the analysis of narrative prose fiction become an effort to fathom sociality? It begins by abandoning the notion of setting as a static framework for narrative action and by accepting the porous and dynamic boundary between setting and character. Then it seeks to identify the sites (much as a textual materialist might identify the *things*) that appear crucial to whatever a given literary text is trying to express. To analyze these sites—to perform a site reading—is to scrutinize an assemblage of humans and nonhumans in the story world with an eye on how the interaction of such figures simultaneously models and theorizes social experience. At times, perhaps owing to the force that Poe dramatizes in "The Man of the Crowd," the boundary between human and nonhuman can seem firm and sharp; yet at other times, owing to the counterforce that we can see clearly in certain segments of *Room* or of *Ulysses*, that boundary is more difficult to discern. Latour would call these two forces, respectively, "purification" and "translation." While purification establishes two distinct "ontological zones," situating humans in one and nonhumans in the other, translation creates mixtures, hybrids, and assemblages of human and nonhuman. The interplay of these two forces, he argues, is constitutive of Western modernity. When he asserts that "we have never been modern," he does not mean to deny the fact of modernization but to suggest that it relies on the mutual reinforcement of purification and translation: one force that establishes and shores up boundaries, another that transgresses them.[76] If this account of modernity also seems like an apt description of how narrative fiction manages the relation between human and nonhuman, then this should come as no surprise given Latour's long-standing engagement with narratology and semiotics.

I track that engagement in "Supermarket Sociology," the first chapter of this book, which provides a kind of vestibular access to *Site Reading* as a whole. By examining the figuration of the supermarket in two very different works—Latour's *Reassembling the Social* and Don DeLillo's *White Noise*—I try to establish the methodological and conceptual stakes of this project, to show how a certain method of interpretation might form the basis for a new sociology of literature. "Supermarket Sociology" seeks in this sense to refine the claims of this introduction through the analysis of a more fully developed case, but it also means to do something more: to assemble a network of cultural artifacts, both literary and visual, that provides a fresh look at postwar and postmodernist culture. To visualize this network is to see the site, the supermarket, as a central node or vertex that not only links Latour and DeLillo but also establishes connections among Andy Warhol, Fredric Jameson, Robert Venturi, Allen Ginsberg, John Updike, and other prominent figures. Thus, even as Latour's sociology enlivens the questions about sociality that I explore throughout this book, it also suggests a particular way of apprehending culture and cultural production. Instead of beginning with a literary text and then situating it in a given cultural context, I always begin with a site and then trace a cultural network that emanates from it, which is really to say that I understand sites as actants in two senses: as determinants of sociality that invite sustained attention from novelists and as material environments that give rise to constellations of cultural artifacts.

This two-part conception of sites animates all the case studies in this book. After "Supermarket Sociology" makes a case for defining the social as a network of humans and nonhumans, the section entitled *Test Sites* considers how that definition ramifies in the writings of several postwar American novelists whose treatments of sites—dumps, roads, ruins, and asylums—amount to meticulous delineations of social form. Concentrating on the work and life of William S. Burroughs, in chapter 2 I propose that *Naked Lunch* constructs something like a nightmare image of Latourian sociality: a collective of human subjects and nonhuman objects governed by the logic of putrefaction, or "translation" run amok. Jack Kerouac and Joan Didion are the key players in chapter 3, where I argue that the postwar American road narrative produces a sophisticated account of the nonhuman social actor through its treatment of the automobile, an entity that is, of course, both a material thing and a social site. The next two chapters both explore the question of limits: If the social is a vast network, they ask, when and where does it end? How do we establish the boundaries that make the social coherent as an object of analysis, representation, or both? In chapter 4, I suggest that Thomas Pynchon addressed such questions when he looked to the ruins and ruination of Malta, to a site where a society was being methodically destroyed, in order to imagine how social relations might withstand destruction and persist through millennia. Turning from temporal to spatial limits, finally, in chapter 5, I propose that Ralph Ellison's career-long interest in asylums—sites where "individuals" are, as Goffman writes, "cut off from the wider society"—suggests a new way of defining his relationship to the discipline of sociology.[77]

While *Site Reading* concentrates on novels and novelists, its point of engagement with sociology shifts from Latour to Goffman as the book unfolds. Goffman has enjoyed something of a resurgence in recent years, partly as a result of what Mark Seltzer calls "the incrementalist turn across a range of recent literary and cultural studies," the new focus on "scaled-down" objects of analysis, such as "minor characters," "little resistances," and "infantile subjects."[78] As I understand him, Goffman set an important precedent for Latour, an influence that Latour himself acknowledges (fleetingly) in *Reassembling the Social* when he cites Goffman as an authority on the "thick imbroglio" of social interaction.[79] Although the two thinkers are incompletely compatible, their respective sociologies share at least three features: a commitment to ethnography and site-specific fieldwork, a sustained interest in nonhuman entities (which Goffman often calls "props"), and a robust relationship to literature and literary theory. *The Presentation of Self in Everyday Life*, for example, redeploys the dramaturgical rhetoric of Kenneth Burke's *A Grammar of Motives*, a study that itself builds on "the philosophy of drama embodied in Henry James's prefaces."[80] Moreover, Goffman's scholarship often uses literary examples to facilitate the production of sociological concepts, as in the case of *Asylums*, his 1961 analysis of psychiatric care, which draws on Melville and other literary authors to develop its claims.[81] The groundwork for *Asylums* was built by a year of fieldwork at St. Elizabeths Psychiatric Hospital, the notorious state institution that housed Ezra Pound from 1945 to 1958, and that by the 1960s had become synonymous with the coldly bureaucratic and even prisonlike impression of asylums that appears in so much cultural production from the period. While I analyze some of that production, mainly to locate both Goffman and Ellison within a wider cultural network, my emphasis falls on how sites of psychiatric treatment came to mediate sociality for (and thus to spark sociological inquiry from) both the sociologist and the novelist.

This is because *Site Reading* is not a cultural history but an experiment in literary criticism whose hypothesis is that writing a novel is a way of knowing about collective life. When I began working on this book, I thought that I was historicizing the postwar US novel, seeking to demonstrate how its treatment of the built environment not only registers major historical events (the rise of suburbia, the construction of the interstates, the uneven development of cities) but also encodes spatial politics—how it manifests a vexed relation to the intertwined ideologies of progress, modernization, neoliberalism, and American exceptionalism that underwrite what Lefebvre calls "the production of space." The more fictions I read, the more sites I found: the home (Marilynne Robinson), the office (Richard Yates, Ed Park, David Foster Wallace), the Indian reservation (Leslie Marmon Silko, Louise Erdrich, Sherman Alexie), and even cyberspace (William Gibson) all warranted some attention, as did site-specific visual art. While I worked to amass an archive of primary sources, both literary and visual, I consulted the rich historicist scholarship on this period, learning how to think about my material by considering how previous scholars had analyzed sites like the suburb, the city, and the border.[82] The literary texts that I had assembled as cases, however, soon began to push back against the ways I wanted to understand them. Their treatments of sites caused me to wonder whether the historicist procedure of contextualizing literature in relation to a *specific* sociohistorical context (postwar America or postmodernity) had foreclosed the more fundamental question of how literature imagines sociality as such. Pynchon's depiction of a ruined Malta, for instance, is not what Jameson describes as "adoptive tourism" meant to satisfy "idle curiosity," which is to say not merely a cultural symptom of the postmodern era but a sophisticated attempt to rethink the temporality of social interaction.[83]

Still, this era is particularly fertile for site reading. Although it can illuminate texts across the full spectrum of literary history, site reading seems like a necessary way of accounting for a broad range of literary and artistic phenomena in the United States after World War II, not least because *site* became a key term in the visual and performing arts at this moment. Three months after Michel Foucault asserted, in the famous "heterotopias" lecture of 1967, that "[o]ur epoch is one in which space takes for us the form of relations among sites," Robert Smithson argued, in the pages of *Artforum*, that "[t]he unknown areas of sites can best be explored by artists."[84] Such exploration was widespread and often highly intelligent, beginning in the late 1960s with the pioneering work of artists such as Smithson, Daniel Buren, Richard Serra, and Mierle Laderman Ukeles, and extending to the more recent projects of Andrea Fraser, Renée Green, Mark Dion, Suzanne Lacy, and a host of others. From what Hal Foster calls "the crux of minimalism," site-specificity emerged to challenge the modernist orthodoxy of the aesthetic object as autonomous, autotelic, and thus indifferent to its site of display.[85] While art historians have developed detailed genealogies and taxonomies of this phenomenon—showing how its different phases have defined sites differently—I understand site-specificity primarily as an investigation of social form, an attempt not merely "to integrate art more directly into the realm of the social" but to theorize sociality itself through artistic practice.[86] Even as Smithson, for instance, aimed to "use the actual land as medium" in earthworks like *Spiral Jetty*, he also sought to analyze "social structures which confine art" and to resist "[t]he function of the warden-curator" whose aim is "to separate art from the rest of society."[87] This is why his work, like that of his fellow practitioners, can be understood as paving the way for the "social turn" of so much contemporary art, especially the recent projects of Maurizio Cattelan, Rirkrit Tiravanija, and Carsten Höller, which take "as their theoretical and practical point of departure the whole of human relations and their social context."[88]

When I turn to the visual arts at various moments in this book, then, I mean to affirm Latour's conviction that "sociologists have a lot to learn from artists." Although the questions about sociality that I examine throughout *Site Reading* are precipitated by narrative prose fiction, my extended accounts of artworks by Warhol, Ukeles, John Chamberlain, Smithson, Gordon Parks, and Jeff Wall are designed to show how visual media reformulate such questions and provide their own answers. Analyzing the paradox of nonhuman agency as DeLillo imagines it, for example, leads to a reading of Warhol's famous *Brillo Boxes* as objects whose formal structure depends on a precise distinction between agency and its figuration. The conversation between literature and visual art in this book, however, is not organized as a conventional history or genealogy. Rather, each chapter traces a network of literary and cultural objects that emanates from a certain generic site, such as the supermarket, whose force as a cultural actant manifests in the array of specific and specifying responses that it has engendered from authors, artists, intellectuals, and other figures. The goal is not to dispute the value of a more traditional historiography but to suggest that site reading might offer a fresh way of seeing the cultural past, something like a new method of data visualization for literary and cultural historians. If how we visualize the past constitutes a way of knowing it, a lesson that is continually reinforced by scholarship in the digital present, then site reading asks what happens when we look closely at sites, when we see them as both social and cultural actants.[89]

To pose this question from the vantage of literary studies is to join the vibrant conversation about critical methodology that currently animates the discipline. These days, a novel like *Room* is just as likely to occasion debate over reading (close versus distant, depth versus surface, critical versus postcritical) as it is to provoke formal and historical interpretation. Such debate should be a reminder that literary critics are pretty good at reflecting on methods of knowledge production, a capability that we bring to our encounters with other disciplines and to our work in the classroom, which, even in the era of massive open online courses (MOOCs), still constitutes the key social site of our discipline. If this era demands that we justify the existence of the brick-and-mortar classroom, while striving to explain the value of literary studies within the political economy of higher education, then part of our message ought to be that literature itself is not only a primary source but also a conceptual resource. As such, *Site Reading* proposes, it capacitates us to think the social, to appreciate the mystery and complexity of collective life.

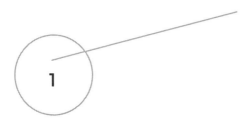

Supermarket Sociology

Émile Durkheim would not live long enough to see the arrival of the super-market in France. Nor would he witness its expansion into the more flam-boyant form of food retailing aptly named the *hypermarché*. It was not until after World War II and during the Marshall Plan, in which food aid was a central component, that American-style supermarkets began to crop up all over Europe.[1] And it was not until 1963 that the Carrefour Company con-structed the first of its hypermarkets just outside Paris. After assimilating the dictates of Bernardo Trujillo, an Ohio-based business educator who was affectionately known as "the pope of modern commerce," Carrefour de-signed a food retailing institution that was unprecedented in both size and style: 2,500 square meters (approximately 1.5 square miles), 450 parking spaces, and a variety of items (clothes, household appliances, low-cost pet-rol) and amenities (a cafeteria, a bakery, a dry cleaner's) that were not aggre-gated in quite the same way anywhere else.[2] Hypermarket grand openings were characteristically hyperreal. They featured circus amusements and games hosted by a TV personality. And they included large-scale binge drinking: ten thousand liters (about 2,641 gallons) of *vin de Touraine* served from a marquee on the parking lot.[3] It is possible that the founder of mod-ern sociology would have had something to say about such a scene, but his death from exhaustion just after World War I leaves us free to speculate on what that might have been. It leaves us on our own, that is, to imagine a supermarket sociology.

Such a speculative fantasy is more serious than it may seem, for it stages a series of instructive encounters: between fin de siècle Europe and postwar America; between high theory and vernacular culture; between the systematicity of social science and the heterogeneity of lived experience; and between one period-imaginary (the industrialization, fragmentation, and anomie of modernity) and another (the globalization, decenteredness, and depthlessness of postmodernity). More specifically, to picture Durkheim strolling the aisles of a supermarket that he never could have visited is to imagine a counterfactual scene in the history of ideas. What kind of sociology might have emerged had he lived long enough to shop for groceries the way most of us do? The answer, this chapter proposes, is the sociology of Bruno Latour. In *Reassembling the Social: An Introduction to Actor-Network-Theory*, Latour proffers a thorough critique of Durkheim, deploying what he calls a "metaphor of the supermarket" as a means of illustrating his argument that the social is best conceived as a network of human subjects and nonhuman objects.[4] Against more familiar ways of conceptualizing and allocating agency, Latour claims that nonhumans must be understood as actors or actants: fully agential participants in the drama of social relations. "How long can a social connection be followed," he asks, "without objects taking the relay?" (*RS*, 78). This conception of the nonhuman has influenced a wide swath of interdisciplinary scholarship—especially the work associated with "thing theory," "posthumanism," "vital materialism," and "speculative realism"—yet it relies on a critical idiom derived from narratology and semiotics.[5] For this reason and others, Latour's sociology is deeply indebted to the enterprise of literary analysis, to the project of developing a critical vocabulary for apprehending the structure and significance of literary texts.

Taking Latour's engagement with the literary as a point of departure, this chapter offers a new model for thinking between the disciplines of literary studies and sociology. At the crux of this model is a site, the supermarket, that dramatizes nonhuman agency as a mundane yet complex fact of social experience, a fact that Latour theorizes throughout his writings and that a host of literary authors, above all Don DeLillo, have sought to explore in different ways. Although extensive critical commentary has positioned DeLillo's *White Noise* (1985) in relation to the theories of Jean Baudrillard, Guy Debord, and, more recently, Ulrich Beck, I read the novel's treatment of the supermarket as a literary exploration of several interlocking questions that animate Latour's thinking.[6] My overarching goal, however, is not merely to offer a reading of the novel in terms of Actor-Network-Theory (ANT) but rather to demonstrate how a site that is crucial to both the novelist and the sociologist could facilitate a new interdisciplinary conversation, a mode of inquiry that would divert from a more traditional sociology of literature whose objective would be to identify the deep significance of literary form in the social forces that subtend aesthetic production.[7] Instead of reading *White Noise* as an epiphenomenon of the social, in other words, I want to understand the novel as a sociological endeavor in its own right, a profound attempt to explore the nature of sociality itself. Insofar as this approach to DeLillo constitutes a sociology *of* literature, then, it seeks to discover the sociology *in* literature. This means emphasizing the former of the two possibilities suggested by Pierre Bourdieu in his influential study of Gustave Flaubert: "In sum, on the one hand, Flaubert's sociology, meaning the sociology which he produces; on the other, the sociology of Flaubert, meaning the sociology of which he is the object."[8] What is the sociology that DeLillo produces? The most compelling answer to this question, I argue, appears in his figuration of the supermarket as a site of interaction between humans and nonhumans.

To make this argument, I deploy the method of site reading that I outlined in the introduction. Although my emphasis falls on how Latour and DeLillo figure the supermarket, the site also plays another part in this chapter, as the central node within a cultural network that includes literature, visual art, design, advertising, and journalism. Inspired by Latour's rethinking of the text/context distinction, as well as by recent calls to reimagine our interpretive procedures, site reading aims to disclose the sociology in literature, while tracing connections between literary and nonliterary phenomena, ultimately to bring otherwise concealed affiliations among literature, art, and mass culture into clear resolution.[9]

THE SUPERMARKET SOCIOLOGIST

Latour's literariness is, in some ways, nothing new. "From the middle of the nineteenth century onwards," writes Wolf Lepenies, "literature and sociology contested with one another the claim to offer the key orientation for modern civilization," yet despite this rivalry, the sociologists of Durkheim's era often looked to literature for inspiration.[10] "What literary sources offered," Susan Mizruchi argues, "were not only characters more richly drawn than those in history books but a common storehouse of culturally specific types—both situational and human—whose properties could resonate in a variety of unpredictable ways, depending on the context."[11] It seems fitting, then, that the most thorough critique of Durkheimian sociology to have emerged in recent years should proceed with and through literary theory. *Reassembling the Social* challenges Durkheim's understanding of the social as autonomous, sui generis, and composed of uniquely social (as opposed to, say, natural) materials.[12] Latour argues, by contrast, that the social is best understood as a constitutively impure and ever-shifting assemblage of humans and nonhumans. For Latour, in other words, there is no "specific sort of phenomenon variously called 'society,' 'social order,' 'social practice,' 'social dimension,' or 'social structure'" that can be defined against other phenomena, such as the material, the psychological, the economic, or the natural (*RS*, 3). Rather, there are only networks of actors in contingent and momentary relationships that must be traced before they can be understood.

Thus, some portion of the real, what Durkheim called "the particular and the concrete," can be considered social only after it has been delineated as such by the work of ANT.[13] Instead of being treated as a preconstituted domain, then, the social is literally *figured out* by ANT: it is given a kind of figural expression in the sociological monograph, not unlike that which is proffered by narrative prose fiction. Hence the reason literary theory is so important to this sociology. "Because they deal with fiction," Latour explains, "literary theorists have been much freer in their enquiries about figuration than any social scientist, especially when they have used semiotics and the various narrative sciences" (*RS*, 54). While Latour frequently acknowledges his debt to Michel Serres, he is referring here to thinkers such as Louis Marin, who exemplifies "the metaphysical freedom of semioticians," and Thomas Pavel, who exhibits "the incomparable freedom of movement of literary theorists" (*RS*, 54–55). It is not that "literary theorists would know more than sociologists," Latour assures, but that "some continuous familiarity with literature" might enable sociologists to "become less wooden, less rigid, less stiff in their definition of what sorts of agencies populate the world" (*RS*, 55).

Agency is a key term in Latour's thought, and its redescription is perhaps the most important contribution of ANT. From his point of view, agency is always figured in one way or another whenever it is conceptualized, regardless of how abstract or concrete that figuration. If agency is, most simply, the capacity for action, then whatever accomplishes an activity is always endowed "with some flesh and features that make [it] have some form or shape, no matter how vague" (*RS*, 53). To preserve the distinction between agency and its figuration, Latour relies on the term *actant*, which he gleans from the narratology of A. J. Greimas, as well as from the more recent work of Jacques Fontanille. In *Semiotics and Language*, Greimas and J. Courtés make clear that "an actant can be thought of as that which accomplishes or undergoes an act, independently of all other determinations," meaning it is "a type of syntactic unit, properly formal in character, which precedes any semantic or ideological investment."[14]

The technology of narrative, according to Greimas and Courtés, includes six actants paired in binary opposition—subject/object, sender/receiver, helper/opponent—and these actants, once "invested" or figured, become *actors*. The narratologists write: "An actor may be individual (for example, Peter), or collective (for example, a crowd), figurative (anthropomorphic or zoomorphic), or non-figurative (for example, fate)."[15] Thus, agency in this narratology is extended to nonhumans, both material and nonmaterial, and it can be rendered either abstractly as an actant or concretely as an actor, which is why Latour tends to use those two terms interchangeably throughout his work: "any thing that does modify a state of affairs by making a difference is an actor—or, if it has no figuration yet, an actant" (*RS*, 71). To observe a change in a "state of affairs," moreover, is to glimpse agency in and as its effect, not to treat it as some mysterious cause. As long as we are inside a narratological framework trying to apprehend a narrative text, this schema of agency, actant, and actor seems reasonable, but it becomes less comfortable when our object of analysis is society and our analytical device is an emergent social theory. We have no trouble understanding "a fable," as Latour puts it, in which "the same actant can be made to act through the agency of a magic wand, a dwarf, a thought in the fairy's mind, or a knight killing two dozen dragons" (*RS*, 54). It is more difficult, however, for us to think of the social as a network comprising both humans and nonhumans as fully agential actors or actants.

Unless we stroll through the supermarket. Latour himself heads there when he needs a familiar environment in which to situate his defamiliarizing claims. What Latour calls the "metaphor of the supermarket" appears at two key junctures in *Reassembling the Social* (*RS*, 65). In both, it serves to distance ANT from traditional sociology while clarifying the distinction between agency and its figuration. There is "a shelf full of 'social ties'"—to be distinguished from the economic, material, psychological, and biological ties that bind the goods on other shelves—in the "imaginary supermarket" of traditional sociology (ibid.). From the point of view of ANT, however, the entire supermarket should be understood as a social whole, a network whose goods serve as actants variously figured by "their packaging, their pricing, their labeling" (ibid.). In the ANT supermarket, the human subject is not only one of the many actants constituting the network but is itself constituted by the nonhuman objects in its environment, the "bewildering array of devices" that buzz and jingle and flash in every aisle and on every shelf (*RS*, 210). In the ANT supermarket, moreover, "when one has to make the mundane decision about which kind of sliced ham to choose," one always benefits from the "dozens of measurement instruments" that capacitate the subject as a consumer (ibid.). Thus, it makes no sense to polarize subject and object in the ANT supermarket, just as it would be impossible to restrict agency in this site to the human particular.

This conception of agency, as distributed among humans and nonhumans, emerges throughout Latour's work, and it has been theorized in various ways by political scientist Jane Bennett, archaeologist Alfred Gell, and media theorist Mark B. N. Hansen, among others.[16] For Latour, this concept has a firm basis in narratology, so it seems reasonable to wonder how a literary narrative might contribute to an understanding of distributed agency as a social phenomenon. "[W]hen everything else has failed," Latour quips, "the resource of fiction can bring . . . the solid objects of today into the fluid states where their connections with humans may make sense" (RS, 82). What happens when *White Noise* is read as a sociological "resource" in this manner?

A NOVEL VIEW OF SUPERMARKETS

"The supermarket is full of elderly people," begins chapter 22 of the novel, "who look lost among the dazzling hedgerows. Some people are too small to reach the upper shelves; some people block the aisle with their carts; some are clumsy and slow to react; some are forgetful, some confused; some move about muttering with the wary look of people in institutional corridors."[17] Depicting the experiential pandemonium of the live supermarket, this passage exemplifies two key features of DeLillo's prose: descriptive precision and deadpan irony. The use of anaphora, moreover, produces a sociological effect insofar as it generates a taxonomy of social types—old shoppers, confused shoppers, clumsy shoppers—that we can all recognize; this is one reason why the novel has been called "a social science fiction" that reads "like an ethnography of sorts."[18] Recognition is central to the humor of *White Noise*, for it includes so many scenes that the reader will have encountered in the real world: "There were two new developments in the supermarket, a butcher's corner and a bakery, and the oven aroma of bread and cake combined with the sight of a bloodstained man pounding strips of living veal was pretty exciting for us all" (WN, 167). Here and elsewhere, though, DeLillo presents familiar details only to defamiliarize them with irony and hyperbole, thereby rendering the supermarket and its sociality both recognizable and strange.

"In *White Noise*, in particular," DeLillo told Anthony DeCurtis in 1988, "I tried to find a kind of radiance in dailiness," and the supermarket seemed like the right place to look: "Imagine someone from the third world who has never set foot in a place like that suddenly transported to an A&P in Chagrin Falls, Ohio. Wouldn't he be elated or frightened? Wouldn't he sense that something transcending is about to happen to him in the midst of all this brightness?"[19] Although DeLillo renders that brightness in original ways, he was not the only postwar American author to focus on the particular details of this site. Just as Ira Levin's protagonist in *The Stepford Wives* (1972) walks through "the market's opening-by-themselves doors" to enter "the usual Saturday morning parade," so too Philip K. Dick's protagonist in *Time Out of Joint* (1959) "passe[s] through the electric eye, causing the door to swing wide for him."[20] Shelves rather than doors caught the attention of Paul Auster, who imagined the supermarket as a setting for psychological drama, depicting a "schizoid break" that causes a character in *The*

New York Trilogy to start "taking those big jugs of apple juice off the shelves and smashing them on the floor."[21] When Joan Didion turned to the supermarket, she too was concerned with pathos. Maria Wyeth, the depressed protagonist of *Play It as It Lays* (1970), "shop[s] always for a household, gallons of grapefruit juice, quarts of green chile salsa, dried lentils and alphabet noodles, rigatoni and canned yams, twenty-pound boxes of laundry detergent." Such items, Maria thinks, "giv[e] off the signs" that she is happy and well adjusted, but for people who have never been to a supermarket, they are completely bewildering, as Spalding Gray suggests in *Swimming to Cambodia* (1987) when he discusses the Laotian Hmong tribes who were relocated after the Vietnam War to immigrant condos in Washington State.[22] "The supermarket confused them totally," he explains. "Thinking it was a bar of soap, they bought a big, yellow block of Velveeta cheese."[23]

Along with DeLillo, these writers have made the supermarket into a meaningful setting for literary fiction, while calling to mind earlier representations of sites such as bazaars, department stores, and grocer's shops. One thinks, for instance, of Honoré de Balzac's *Le Peau de Chagrin* (1831), with its variety shop showcasing "a chaotic medley of human and divine works," or of Émile Zola's *Au Bonheur des Dames* (1883), with its long, descriptive passages detailing the "giant fairground display" of the Parisian department store.[24] More relevant for DeLillo, perhaps, are Theodore Dreiser's *Sister Carrie* (1900), whose protagonist "feel[s] the claim of each trinket and valuable upon her personally," and James Joyce's "Araby" (1914), with its bazaar that fascinates and obsesses its narrator, casting "an eastern enchantment" over him.[25] It was Charles Dickens, however, who set the most important precedent for DeLillo. *A Christmas Carol* (1843) includes this lavish description:

> The Grocers'! oh, the Grocers'! nearly closed, with perhaps two shutters down, or one; but through those gaps such glimpses! It was not alone that the scales descending on the counter made a merry sound, or that the twine and roller parted company so briskly, or that the canisters were rattled up and down like juggling tricks, or even that the blended scents of tea and coffee were so grateful to the nose, or even that the raisins were so plentiful and rare, the almonds so extremely white, the sticks of cinnamon so long and straight, the other spices so delicious, the candied fruits so caked and spotted with molten sugar as to make the coldest lookers-on feel faint and subsequently bilious. Nor was it that the figs were moist and pulpy, or that the French plums blushed in modest tartness from their highly-decorated boxes, or that everything was good to eat and in its Christmas dress; but the customers were all so hurried and so eager in the hopeful promise of the day, that they tumbled up against each other

at the door, crashing their wicker baskets wildly, and left their purchases upon the counter, and came running back to fetch them, and committed hundreds of the like mistakes, in the best humour possible.[26]

As Dickens catalogs foodstuffs, almost as though he is composing a shopping list, he renders a site that is not only suffused with sounds and smells but also humming with life. Both humans and nonhumans animate this grocery: scales strike countertops, twine splits from its roller, customers crash baskets. "The Grocers'! oh, the Grocers'!"—nearly closed, yet pulsing with the energy of Christmas in London.

DeLillo's supermarket is no less animated, but it pulses with a different sort of energy: the buzzing currents of "waves and radiation" (*WN*, 103). Indeed, the descriptions of the supermarket in *White Noise* read like subtle revisions (or postmodernizations) of this passage in Dickens. Early in the novel, the narrator, Jack Gladney, brings his family there to undertake the mundane task of purchasing the groceries, but the site is also a kind of holy temple demanding pilgrimage: "This place recharges us spiritually," one of the characters remarks; "it prepares us, it's a gateway or pathway. Look how bright. It's full of psychic data" (*WN*, 37). After exchanging pleasantries with the eccentric Murray Jay Siskind, a professor of American environments at the college where Jack teaches Hitler studies, Jack and his daughter coast down the generic food aisle and over to the produce:

> Steffie took my hand and we walked past the fruit bins, an area that extended about forty-five yards along the wall. The bins were arranged diagonally and backed by mirrors that people accidentally punched when reaching for fruit in the upper rows. A voice on the loudspeaker said: "Kleenex Softique, your truck's blocking the entrance." Apples and lemons tumbled in twos and threes to the floor when someone took a fruit from certain places in the stacked array. There were six kinds of apples, there were exotic melons in several pastels. Everything seemed to be in season, sprayed, burnished, bright. People tore filmy bags from racks and tried to figure out which end opened. I realized the place was awash in noise. The toneless systems, the jangle and skid of carts, the loudspeaker and coffee-making machines, the cries of children. And over it all, or under it, a dull and unlocatable roar, as of some form of swarming life just outside the range of human apprehension. (*WN*, 36)

This passage simultaneously recalls and reimagines Dickens's grocery. Like his predecessor, DeLillo develops a panoramic view of foodstuffs as he conveys the commotion of the food-retailing environment, emphasizing both sounds and movements, and he portrays his customers as a clumsy and distracted lot, "commit[ing]" what Dickens calls "hundreds" of little "mistakes" as they punch the mirror and fumble with bags and skid their carts. *White Noise* goes a step further in its treatment of animation, however, suggesting that the "dull and unlocatable roar" of the supermarket indicates something like the "swarming life" of the nonhuman, which Jack can intuit but not exactly apprehend. Before Jack speculates about what he cannot apprehend, though, he provides a detailed description of his phenomenal realm, rendering both human subjects and nonhuman objects as actors in the sense that Latour derives from Greimas. What Latour would call the "state of affairs" is fluid and frenetic, and both humans and nonhumans participate in its ongoing modification.

The narration achieves this effect partly by treating objects (fruits, filmy bags, carts) as material entities rather than symbols. In this sense, they are similar to the objects of the *nouveau roman*. "Their surfaces," as Alain Robbe-Grillet wrote of the objects in his own work, "are distinct and smooth, *intact*, neither suspiciously brilliant nor transparent," but nonetheless "burnished" and "bright" like nearly everything in "the neon fruit supermarket," as Allen Ginsberg named it in his well-known poem "A Supermarket in California" (1956).[27] Ginsberg's poem, in contrast to this portion of DeLillo's novel, deploys food-objects as potent symbols. As the speaker ambles through the store, he encounters Walt Whitman, a "childless, lonely old / grubber, poking among the meats in the refrigerator / and eyeing the grocery boys." Both humorous and sad, this image uses supermarket meats to symbolize anal eroticism, as Whitman "pokes" at them while ogling the young men in his midst. These meats are situated amid a wide array of comestibles—including produce ("What peaches and what penumbras!"), "brilliant stacks of cans," and so many "frozen delicac[ies]"—that conjure the plenitude of postwar America while ironically underscoring a certain lack, since the poem ends on a note of longing for Whitman's "lost America of love."[28] Although DeLillo's supermarket is also well stocked with dazzling items, he is less interested in symbolizing plenitude than in describing a flux of interactions between humans and nonhumans.

These descriptions render mundane events—"Apples and lemons tumbled in twos and threes to the floor when someone took a fruit from certain places in the stacked array" (*WN*, 36)—while intimating that a mysterious vitality underlies the apprehensible realm of objects. Striving to convey "a kind of radiance in dailiness," DeLillo not only shares Bennett's "sensuous enchantment with the everyday world" but also expands a familiar claim of modernist literature and visual art, a claim of surrealism in particular.[29] According to Juan A. Suárez, citing Walter Benjamin, the surrealists "demonstrated that, despite its homogenous, standardized façade, the material life of modernity was a porous terrain pitted with enigmas, pregnant with repressed histories, and driven by its own forms of automatism independent of consciousness and intention."[30] André Breton, for instance, explored what Suárez calls "the feasibility of objective automatism" by venturing to the flea market, "searching for objects," as he writes in *Nadja* (1928), "that can be found nowhere else: old-fashioned, broken, useless, almost incomprehensible, even perverse."[31] For Breton and other surrealists, the flea market contained objects that could provoke wonder and foster creativity by interrupting the ordinary routines of perception and cognition.[32] DeLillo is more a realist than a surrealist, but his supermarket is no less a site of wonder. As Jack looks around, he sees a "standardized façade," but he also begins to marvel at what might be beyond or beneath the surface, sensing the presence of what could be called a semiautonomous nonhuman sphere.

This sphere is figured throughout the novel in two ways. Short sentences describe actions that involve but do not exactly include human beings: "Blue jeans tumbled in the dryer" (*WN*, 18). These actions—"The radio came on" (*WN*, 203)—occur alongside the main action of the plot, the various dramas involving Jack, Steffie, Murray, Jack's wife, Babette, and the other human actors. In addition, DeLillo endows the nonhuman with something like its own voice, regularly interrupting Jack's narration with lists of consumer brands—"Dacron, Orlon, Lycra, Spandex" (*WN*, 18)—as though the "dull and unlocatable roar" were transformed momentarily into commodities naming themselves. And yet, even as certain narrative strategies separate human from nonhuman, others underscore their interpenetration. "A voice on the loudspeaker said: Kleenex Softique, your truck's blocking the entrance" (*WN*, 36). To whom is this utterance addressed? The ambiguity here is crucial. On the one hand, DeLillo is merely representing a familiar occurrence: a supermarket employee broadcasting a message to the delivery personnel. On the other hand, he is calling attention to the strangeness of an utterance wherein a disembodied, electronic voice notifies a commodity about its truck. As in "Blue jeans tumbled in the dryer," the grammar of the sentence implies, but does not exactly include, a human subject. At these moments and others, then, it is not that DeLillo is erasing the human but that he is blurring the distinction between human and nonhuman by calling attention to their mutual entanglement.

Understood like this, *White Noise* engages a central tension within Western modernity as Latour has defined it. For Latour, modernity is characterized by two sets of practices: translation and purification. The first "creates mixtures between entirely new types of beings, hybrids of nature and culture," whereas the second "creates two entirely distinct ontological zones: that of human beings on the one hand; that of nonhumans on the other."[33] In Latour's view, therefore, modern epistemology scrupulously maintains a whole set of binaries—human/nonhuman, subject/object, society/nature, mind/matter—despite the widespread proliferation of entities such as cyborgs, hybrids of human and machine. Such hybrids attained prominence in the mid-1980s. DeLillo was putting the finishing touches on *White Noise* when Donna Haraway's now-canonical "Manifesto for Cyborgs" (1985) was under consideration at the *Socialist Review*. One of the earliest attempts to conceptualize the posthuman, the "Manifesto" would go on to inspire later works, by thinkers such as Katherine Hayles and Cary Wolfe, that challenge the logic of purification, the axiomatic distinction between human and non-human, as Latour has described it. "So my cyborg myth," Haraway writes, "is about transgressed boundaries, potent fusions, and dangerous possibilities."[34] *White Noise* is not a story of cyborgs, but its send-up of American suburbia nonetheless troubles the neat division between human and non-human, especially in its supermarket scenes, which depict nonhumans as social actors whose agency Jack is just beginning to fathom.

AGENCY IN THE SUPERMARKET

Still, Jack's observations do not amount to anything like a fully formed sociology. He sees the interactions all around him, and he speculates about the possibility of nonhuman agency, but he never develops a theory to account for what he observes and intuits. Jack, in other words, is no Bruno Latour. Conversely, when the sociologist turns to the supermarket, he does not mean to construct a dense, novelistic impression of the site but to illustrate two of his most challenging theoretical claims: that the social includes the nonhuman and that agency is irreducible to subjective intentionality. Yet DeLillo and Latour nevertheless appear to be exploring similar questions. Rather than treating *Reassembling the Social* as a theoretical framework for interpreting *White Noise*, therefore, I want to imagine the sociologist and the novelist as collaborators, attempting to apprehend the sociality of the same site with very different disciplinary and discursive tools. How might their respective approaches to the supermarket become mutually illuminating?

The supermarket that Jack inhabits, circa 1985, evolved from the nineteenth-century grocery store. Before Clarence Saunders, the proprietor of Piggly Wiggly, developed the concept of self-service retail, shoppers relied on a clerk to fetch merchandise from behind the counter. While this practice helped to forge amiable and loyal relationships between customers and employees, it was terribly inefficient, so grocers sought an alternative. Following the model of Piggly Wiggly, which opened in 1916, the Great Atlantic and Pacific Tea Company (A&P) transferred the task of selecting goods and products to the customers themselves. A&P stores spread throughout North America during the 1920s, but the first true supermarket did not appear until 1930, when Michael J. Cullen, a former Kroger Company employee, opened King Kullen (whose name is a riff on "King Kong") in an abandoned garage in Jamaica, Queens, just east of Manhattan. "Pile it high, and sell it low" was his slogan. Combining Saunders's self-service paradigm with other innovations—separate product departments, discount pricing, heavy marketing, and volume selling—made King Kullen a great success, especially during the Great Depression, as consumers grew increasingly sensitive to food prices.[35]

Supermarkets proliferated wildly across the United States during the postwar era. Car friendly and bountifully stocked, they were the right food-retailing establishment for the developing suburbs. Today, with ample parking lots and great selection, they lure us with the promise of one-stop shopping. They also lure us with their design, layout, and selling techniques, all of which have some basis in the academic social sciences. In fact, when the 1959 meeting of the Super Market Institute took place in Atlantic City, it could have been mistaken, according to *Time* magazine, for "a meeting of circus showmen or of sociologists." Amid cutthroat competition, *Time* suggests, "today's supermarket operators must be both showmen and sociologists to sell their goods." For Kroger, this meant "putting lounges in all its new supermarkets, with foam-rubber sofas, partitions to dampen noise, vending machines that serve drinks and food." Other companies invested in "easy-touch cash register[s]" or "circuslike kiddy corners and amusements," including a "cartoon theater." In addition, staff went back to school. Both independent and chain retailers put their checkout clerks through an obligatory training course at the University of Houston—"Grocery Checking with Charm"—that emphasized the fundamentals of "personality and poise, how to dress and make up properly, how to discuss problems with customers, how to stand on a hard floor all day without becoming grouchy."[36] Within the booming postwar economy, the success of any supermarket depended on a carefully orchestrated performance that was informed, from beginning to end, by the insights of marketing science and motivational research, enterprises that drew extensively from the resources of academic sociology and psychology.[37]

It is this triangulation of sociological thought, everyday-life practice, and quotidian spectacle that makes the supermarket an ideal site for investigating the problematic of nonhuman agency. I have been suggesting that an interest in this problematic brought DeLillo and Latour there, but they were not alone. In fact, consumer advocates often worry that human intentionality is being overwhelmed at the supermarket by the pernicious forces of retail marketing and design. Vance Packard, in his best-selling *Hidden Persuaders* (1957), was among the first to sound the alarm: "Large-scale efforts are being made, often with impressive success, to channel our unthinking habits, or purchasing decisions, and our thought processes by the use of insights gleaned from psychiatry and the social sciences."[38] These efforts included innovative packaging meant to "hypnotize the woman," as well as floor plans meant to encourage the casual, dazed ambling that is so crucial to "impulse buying."[39] Following Packard, it became commonplace to lament the plight of the supermarket shopper, especially the housewife. For William D. Zabel, a lawyer and former humanities professor at MIT, she was "the most exploited American consumer," thoroughly incapable of making rational choices, always drawn to the unreasonably marked-up item, and ill equipped to outmaneuver the corporate marketeers. "She may as well close her eyes and pick a package at random," he asserts. "She probably often does just that." (By contrast, Zabel notes, "The most pampered American consumer"—the American man buying booze—"has no such problems in his liquor store.")[40]

As one might expect, the supermarket has fared just as poorly in literary and cultural criticism, where it is often figured not as a site of corporate conspiracy and hapless consumption but as a symbol of American cultural degradation and anti-intellectualism. In *A Sad Heart at the Supermarket*, a collection of essays published in 1965, Randall Jarrell articulates a firm opposition between the culture of intellectuals, whom he describes as a "looked-down-on-class," and the culture of rapacious consumers.[41] Jarrell maintains the opposition between high culture and everything else, an expanding middlebrow. Leslie Fiedler provides a somewhat more nuanced perspective:

> For a long time the index of literacy has crept inexorably upward, the paperbacks in supermarkets have proliferated until there is scarcely room for bread and milk; and the boards of directors of large corporations have invited intellectuals to lecture their junior executives on Dostoevski and Kierkegaard and Freud. Most appalling of all, in the past couple of years, for the first time in our history, more Americans have attended cultural events than have paid to watch sports.[42]

What is obvious here is that Fiedler understands the rise of middlebrow literature, represented by the supermarket paperback, to be an indication of cultural stasis marked by the retreat of a well-developed literary vanguard and the advance of junior executives casually consuming the classics. What is less clear, however, is that Fiedler is implicitly channeling Dwight Macdonald, who published a theory of middlebrow culture several years earlier in *Partisan Review*.[43] Macdonald memorably described the "tepid ooze of Midcult" as a falsification and exploitation of highbrow art by the industries of culture, a process whereby the formal innovations of the avant-garde are repackaged as mere entertainment.[44] Midcult was neither authentic (like the folk tradition) nor ambitious (like highbrow art) but an inauspicious combination of the two that, by virtue of being generally tolerable, eventuated in a tepid ooze across otherwise disparate spheres of American society. Like Fiedler, Macdonald understood the supermarket to play a crucial role in the literary manifestation of middlebrow culture. "This is a magazine-reading country," he explains. "When one comes back from abroad, the two displays of American abundance that dazzle one are the supermarkets and the newsstands. There are no British equivalents of our Midcult magazines like *Atlantic* and *The Saturday Review*."[45]

While foreign travel seems to have given Macdonald the capacity to be newly, if also ironically, "dazzled" by the American supermarket, foreigners themselves were not uniformly receptive to its arrival.[46] In France, local butchers who were being driven out of business by *la méthode américaine* referred to the influx of supermarkets as "the plague."[47] In Japan, the first supermarkets took on "the appearance of monsters" descending on local grocers and "spreading over the country like wildfire."[48] Yet not all cultures were so alarmed by this monstrosity. In parts of Italy, for instance, the supermarket was welcomed with open arms. When the Minimax chain opened a Rome store in 1965, *Time* reports, "it might have been the premiere of a new Fellini film."[49] Like hypermarket grand openings in France, Minimax grand openings were spectacular events: "Row after row of limousines pulled up, cameras clicked on all sides, and the chic, smartly dressed guests sipped Scotch and martinis as they ogled a pop art exhibition that included plastic turkeys, fish, steaks and a display of Andy Warhol's stacked Brillo Boxes."[50] Following the success of events like these, the mid-1960s saw the full realization of the supermarket's entertainment potential. Thanks to ABC, the 1966 television season included *Supermarket Sweep*, a game show involving the fast-paced, competitive pilfering of foodstuffs, which was "reminiscent," as one review describes it, "of the late Roller Derby."[51] Eventually *Supermarket Sweep* would become, like the site from which it takes both its name and its mise-en-scène, an international sensation, with a London Tesco staging a mock-up of the show featuring former contestants trying to duplicate their feats of theatrical pseudoconsumption.

Would it be extreme to call this the origin of postmodernism? This question, taken literally, is tantamount to asking whether an entire theory and practice of cultural production in the late twentieth century has emerged out of a food-retailing institution. And yet, it is far from absurd given the supermarket's influence on canonical postmodern theory. *Learning from Las Vegas*, arguably the most influential manifesto of architectural postmodernism, began as a field study of A&P parking lots. This manifesto plays a major role in Fredric Jameson's *Postmodernism; or The Cultural Logic of Late Capitalism*, a book that continues to define the topic, and Jameson's work has been described by Terry Eagleton as "some great Californian supermarket of the mind."[52] Before getting to work on what would become *Learning from Las Vegas*, Robert Venturi, Denise Scott Brown, and Steven Izenour published "A Significance for A&P Parking Lots, or Learning from Las Vegas" in the March 1968 issue of *Architectural Forum*. This article, the authors explain, "formed the basis for the research program" that would lead, first, to a more comprehensive study of the Vegas strip and, later, to the proclamations about "the ugly and ordinary in architecture" meant to interrupt the modernist orthodoxy of Le Corbusier and the International school.[53]

The claims in *Learning from Las Vegas*, which includes the "A&P Parking Lots" article in its first section, mostly concern the outdoor built environment. The "vulgar extravaganza" of the street sign, for instance, exemplifies the new postmodernist tendency toward symbolic structures and "bold communication."[54] When the architects do briefly venture indoors, though, they discover that the A&P is a reversion to the bazaar form, "except that graphic packaging has replaced the oral persuasion of the merchant."[55] At this moment, the architects are noticing a significant displacement of agency from human to nonhuman. With the rise of self-service retailing—a phenomenon that has been dubbed the "revolution in distribution" for the twentieth century[56]—the role of the salesperson has diminished to the degree that its nonhuman counterpart, the commodity package, has acquired the function of enticing, persuading, and ultimately overpowering the customer.[57] "Commodities are designed," argues Wolfgang Fritz Haug, "to stimulate in the onlooker the desire to possess and the impulse to buy," and "[c]ommodity aesthetics," as he defines it, "is one of the most powerful forces in capitalist society."[58] This explains why consumer advocates, such as Packard and Zabel, were so alarmed by packaging-design strategies, and this might explain why Latour locates the paradox of nonhuman agency in the supermarket, a site where the "powerful forces" of the "silent salesman" are so prominently displayed.

THE DISPLAY OF AGENCY AND THE AGENCY OF DISPLAY

Yet commodity display is not a central concern of Latour's work, even though the supermarket shelf could be considered a highly developed network of nonhuman actants. DeLillo, on the other hand, exhibits dozens of commodities throughout *White Noise*, especially in the supermarket scenes featuring Murray Jay Siskind, one of the novel's more eccentric characters. Murray's observations of this site are, at first, autobiographical: "Supermarkets this large and clean and modern are a revelation to me. I spent my life in small steamy delicatessens with slanted display cabinets full of trays that hold soft wet lumpy matter in pale colors. High enough cabinets so you had to stand on tiptoes to give your order. Shouts, accents" (*WN*, 38). In contrast to the local, vaguely European grocery store that Murray recalls here, the postmodern American supermarket is a carefully designed system of display in which the customer's attention is always directed toward the packages that give undifferentiated matter an individuating figuration:

"Krylon, Rust-Oleum, Red Devil" (*WN*, 159). Furthermore, while Murray's grocery store is dense with inelegant human interaction—awkward tiptoeing and brash shouting—the postmodern supermarket is full of human-to-nonhuman contact and all but devoid of any interfacing between humans.

John Updike was the first American fiction writer to explore what this might mean. In his much-anthologized short story "A&P," a psychosexual conflict is prompted by the intrusion of the human body into a site designed to foreground the nonhuman one: "In walks these three girls in nothing but bathing suits," the story begins.[59] For the narrator, Sammy, a clerk manning the third checkout slot, these girls become an object of attention; he anatomizes their bodies ("She was a chunky kid, with a good tan and a sweet broad soft-looking can with those two crescents of white just under it"), which spurs his fantasies about their individual lives and his speculations about their shared lifeworld.[60] But the interior monologue of the clerk is not exactly what Updike means to explore. "A&P" is less about the private drama in Sammy's mind than the social conventions of the supermarket, which have been altogether upended by the presence of these girls. "I bet you could set off dynamite in an A&P," Sammy asserts, "and the people would by and large keep reaching and checking oatmeal off their lists and muttering, 'Let me see, there was a third thing, began with A, asparagus, no, ah, yes, applesauce!' or whatever it is they do mutter." By contrast, "there was no doubt" that the presence of the girls "jiggled them."[61] Not even a bomb could distract the customers away from their attention to the stuff on the shelves; it takes the scandal of scantily clad adolescents, Sammy's hyperbole suggests, to disrupt business-as-usual in the supermarket.

And yet, in a different site these girls would be no scandal whatsoever. "[I]t's one thing to have a girl in a bathing suit down on the beach," Sammy opines, "and another thing in the cool of the A&P, under the fluorescent lights, against all those stacked packages, with her feet padding along naked over our checkerboard green-and-cream rubber-tile floor." These girls are not merely out of place but out of place in a site where human attentiveness is intensely directed toward the nonhuman body. When the girls enter the supermarket with their bodies exposed, however, the technology of display (its fluorescent lights, its cool interior, its muted floor) serves to exhibit them in a way that the beach never could. Their presence is staged by their environment, which is why they are more effective than "dynamite" at distracting customers away from foodstuffs ready-to-hand. The scandal of these girls, then, is not their premature sexuality but their unwitting seizure of a display technology intended to ensure that nonhumans are always constituted as the objects of human attention. Furthermore, they reassert both human agency and human embodiment, however unaware they are of their effect on the other shoppers, in a site where non-humans are the proper agents of seduction.

The seductive power of the nonhuman body is precisely what DeLillo's Murray means to avoid when he decides to start purchasing "nonbrand items in plain white packages with simple labeling" (*WN*, 18). He explains to Jack that "[f]lavorless packaging" is the "new austerity" and that his consumption practices are deeply patriotic: "I feel I'm not only saving money but contributing to some kind of spiritual consensus. It's like World War III. Everything is white. They'll take our bright colors away and use them in the war effort" (ibid.). Likewise, Murray expresses a certain ambivalence about his colleagues' objects of study in the American Environments Department: "I understand the music, I understand the movies, I even see how comic books can tell us things. But there are full professors in this place who read nothing but cereal boxes." Not without some ambivalence of his own, Jack replies, "It's the only avant-garde we've got" (*WN*, 10). This exchange, which continues as the topic shifts, sets the stage for Murray's performance of "austerity" with nonbrand items in the supermarket a few days later. Although Murray seeks to mitigate the power of packaging in the hope of contributing to some greater "spiritual consensus," he nonetheless appreciates the aesthetics of the supermarket shelf: "Most of all I like the packages themselves. You were right, Jack. This is the last avant-garde. Bold new forms. The power to shock" (*WN*, 19).

In this conversation, which parodies the logic of the avant-garde, the two characters challenge the distinction between art and kitsch that thinkers such as Clement Greenberg and Theodor Adorno took to be axiomatic, and their dialogue is at once humorous and serious. On the one hand, we laugh at the self-important academics for their clumsy application of art-critical jargon to the objects of mass culture. Defining "packages" as "[b]old new forms" with "[t]he power to shock," they exemplify the satire of academic sociality that appears throughout the novel: "You've established a wonderful thing here with Hitler," Murray tells Jack. "You created it, you nurtured it, you made it your own. Nobody on the faculty of any college or university in this part of the country can so much as utter the word Hitler without a nod in your direction, literally or metaphorically" (*WN*, 11). On the other hand, DeLillo seems to be making a serious claim, highlighting the instability of the art/kitsch division by focusing on the stuff at the supermarket, dramatizing the central concern of pop art and calling to mind the work of Andy Warhol in particular.[62] Employing the iconography of the supermarket—the "bold new forms" of Campbell's, Brillo, Coke, Heinz, Del Monte, and other brands—Warhol did more than anyone else to complicate the dichotomy between high and low culture; as DeLillo himself put it, Warhol "obliterate[d] distinctions" between "consumerism" and "the mass production of art." This project impressed the novelist: "Interesting work," he called it, "and judging from its extraordinary reception, perhaps a little frightening as well."[63]

Warhol was drawn to supermarkets throughout his life. On January 5, 1985, about three weeks before *White Noise* appeared, he joked about "switching the price stickers" as a sly "way to shoplift."[64] Ten years earlier, he reveled in the pleasures of the site: "I lived next to a Gristedes grocery for twelve years," he wrote in *The Philosophy of Andy Warhol* (1975), "and every day I would go in and drift around the aisles, picking out what I wanted—that's a ritual I really enjoy."[65] At stores like Gristedes, a New York chain, Warhol found the imagery for some of his best-known paintings and sculptures, such as *Campbell's Soup Cans* and *Brillo Boxes*. For John Cage, these works should be understood within a certain trajectory of twentieth-century art:

> In Paris in the 20's we had Dada first, and it was followed by Surrealism. In Dada is a certain self-abnegation; in Surrealism is a certain self-pronouncement. Now, neo-Dada, which is what we have in New York in the work of Robert Rauschenberg and Jasper Johns, is followed by what's called Pop art, which is, in another sense, Surrealism. But it is not Surrealism as related to the individual, but Surrealism as related to society, so that Andy Warhol's work is like Andre Breton's, and we can equate Breton's interest in sex with Warhol's interest in supermarkets.[66]

While Cage is being somewhat elliptical, it is clear that he sees pop as an extension of surrealism, aligning Warhol's "interest in supermarkets" with Breton's "interest in sex." By doing so, he suggests a new way of thinking about both Warhol and the relationship between Warhol and DeLillo. Surrealism, as Suárez persuasively argues, pursued the question of "objective automatism" by concentrating on the enigmas of the material everyday at sites like flea markets. This "surrealist-object research," as he terms it, "foreshadowed the ideas of a number of contemporary theorists of science," namely, Bruno Latour.[67] Above all, Breton and his cohort challenged the division between subject and object that Latour takes to be artificial. Casting Cage's statement in light of Suárez's argument, then, I want to suggest that Warhol's "interest in supermarkets" takes up the problem of nonhuman agency, which is so important both to DeLillo and to ANT.

Two years after Irving Blum exhibited *Campbell's Soup Cans* at the Ferus Gallery in Los Angeles in 1962, and three years after Claes Oldenburg opened *The Store* in New York's Lower East Side, Warhol participated in the *American Supermarket* exhibition at the Bianchini Gallery (figure 1.1). In that show—which featured a half-dozen pop artists, a commercial designer specializing in food replicas, and a gallerist taking orders on a grocer's

1.1. *The American Supermarket at the Bianchini Gallery*, New York, 1964. Unidentified photographer. Held in the Lucy R. Lippard Papers, Archives of American Art, Smithsonian Institution.

pad—Warhol exhibited a readymade, a stack of autographed Campbell's soup cans; a painting from the *Campbell's Soup Cans* series; and an installation of various box sculptures, including the famous *Brillo Boxes*. A few months prior to this, the *Brillo Boxes* had been unveiled at the Stable Gallery in New York, occasioning a powerful, and still-influential, interpretation from Arthur Danto in his address to the American Philosophical Association. Danto's address, entitled "The Artworld," grapples with a question ("What makes it art?") that has been a persistent concern ever since Marcel Duchamp introduced the readymade.[68]

But what happens when the *Brillo Boxes*, hollow wooden sculptures whose surfaces were painted and silk-screened to replicate the appearance of their prototype, are displayed in a gallery that is designed to *mimic* a supermarket? Certainly they raise questions that are not exactly Duchamp's questions, however comfortably they fit into the anti-aesthetic tradition. In fact, their juxtaposition with an actual readymade, the autographed soup cans, serves only to emphasize their contrast with Duchamp's *Fountain*, and their inclusion in the supermarket art gallery—a site where the contextual differences between art-world consumption and mass consumption have been mitigated—denies them the reflexive specificity of Duchamp's objects. This is why Martha Buskirk has called the box sculptures "remade readymade[s]": they appropriate a readymade icon, yet they themselves are original creations. In this sense, they echo what Buskirk calls "Duchamp's declared indifference." Their fabrication required a certain measure of artistic skill (the techniques of carpentry, silk-screening, and painting) to become sufficiently artless.[69] And yet, as Buskirk acknowledges, Warhol's Duchampianism stages problems that Duchamp's practice never did. Perhaps the most significant difference between the *Brillo Boxes* and the actual boxes of Brillo is that the former contain no Brillo pads. Their surface suggests a false interior; in Latourian terms, their figure is misaligned with their agency. On the surface, the *Brillo Boxes* promise to be able to do something—"SHINES ALUMINUM FAST"—that is totally betrayed by their empty insides. They figure an agency that is not their own.

In the actual supermarket, we call this false advertising. Warhol was as interested in this problem as consumer advocates like Packard. In 1963, one year after he first exhibited *Brillo Boxes* in Los Angeles, he did a series of pictures titled *Tunafish Disaster*. These pictures repeat the image of a commodity package, containing what should be ordinary A&P tuna, above newspaper copy and photos of two women, Mrs. McCarthy and Mrs. Brown (figure 1.2). Warhol took his material from a case of food poisoning in Detroit; the two women died after they had consumed contaminated fish. By concentrating on this tragedy, Warhol was engaging the widespread concern during the era that a modernizing agribusiness was producing foodstuffs unfit for human consumption. As Thomas Crow puts it, "[T]he pictures commemorate a moment when the supermarket promise of safe and abundant packaged food was disastrously broken."[70] They identify the fear, prominently expressed in 1962 by environmentalist Rachel Carson, that the efficiency of large-scale food production and distribution was masking an "ever-widening wave of death" caused by the extensive use of pesticides and other contaminants.[71]

The *Tunafish Disaster* pictures, however, are not just macabre illustrations of a debacle in food safety. Like the *Brillo Boxes*, only more severe, they visualize the subtle distinction between agency and its figuration. They do so by establishing a literal and figurative parallel between the human face and the nonhuman package: just as the smiles of McCarthy and Brown belie their tragic demise, so too the ordinary can of tuna fails to disclose its deadly contents. The package promises safe food, but it actually contains lethal poison. This tuna can kill you, but you would never know that by looking at it. While DeLillo implies that generic foodstuffs—"a white package of bacon without a plastic window for viewing a representative slice" (*WN*, 18)—do not possess the same aesthetic appeal as brand-name items with "[t]he power to shock," Warhol is not making a

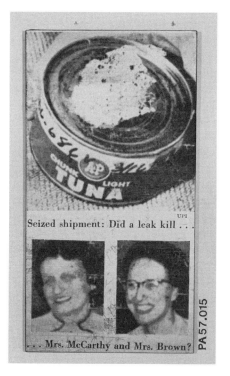

1.2. Andy Warhol, *Tunafish Disaster*, 1963. © 2014
The Andy Warhol Foundation for the Visual Arts,
Inc./Artists Rights Society (ARS), New York.

point about commodity aesthetics. Rather, he is drawing attention to the *spectrum* of agency, or to what Latour calls the "many metaphysical shades between full causality and sheer inexistence" (*RS*, 72). Who or what is the agent of death in the *Tunafish Disaster*? It is not the contaminated tuna itself, nor the unknowing consumers or producers of this food item, but a combination of all these actors, and more. Death was the unfortunate result of a course of action that included both human and nonhuman participants. Even as Warhol traces the distinction between agency and its figuration, therefore, he also mediates the notion of distributed agency as it has been conceptualized by both Latour and Bennett. "Action is not simply a property of humans," Latour writes, *"but of an association of actants,"* a claim echoed by Bennett when she argues that the "locus of agency is always a human-nonhuman working group."[72] The disaster of the *Tunafish Disaster* was effected by such a working group.

Following Latour and Gilles Deleuze, Bennett often calls such working groups *assemblages*, a term denoting an ad hoc concatenation of actants whose agency exceeds that of its individual constituents. Assemblages arise in particular historical circumstances, and they are not governed by a central authority but rather appear as uneven distributions of power. The electrical grid, for instance, is "a volatile mix of coal, sweat, electromagnetic fields, computer programs, electron streams, profit motives, heat, lifestyles, nuclear fuel, plastic, fantasies of mastery, static, legislation, water, economic theory, wire, and wood."[73] It is perhaps easiest to appreciate the agency of this assemblage when it breaks down, a point that Bennett makes by examining the 2003 North American blackout. When the grid ceased to function on August 14, leaving millions in the dark, its agency was felt far and wide.

DeLillo concludes *White Noise* by considering the agency of a much simpler assemblage: supermarket shelving. The latter is not exactly "volatile" like the grid, but it does comprise multiple constituents—wood, metal, plastic, marketing science, interior design, corporate greed, laboring bodies, and so on—in a contingent setup that could be disrupted at any moment. "The supermarket shelves have been rearranged," begins the final paragraph of the novel. "It happened one day without warning" (*WN*, 325). The effects ramify throughout the site:

> There is agitation and panic in the aisles, dismay in the faces of older shoppers. They walk in a fragmented trance, stop and go, clusters of well-dressed figures frozen in the aisles, trying to figure out the pattern, discern the underlying logic, trying to remember where they'd seen the Cream of Wheat. They see no reason for it, find no sense in it. The scouring pads are with the hand soap now, the condiments are scattered. The older the man or woman, the more carefully dressed and groomed. Men in Sansabelt slacks and bright knit shirts. Women with a powdered and fussy look, a self-conscious air, prepared for some anxious event. They turn into the wrong aisle, peer along the shelves, sometimes stop abruptly, causing other carts to run into them. Only the generic food is where it was, white packages plainly labeled. The men consult lists, the women do not. There is a sense of wandering now, an aimless and haunted mood, sweet-tempered people taken to the edge. (*WN*, 325–26)

Like much of the novel, this final scene somehow manages to be both hyperbolic ("panic in the aisles") and realistic, both ludicrous and poignant. We smile at these shoppers, anonymous men and women who "scrutinize the small print on packages, wary of a second level of betrayal" (*WN*, 326).

But it also seems that DeLillo wants to capture the subtle yet definite power of shelving. The way that shelving facilitates the shopping experience becomes fully apparent at the moment of its unexpected rearrangement; its agency manifests in and as its effect on the discombobulated and distressed customers who "try to work their way through confusion" (ibid.). *White Noise* concludes, then, by dwelling on how the material environment mediates both subjectivity and sociality. The transformed site produces a new set of consuming subjects, shoppers who are not just clumsy and distracted, as in earlier episodes, but agitated, dismayed, on the brink of lashing out. The site in this scene is not a passive background for narrative action; it is active in the Latourian sense. While DeLillo tacitly acknowledges the role of human agency by opening the description with a passive-voice construction—"The supermarket shelves have been rearranged"—he makes no mention of supermarket employees; rather, his emphasis falls on the shelves themselves. They surprise the shoppers, prompt a range of affective reactions, and fundamentally reorient the social experience.

"But in the end," the narrator ultimately decides, "it doesn't matter what [the shoppers] see or think they see. The terminals are equipped with holographic scanners, which decode the binary of every item, infallibly" (*WN*, 326). A paranoid reading would take DeLillo to be implying that humans are being displaced, rendered obsolete by thinking machines, yet he appears to be making a somewhat different point. Focusing on the interface between the scanner and the bar code, he reminds us that humans are not the only actors interacting at the supermarket. Something like nonhuman sociality is everywhere. The bar code enables the scanner and the package to speak a "language of waves and radiation" that is "just outside the range of human apprehension" (*WN*, 326, 36). *White Noise* strives to acknowledge that language—not to make it apprehensible, exactly, but to mark its presence. If you pause to listen, you will hear it, the "ambient roar" (*WN*, 326) of everyday life, the white noise all around you, a low drone signaling that you are, as Latour puts it, "folded into nonhumans."[74] To glimpse this enfolding by DeLillo's light, to see it as an implacable fact of our modernity or postmodernity, is not just to acknowledge that "[s]ocialness is shared with nonhumans in an almost promiscuous way" but also to appreciate Latour's more radical claim that there can be "no relation whatsoever between 'the material and the social world,'" precisely "because it is this very division which is a complete artifact," an invention of our epistemology.[75]

This claim, which rejects a fundamental dichotomy in both philosophical thought and common sense, exemplifies how Latour's work, from his early ethnographies of science to his most recent anthropology of the modern, functions as a "canny provocation to our entrenched ways of thinking."[76] Inspired by Latour's engagement with the literary—his adaptation of narratology as well as his faith in "the resource of fiction"—the next four chapters of this book examine a cluster of provocations that his writings offer to literary studies, not to apply ANT as an interpretive framework for literature but in an effort to grasp how novels and novelists explore the nature of sociality. While Latour pursues such exploration through the methods of the social sciences, through ethnographic research and site-specific fieldwork, novelists have their own techniques for figuring and investigating the social, especially as in the case of DeLillo, when they define particular zones of action and interaction, when they engage in what could be called site specification, endowing generic locales (the supermarket) with particular properties ("swarming life just outside the range of human apprehension"). The section that follows, then, considers four "test sites" of postwar American fiction—dumps, roads, ruins, and asylums—that raise different yet related questions about the social and its constituents.

The first of these sites, the dump, is in many cases the final resting place of the goods on the supermarket shelf, the Krylon and Rust-Oleum, now spent, that constitute the residue of mass consumption. While DeLillo thematizes the link between consumption and waste throughout his work, the emphasis of chapter 2 falls on a more radical project, William S. Burroughs's *Naked Lunch* (1959), a novel so littered with excrement and detritus that it earned the label "literary sewage," in full recognition that consumption and waste go hand in hand. "Two aspects of American civilization strike almost everyone," wrote John A. Kouwenhoven in *Harper's* the year that *Naked Lunch* was first published, "the abundance it enjoys and the waste it permits (if it does not enjoy that too)."[77]

Test Sites

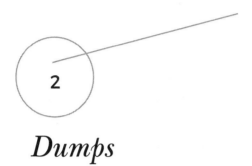

2

Dumps

When Mierle Laderman Ukeles, artist-in-residence at New York City's Department of Sanitation, refers to the Fresh Kills Landfill as "the city's most comprehensive, democratic social sculpture," she directs attention to the fact that dumps are collective constructions.[1] "Each of us living or working in or passing through New York City between early 1951 and March 2001," she explains, "has made this place. It is ours."[2] Don DeLillo completes the chiasmus: his best-selling *Underworld* (1997) argues not only that it is ours but also that *we are its*. "[G]arbage rose first," asserts Jesse Detwiler, the self-proclaimed "garbage archaeologist" in DeLillo's novel, "inciting people to build a civilization in response, in self-defense."[3] According to Detwiler, we can thank waste for what we call culture as well. "We had to find ways to discard our waste," he elaborates in his "talk show" manner, "[a]nd it forced us to develop the logic and rigor that would lead to systematic investigations of reality, to science, art, music, mathematics" (*UW*, 287). This remarkable assertion provokes incredulity: "Do you really believe that?" asks protagonist Nick Shay, a waste management executive. "Bet your ass I believe it," Detwiler retorts. "I teach it at UCLA. I take my students into garbage dumps and make them understand the civilization they live in" (ibid.). Yet the novel suggests that these field trips, although led by an archaeologist, involve no archaeological work, no excavation. The dump is not a massive trove of data for Detwiler, but a dramatic setting for him to hammer home his thesis: "We make stupendous amounts of garbage, then we react to it," he declaims. "Garbage comes first, then we build a system to deal with it" (*UW*, 288).

Actual garbage archaeologists, by contrast, undertake painstaking excavations of dumps. "Taken as a whole the garbage of the United States," write William Rathje and Cullen Murphy of the Garbage Project, "is a mirror of American society."[4] Because landfills "are not vast composters" but "vast mummifiers," the Garbage Project, an archaeological initiative headed by Rathje at the University of Arizona, has been able to unearth "such preserved perishables as heads of lettuce, Kaiser rolls, hot dogs, corncobs with their kernels intact, guacamole, and literally tons of datable, readable newspapers," all of which contribute to an understanding of "changing lifeways" in the United States since the end of World War II, when so-called sanitary landfills became the dominant mode of refuse disposal.[5] These archaeologists, who share with Ukeles a sense of the dump as a great collective construction, assume that our trash can teach us both who we are and how we have changed; for them, and for DeLillo as well, the dump speaks eloquently about the society that created it, which is why Fresh Kills is such a key figure in *Underworld*. Beholding "acres of mountained garbage," Nick's colleague Brian Glassic feels a sudden "sting of enlightenment," for he finally understands the American "mass metabolism," the way that all our "appetites and hankerings [and] sodden second thoughts" are fully materialized in this "mountain of wrack" (*UW*, 184–85).

More than a recurring motif in *Underworld*, the dump is DeLillo's answer to the White Whale, a densely symbolic figure within a Great American Novel, as Lawrence Buell has defined the genre, one of those "doorstop books" from the late 1990s that "tried to sum up the century" while representing the whole of American society.[6] But what form would the novel take if, instead of merely including the dump as a setting or a symbol, it aspired *to be* a kind of dump itself—the literary counterpart to an actual landfill? The answer, I want to propose, would look something like William S. Burroughs's *Naked Lunch* (1959). The latter not only visualizes a welter of "literal garbage" decomposing in a dumpsite, which Burroughs names the "junk world," but also assumes the formal structure of a landfill, a site governed by the logic of putrefaction.[7] Rather than simply representing the dump, in other words, Burroughs enacts a mimetic relation to it, thereby converting spatial into literary form. This conversion, which relies on a set of experimental techniques that flout the conventions of realism, draws a very peculiar image of sociality—a network, in Latourian terms, composed of numerous actors surrounded by a "gelatinous substance" (variously termed "rotten ectoplasm," "green slime," and, most often, "flesh") that they themselves produce as they decompose (*NL*, 5, 37, 15, 185). To move through the "junk world," then, is to encounter heaps of waste matter, as well as a rather stark example of what Latour calls "translation," the process whereby subjects and objects, humans and nonhumans, congeal into "entirely new types of beings," ontological hybrids that only Burroughs could have invented.[8] Burroughs offers us, in this sense, an extreme vision of the social, an "exacerbated, morbid, and perverted" account, as one early reader described it, of the social as an association of humans, nonhumans, and monstrous beings otherwise defined.[9] Indeed, while *Naked Lunch* can still scandalize readers with its frenzied adumbrations of filth, its most radical contribution to literary history is its sociology—its depiction of a social site where discrete entities are constantly translating into hybrids, undergoing a process of putrefaction whose end result is to render everything as a single substance.

A garbage archaeologist reading *Naked Lunch* might call this substance *leachate*. This term, in the lexicon of waste management, refers to the "watery potage that drools to the bottom" of every landfill and eventually seeps out in staggering quantities. Fresh Kills, for instance, pours at least a million gallons of leachate into New York Harbor on a daily basis.[10] Alternatively, she might think of it as either *slops*, the "stew of such things as coffee grounds, fruit parts, rotten vegetable bits, cigarette butts, grit of unknown origin, and the sort of gooey canned mush epitomized by Chef Boyardee ravioli," or *fines*, "the vast connecting mixture of tiny bits of paper, metal, glass, plastic, dirt, grit, and former nutrients that suffuses every landfill like a kind of grainy lymph."[11] In any case, she would be noticing that, without deploying the jargon of waste management, Burroughs portrays a network of actors in various states of decay and disarray: "His flesh turns viscid, transparent jelly that drifts away in a green mist" (*NL*, 87). Such imagery came to Burroughs while he was living in Tangier—the site where most of *Naked Lunch* was composed—yet still contemplating (and, quite often, reviling) American society and culture.[12] Historians have demonstrated that postwar America was both a "consumers' republic" and a "throwaway society," suggesting that the rise in mass consumption generated unprecedented amounts of waste and thereby created new problems in both sanitation and waste management.[13] Without addressing these problems explicitly, Burroughs imagined his own version of a "throwaway society" while living beyond the geographical borders of the United States. "I have a strange feeling here of being outside any social context," he wrote to Allen Ginsberg from Tangier on October 29, 1956.[14] There, at times feeling isolated from society, he produced a striking contribution to sociological thought.

WRITING AND DUMPING

To develop some sense of that contribution, you could start by envisioning the material context of its production, the site where Burroughs composed *Naked Lunch*. Although the novel, as two prominent Burroughs scholars explain, "accumulated through a decade of travel and turmoil on four con-tinents," it was written mostly in Tangier between 1953 and 1958 (*NL*, 233). Officially an international zone from 1923 to 1956, Tangier was controlled by a committee of eight countries, including the United States, which meant that its central governing body was, as historian Iain Finlayson writes, "inherently weak [and] fundamentally flawed by constant and recur-ring disputes between the various nations concerned."[15] Moreover, by the 1950s, the city had earned a reputation, not entirely unjustified, of being "seedy, salacious, decadent [and] degenerate," the ideal place for Burroughs, as he himself put it, to be "shitting out all [his] educated Middlewest back-ground once and for all."[16] However, the material context for *Naked Lunch* that I have in mind is not the city per se, but the small room in the Villa Muniria where its author sat at his typewriter. Alan Ansen suggests that Burroughs's "living quarters [were] tantamount to the worst inn's worst room," and Paul Bowles reports that this room was, literally, a dump:

> There were hundreds of pages of yellow foolscap all over the floor, month after month, with heel prints on them, rat droppings, bits of old sandwiches, sardines. It was filthy. I said, "What is all that Bill?" He said, "That's what I'm working on." "Do you have a copy of it?" I asked. "No," he said. I couldn't help myself from saying, "Why don't you pick it up?" Candy bar in hand, he said, "Oh, it'll get picked up someday." As he finished a page, he'd just throw it on the floor.[17]

Surrounded by "literal garbage," Burroughs first issued the *Naked Lunch* manuscript in a series of "deposition episodes," to borrow the language of waste management, ripping sheets from the typewriter and tossing them onto the floor amid half-eaten sandwiches and rotting fish.[18] If, as Diana Fuss has argued, "interiors shape imagination," then this room surely influ-enced the creation of what Burroughs called his "saleable product," the "ex-treme material" that eventually made its way into the novel (*LG*, 21).[19] He did argue, after all, that "[t]here is only one thing a writer can write about: *what is in front of his senses at the moment of writing*" (*NL*, 184; italics in origi-nal). At such moments, and during periods of procrastination, garbage so-licited his attention:

> All day I had been finding pretexts to avoid work, reading magazines, making fudge, cleaning my shot-gun, washing the dishes, going to bed with Kiki, tying the garbage up in neat parcels and putting it out for the collector—(if you put it out in a waste basket or any other container they will steal the container every time. I was going to chain a basket to my doorstep but it's like too much trouble. So I put it out in packages—buying food for dinner, picking up a junk script.

So finally I say: "Now you must work" and smoke some tea and sit down and out it comes all in one piece like a glob of spit. (*LG*, 17)

This passage begins the letter to Ginsberg on February 7, 1954, that contains the celebrated "talking asshole" episode in *Naked Lunch*.[20] After detailing his consternation regarding domestic garbage disposal, Burroughs likens his prose to a "glob" of saliva and phlegm. Paired with Bowles's account of what Fuss terms the "theater of composition," this description defines *Naked Lunch*, or at least its mid-1950s manifestation, as an admixture of bodily wastes, spit coughed into the dumpsite that was Burroughs's writing space.[21] Burroughs regularly identified writing with expectorating—with expelling a "hoard" of "verbal garbage."[22] No wonder he would complain to Ginsberg less than a year later: "[E]verything I write disgusts me … I really feel *awful*" (*LG*, 86–87). Of course, whatever disgust he felt at the time—"coughing and spitting in the junk-sick dawn" (*NL*, 5)—pales in comparison to the experience of some notable early readers.

"I have read the book," wrote Justice Paul C. Reardon of the Massachusetts Supreme Court, "and found it to be a revolting miasma of unrelieved perversion and disease … It is, in truth, literary sewage."[23] Reardon wrote the dissenting opinion for the court decision that cleared *Naked Lunch* of obscenity charges in 1966. Burroughs's text, considered "sewage" by Reardon and often treated as a kind of waste by its author, was put on trial numerous times during the early 1960s in order to determine whether it was "worthless trash," utterly without redeeming social value.[24] After its first trial in 1960, Justice Julius J. Hoffman wrote that it was "not exactly a wild prose picnic in the style of Kerouac," but nevertheless not obscene, even though it depicted "exacerbated, morbid, and perverted sex."[25] Kerouac himself, an early champion of Burroughs's work, had his own struggles with *Naked Lunch*; in the winter of 1957, when he visited his friend in Tangier, he had to stop transcribing the manuscript after the first two chapters because "he had nightmares of great long balonies coming out of [his] mouth."[26]

Still, the most visceral reaction to the novel came from an anonymous reviewer, later identified as John Willett, writing for the *Times Literary Supplement* in 1963. "Struggling upstream through [*Naked Lunch*] is not unlike wading through the drains of a big city," he wrote in a piece simply titled "UGH."[27] Anticipating Reardon, he likened the reading process to swimming in raw sewage and complained that the novel's "stereotyped debris" seems to have the "texture" of "grey porridge," not unlike what landfill operators call fines.[28] Donald Malcolm, writing for the *New Yorker* the same year that Willett published "UGH," also criticized the novel's texture, what he termed its "thickening welter of degradations," finally arguing that the text, considered trash, "might as fittingly have been issued in a paper bag as between hard covers."[29] And when the text was initially presented to the man who would be the first to issue it, Maurice Girodias of Olympia Press in Paris, he turned it down, for he "couldn't physically read the stuff," as it appeared that "[t]he ends of the pages [had been] eaten away by the rats or something."[30]

Thus, if one were to ask what the text of *Naked Lunch* is, as Carol Loranger does,[31] this archive would provide variations on a single answer: trash, waste, a glob of spit, literary sewage, and verbal garbage. Following the precedent set by this archive, while avoiding the irritation expressed by some of Burroughs's early readers, I want to suggest that *Naked Lunch* is, or aims to be, the textual manifestation of a dumpsite, even as it represents a throwaway society. By this I do not mean that it is "trash" by a "mentally sick" author, as it was described by Justice Eugene A. Hudson during its trial in Boston, but that it gives literary form to the physical processes of decomposition and unformation.[32] These processes generate an effluvial by-product that can be likened to "grey porridge" while effecting a strange sort of disfiguration throughout the novel: embodied subjects dissipating into whorls of flesh, as well as physical objects degrading from brand-name commodities (Kotex, K-Y) into waste matter. It would not be an exaggeration to say that during the 1950s—when he felt "a great formless menace pressing on" him (*LG*, 43)—Burroughs was obsessed with form, the dynamic of unformation, and the relation between form and material. "When I try to pressure myself into organizing production, to impose some form on material," he wrote to Ginsberg on February 7, 1954, "the effort catapults me into a sort of madness" (*LG*, 21). Indeed, attempting to shape the manuscript into a novel exacted a great psychological toll: "Trying to write novel. Attempt to organize material is more painful than anything I ever experienced" (*LG*, 27). Occasionally, this pain yielded to dejection: "Everything I have written reads like notes for a novel, fragments. The final effort of creation, the novel itself, I can't achieve. I can't force it, and it won't come to me ... All I can write is pieces of a novel, and the pieces don't fit together" (*LG*, 73–74, 76). To be sure, "how to weave it all together," as Ginsberg recalls, was the major compositional problem facing Burroughs during much of the 1950s (*LG*, 9).

By the end of the decade, though, he had settled on the *routine* as his primary formal and organizational device. "Routines," he explains, "are completely spontaneous and proceed from whatever fragmentary knowledge you have. In fact, a routine is by nature fragmentary, inaccurate. There is no such thing as an exhaustive routine, nor does the scholarly-type mind run to routines" (*LG* 78). *Naked Lunch* is a collection of routines, "fragmentary" episodes that are, as Frederick Whiting puts it, "locally coherent (if utterly fantastic) but exceedingly difficult to synthesize into a coherent whole."[33] Each routine, in other words, includes the key components of a coherent chapter—characters, conflict, causality—but the collection of routines does not add up to a novel, at least not in the conventional sense. The result is a text that appears to be less aspiring to the novel form than devolving from it, manifesting in its narrative structure the dynamic of unformation that it so frequently depicts: "Some way he make himself all soft like a blob of jelly and surround me so nasty . . . and he stink like an old rotten cantaloupe" (*NL*, 15). Given that garbage has been conceptualized as "the formlessness from which form takes flight," it is plausible that this dynamic suggested itself to Burroughs as he tidied his "filthy" apartment, avoiding the manuscript by "tying the garbage up in neat parcels," imposing form on a different sort of unruly material.[34] Or it may have become apparent to him as he sauntered around Tangier, a city that he understood, in contrast to "the grey horror of a Midwest suburb," to be "unstable" (*LG*, 27, 53).

After "a series of Kafkian incidents," presumably hallucinatory metamorphoses, he began to appreciate the unformation and decomposition all around him: "There is something special about Tanger [*sic*]. It is the only place when I am there I don't want to be anyplace else. No stasis horror. And the beauty of this town that consists in changing combinations" (*LG*, 154). By contrast, the United States during this period provoked in him nothing but the horror of stasis: "When I was home I fell into a disgusting state of stagnation, ate and slept to excess . . . It's like I can't breathe in the U.S., especially in suburban communities. Palm beach is a real horror. No slums, no dirt, no poverty. God what a fate to live there!" (*LG*, 79). Burroughs was horrified by what we have come to call postwar containment culture; 1950s America was defined in his estimation by stagnation and sloth, particularly in the wealthy, white suburbs, where each home, as Elaine Tyler May argues, "was planned as a self-contained universe."[35] Growing up in St. Louis, the "subdivided lots" always made him feel "the impact in stomach of final loneliness and despair," so his "filthy" living conditions in Tangier, where he experienced "Kafkian incidents" and avoided "stasis horror," offered an alternative to the intolerable conditions back home: "I don't realize what a drag the U.S. can be until I hit a free country and get relief in every direction" (*LG*, 27, 76). While Burroughs was living in Tangier, then, he was still reflecting on postwar America, a society that he found deeply antipathetic. *Naked Lunch* constitutes a response to this society that is more complicated than his letters may suggest.

WASTE OBJECTS

"[N]o society," write Michael Shanks, David Platt, and William Rathje, "has ever invested more thought and resources into 'getting rid' of its unwanted remains than contemporary America."[36] Waste-management technologies pioneered in the fifties and sixties, such as the sanitary landfill, address the "ubiquity" of garbage while keeping it far from view, which is partly why, even though garbage is "everywhere, most people don't see it."[37] Burroughs's ambition, at its most fundamental, was to make garbage visible:

> An old garbage collector, face fine and yellow as Chinese ivory, blows The Blast on his dented brass horn, wakes the Spanish pimp with a hard-on. Whore staggers out through dust and shit and litter of dead kittens, carrying bales of aborted foetuses, broken condoms, bloody Kotex, shit wrapped in bright color comics. A vast still harbor of iridescent water. Deserted gas well flares on the smoky horizon. Stink of oil and sewage. Sick sharks swim through the black water, belch sulphur from rotting livers, ignore a bloody, broken Icarus. Naked Mr. America, burning frantic with self bone love, screams out: "My asshole confounds the Louvre! I fart ambrosia and shit pure gold turds! My cock spurts soft diamonds in the morning sunlight!" He plummets from the eyeless lighthouse, kissing and jacking off in face of the black mirror, glides obliquely down with cryptic condoms and mosaic of a thousand newspapers through a drowned city of red brick to settle in black mud with tin cans and beer bottles. (NL, 63–64)

This old garbage collector certainly has his work cut out for him. "Don't you see that everywhere's littered with waste and garbage," could be his refrain, echoing the title character of John Dos Passos's *The Garbage Man*.[38] This place is a dump; there are no "neat parcels" here. The streets are littered with shit, dead kittens, aborted fetuses, broken condoms, tin cans, old newspapers, and bloody Kotex. The harbor might be "iridescent," but it reeks of "oil and sewage" and swarms with sharks whose "rotting livers" belch sulfur as they swim past a corpselike Icarus. Infatuated with his own excrement, Mr. America is in better shape, although the narrator assures us that "the slow striptease of erosion" will transform him, too, into a depleted version of himself (NL, 64). While these images are vivid, their relations to one another are somewhat opaque. On the one hand, this passage, like the routine in which it appears, is meant to be "fragmentary" and thus frustrating to "the scholarly-type mind" that would seek synthesis. On the other hand, it presents a fairly coherent "mosaic," something like the full spectrum of waste objects, a spectrum that not only includes a variety of solid wastes (human excrement, raw sewage, dead or dying bodies, fouled environments, sick creatures) but also points to shit art—"My asshole confounds the Louvre!"—anticipating the work of a contemporary painter like Chris Ofili.[39] This is a perfect example of what has been termed the "anal economy" of *Naked Lunch*, its "radical incorporation of all waste."[40]

A long tradition of anthropological thought has demonstrated that the category of waste is both unstable and contingent, produced by classification systems that are specific to a given society and culture. Mary Douglas was the first to argue that "dirt" is essentially "matter out of place," and Gay Hawkins reiterates this point in her more recent work on "the ugly, shit end of capitalism." Rather than "a fixed category of things," Hawkins asserts, waste is "an effect of classification and relations."[41] Waste and not-waste, in other words, are mutually constitutive, although Burroughs seems less interested in this dynamic than in itemizing all the objects that are categorized as waste by Western modernity. Indeed, Burroughs's old garbage collector confronts garbage, trash, rubbish, junk, offal, and excrement. The first waste objects to appear in *Naked Lunch*, the "condoms and orange peels" floating in New York City's East River, represent two different subcategories: biohazardous medical waste and compostable food (*NL*, 5). The river itself is polluted by a "silent black ooze" and "a mosaic of floating newspapers" (ibid.); here we have an industrial contaminant, an oil slick, as well as postconsumer wastepaper. Together, the sodden condoms, orange peels, and newspapers constitute *garbage*, which refers technically to both wet and dry discards, rather than *trash*, which names only the dry.[42] At other moments, though, there is plenty of trash: "broken bottles and tin cans," for instance, or "H caps and K.Y. tubes squeezed dry as bone meal in the summer sun" (*NL*, 13, 43). At still other moments, Burroughs describes "islands of rubbish," which, based on the technical definition of *rubbish*, denotes islands composed of garbage and trash, as well as the debris from construction and demolition, both of which occur often in the "shabby junk quarters" of the junk world (*NL*, 13, 7). And since *junk* indicates waste with a potential to be reclaimed, "junk quarters" refers simultaneously to sites of rampant heroin use and to the dilapidated buildings that have been repurposed by junkies.[43]

Furthermore, *Naked Lunch* depicts no shortage of wasted subjects, both junkies and cadavers, along with even stranger "mosaics" of waste, such as the *offal* that is branded "Transcendental Cuisine" at *Chez Robert*: "After-Birth Suprême de Boeuf cooked in drained crank case oil" (*NL*, 125). These mosaics often appear to be floating in some kind of waste stream—"a purulent stringy discharge streaked with blood and putrid lymph" (*NL*, 37)— flowing from disembodied "rectums" that "open, defecate and close" (*NL*, 9). It is easy to see why some of Burroughs's early readers were so disgusted, and why, much more recently, "the desire to shock, to rub one's face in human ordure" has been described by the editors of the fiftieth anniversary edition as "the book's strategic, perpetual motor."[44] *Naked Lunch* is extreme in this sense, but there are several key precedents for its treatment of waste, including American realism and naturalism. "On top of this were the rooms where they dried the 'tankage,'" begins a famous description in Upton Sinclair's *The Jungle* (1906), "the mass of brown stringy stuff that was left after the waste portions of the carcasses had had the lard and tallow dried out of them."[45] Another, perhaps more influential model was furnished by James Joyce. *Ulysses* not only taxonomizes waste objects ("waste paper, fells of sewer rodents, human excrement") but also renders wasted landscapes: "A barren land, bare waste. Vulcanic lake, the dead sea: no fish, weedless, sunk deep in the earth. No wind could lift those waves, grey metal, poisonous foggy waters ... the grey sunken cunt of the world."[46] As Joyce traces the line between sense and nonsense, moreover, he also treats language itself as a kind of detritus, which Burroughs called "verbal garbage" and Samuel Beckett called "wordshit."[47]

Both Burroughs and Beckett were influenced by the Joycean take on the materiality of language—"These heavy sands," observes Stephen Dedalus, "are language tide and wind have silted here"—yet Burroughs was more keenly interested in the brute physicality of garbage.[48] (Although *Endgame* [1957] features two characters living in ashbins, Beckett was known for his hygienic temperament. When Burroughs and Susan Sontag went to visit him in Berlin, for instance, his "beautiful atelier," Sontag reports, "was very clean and bare and white," absolutely nothing like the novelist's filthy room in Tangier.[49]) *Naked Lunch* also resonates (faintly) with another strain of twentieth-century writing: the lyrical tradition extending from T. S. Eliot to A. R. Ammons. *The Waste Land* names a wide array of waste objects—"empty bottles," "sandwich papers," "cigarette ends," "broken fingernails"—and it describes a "dead land" whose "river sweats oil and tar," which is why it has been called "one of the most abject texts in English literature."[50] These objects and this land, however, seem always to stand for something else, as critics have been suggesting since its initial publication: "Now Mr. Eliot uses *The Waste Land* as a concrete image of a spiritual drought," wrote Edmund Wilson in 1922.[51] The poem, in this sense, contains no "literal garbage" but rather resembles Wallace Stevens's dump, which is "full / [o]f images" functioning as symbols.[52] Like Eliot, Ammons was drawn to the symbolic dimension of material waste—"garbage has to be the poem of our time because / garbage is spiritual"—although the main sentiment of *Garbage* (1993) allies him more closely with William Carlos Williams. "[T]hings," Williams writes, "are awash in / ideality."[53]

Burroughs, by contrast, depicts things that are awash in "putrid lymph." These things may serve to symbolize "the malaise [that] underlies all existing societies," as John Calder put it in his response to Willett's "UGH," but it seems Burroughs is less committed to symbolizing malaise than to cataloging every conceivable waste object in relentless and almost maniacal fashion. This technique makes the materiality of waste feel omnipresent and indeed overwhelming. It is as though he means to put his readers in the position occupied by "The President of the Island," a character in *Naked Lunch* who, upon meeting his constituents at the municipal dump, "is required by custom to crawl across the garbage on his stomach" (*NL*, 152–53). By relentlessly cataloging waste objects, in other words, Burroughs strives to broker something like direct access, unmediated by "ideality" and symbolic significance, to what Georges Bataille termed "everything rejected," by which he meant "the waste products of the human body and certain analogous matter."[54] Bataille's thinking (which he called either "heterology" or "scatology") posed a challenge both to idealism and to traditional materialism. "When the word *materialism* is used," he writes, "it is time to designate the direct interpretation, *excluding all idealism*, of raw phenomena, and not a system founded on the fragmentary elements of an ideological analysis, elaborated under the sign of religious relations."[55] For Yve-Alain Bois and Rosalind Krauss, deploying Bataille to rewrite the history of twentieth-century art, the key term in his work is *formless*, and they contend that this term is best understood as an "operation" rather than a concept, which effects both "lowering" and "taxonomic disorder."[56] This operation, they argue, has enabled many artists to make formal objects that appear to be exceeding their forms.

To this history of art we might add Burroughs. *Naked Lunch* is hardly formless, but it does stage several dramas of unformation, including that of the commodity becoming waste. As it unfolds, this drama constitutes a response to postwar American society that has so far eluded critical commentary. Although the novel itemizes many waste objects, it singles out one—used Kotex—for special attention. Kotex appears in a variety of scenarios. It is strewn in the street among other discards, heaped in a hospital bedpan, left on the floor of a pub, and served by "ordinary men and women" as an entrée: "Dinner is Lucy Bradshinkel's cunt *saignant* cooked in Kotex *papillon*" (*NL*, 64, 52, 107, 109). Most often, it is soiled and bloodied: "I am passing room 10 they moved me out of yesterday . . . Maternity case I assume . . . Bedpans full of blood and Kotex and nameless female substances, enough to pollute a continent" (*NL*, 52–53). There are several ways to make sense of this image. It certainly evokes what Mary McCarthy termed "the horror of female genitalia" in her 1963 review of *Naked Lunch*, a fear of female corporeality that calls to mind Klaus Theweleit's study of the male imaginary.[57] But the image of bloody Kotex also expresses a more general horror of waste, the fear that all the new commodities produced in the booming postwar decades—all the packaged goods invented and distributed by corporations like Kimberly-Clark, the manufacturer of both Kotex and Kleenex—were turning into a massive quantity of garbage ("enough to pollute a continent") and thereby making America into a dump.

Kotex was not just any commodity. It was, as Thomas Heinrich and Bob Batchelor explain, among the very first self-service items in the history of retail. Typically displayed on countertops near the cash register, it "enabled the customer to take a box and pay for it with minimal communicative action."[58] This box, which points to the cultural taboo of menstruation, did not need to be *discussed* but only *selected*, and in this regard it paved the way for the myriad packaged goods that sit on the shelves of every supermarket and drugstore. Latour would understand such goods, as I suggested in chapter 1, as fully agential participants in the social, actors in a network that extends from the point of purchase. Here I would add that without them, what historians call the consumers' republic would look very different, and what we experience as an ordinary form of shopping (i.e., strolling the aisles sans intervention from a clerk) would be impossible, because the success of self-service retailing depends on objects that sell themselves. Kotex sold itself remarkably well during the postwar era: its sales, along with those of Kleenex, grew twentyfold between 1945 and 1971, reaching almost $1 billion in the latter year.[59]

When Burroughs depicts "bloody Kotex," however, he is not portraying a pristine commodity with a striking package but a soiled waste object destined for the dump, where, of course, it could be recommodified, as DeLillo frequently points out: "How's the waste business? Booming. The waste business. Bigger by the minute" (*UW*, 205). Appearing no fewer than five times in *Naked Lunch*, "bloody Kotex" serves as a synecdoche of two sites: both the retail outlet where it was once prominently displayed and the dump where it is or will soon be deposited. Conjuring these two sites, it mediates a convergence between consumption and waste, underscoring that the "consumers' republic," which produced unprecedented quantities of so-called consumer nondurables like Kotex and Kleenex, was also a "throwaway society," where widespread affluence, plus an ethos of convenience and disposability, spurred what Martin V. Melosi calls "the relentless production of solid waste."[60] Indeed, the explosion of packaged goods during the period exacerbated both a "garbage crisis" (a national anxiety over where and how to jettison an increasing number of discards) and a "litter problem" (a growing concern that "litterbugs" were befouling national space).[61]

By repeating the image of the "bloody Kotex," *Naked Lunch* registers both this crisis and this problem ahead of the sweeping changes to sanitation, conservation, and waste management that would come in the 1960s and 1970s. In 1965, three years after the novel was first published in the United States, President Johnson called for "a new conservation" to address "entire[ly] new categories of waste [that] ha[d] come to plague and menace the American scene."[62] He was referring specifically to "the technological wastes—the by-products of growth, industry, agriculture, and science" —that had been examined by best-selling writers like Rachel Carson and Vance Packard some years before.[63] *Naked Lunch*, with its relentless itemization of both old and "entire[ly] new" categories of waste, can be understood to anticipate the work of these writers, although it is certainly stranger than either *Silent Spring* (1962) or *The Waste Makers* (1960). Indeed, it presents "mosaics" that only Burroughs could have fathomed, not only bloody Kotex and other examples of commodity waste but also "pink convolutions of gristle laced with crystal snot, time shit and black blood filters of flesh" (*NL*, 9).

WASTED SUBJECTS

These "mosaics" include both waste objects and wasted subjects, yet the latter are not always junkies. Although *Naked Lunch* features many "junk-sick" characters, and although Burroughs himself struggled for many years with drug addiction, suffering intensely from the cycle of dependence and withdrawal in Tangier, the subjects in the novel are also *wasted* in a different sense. Like the objects, such as the bloody Kotex, they participate in various dramas of unformation and decomposition. "The Dream Police," for instance, "disintegrate in globs of rotten ectoplasm swept away by an old junky, coughing and spitting in the sick morning" (*NL*, 46). Likewise, the "Liquefactionists" pursue a program that "involves protein cleavage and reduction to liquid which is absorbed into someone else's protoplasmic being" (*NL*, 69). Although not a Liquefactionist, Lee, the closest character in the novel to a protagonist, has a body composed of "yellow-pink-brown gelatinous substance," which is "so soft" that it is "cut to the bone by dust particles" (*NL*, 60). At any moment, it seems, his "tentative" flesh might disintegrate into "faint, iridescent whorls of slime" (*NL*, 169). Still, it is not Lee but "the Vigilante" who is at the center of the novel's most striking scene of bodily disintegration:

> I saw it happen. Ten pounds lost in ten minutes standing with the syringe in one hand holding his pants up with the other, his abdicated flesh burning in a cold yellow halo, there in the New York Hotel room ... night table litter of candy boxes, cigarette butts cascading out of three ashtrays, mosaic of sleepless nights and sudden food needs of the kicking addict nursing his baby flesh ... The Vigilante is prosecuted in Federal Court under a lynch bill and winds up in a Federal Nut House specially designed for the containment of ghosts: precise, prosaic impact of objects ... washstand ... door ... toilet ... bars ... there they are ... this is it ... all lines cut ... nothing beyond ... Dead End ... and the Dead End in every face ... The physical changes were slow at first, then jumped forward in black klunks, falling through his slack tissue, washing away the human lines. In his place of total darkness mouth and eyes are one organ that leaps forward to snap with transparent teeth ... but no organ is constant as

regards either function or position ... sex organs sprout everywhere
... rectums open, defecate and close ... the entire organism changes
color and consistency in split-second adjustments. (*NL*, 9)

This fragmentary passage, punctuated by numerous ellipses, depicts a drug
addict, the Vigilante, who was "copped out as a schizo possession case" and
who is now serving his sentence in an asylum (*NL*, 8). Prior to his conviction in "Federal Court," he spent many "sleepless nights" taking drugs in a
New York hotel room, where the narrator witnessed his unformation and
subsequent transformation. Surrounded by trash—"candy boxes" and "cigarette butts cascading out of three ashtrays"—he appears suddenly to ema-
ciate right before the narrator's eyes: "I saw it happen. Ten pounds lost in
ten minutes." At first, his flesh looks "abdicated," as though it has been relinquished from his body, free to dissipate like the light of "cold yellow halo."
Then the "physical changes" become more intense, until, finally, he is losing
and acquiring bodily forms in "split-second adjustments." By the end of
the passage, he is no longer an emaciated human subject, but an "organism,"
or a chaotic jumble of "organs," constantly changing in both "color and
consistency."

All this occurred at some unspecified moment in the past. Now the presumably sober Vigilante spends his time "in a Federal Nut House," where he
feels the "precise, prosaic impact of objects." This passage, therefore, not
only renders the unformation of a human subject, and his subsequent
transformation into a monstrous organism, but also contrasts two images
of the *relation* between subject and object. On the one hand, there is the
drug-taking Vigilante, "washing away the human lines," who abandons his
subjective form, in a sense miming the unformed objects scattered around
him, the commodities that have become waste matter. Here Burroughs
seems to be suggesting that, through a mutual decomposition, object and
subject can congeal, like the contents of a landfill, into a "stew" or a "watery
potage" of waste matter and abdicated flesh, at least until that flesh suddenly forms itself into a new organism. On the other hand, this passage
depicts a fully embodied subject, the sober Vigilante in the asylum, making
contact with solid objects and registering their precise and prosaic impact,
without ever sensing that "they wanta merge with [his] protoplasm" (*NL*,
105). The Vigilante's experience of the physical object world in the asylum,
in other words, is antithetical to the experience of those characters in the
novel that do "merge" with that world. "The Zone," Burroughs writes, "is a
single, vast building. The rooms are made of a plastic cement that bulges to
accommodate people, but when too many crowd into one room there is a
soft *plop* and someone squeezes through the wall right into the next house"
(*NL*, 149). The onomatopoeia in this description—*plop*—conveys the sound

of physical and ontological congealing: the lurid fusion of subject and object that Burroughs depicts here and throughout the novel.

This fusion constitutes a fantastic example of what Latour calls "translation," the process of conjoining discrete entities to create "entirely new types of beings," which is why *Naked Lunch* has been so important to posthumanist thought. Contemporary critics, such as Katherine Hayles and Marianne DeKoven, have attended to the novel's hybrid subjects—what DeKoven, referring to Donna Haraway's "Manifesto for Cyborgs," calls "quintessentially postmodern, boundary-crossing, Harawayan cyborgs"— yet these critics were anticipated by an earlier generation of readers that includes both Leslie Fiedler and Marshall McLuhan.[64] Fiedler argued, in a 1965 lecture titled "The New Mutants," that Burroughs's novel is "no mere essay in heroin-hallucinated homosexual pornography—but a nightmare anticipation (in Science Fiction form) of post-humanist sexuality."[65] This sexuality, he asserted, is a marker of "the post-male post-heroic world," meaning the world of the American 1960s, which he took to be characterized not only by revolutionary social changes but also by "the prospect of the radical transformation (under the impact of advanced technology and the transfer of traditional human functions to machines) of homo sapiens into something else."[66] With his reference to "advanced technology," Fiedler echoed McLuhan, who had argued only a few months earlier that "*Naked Lunch* records the private strategies of culture in the electric age."[67] According to McLuhan's "Notes on Burroughs," which appeared in the *Nation* the same year that *Understanding Media* was first published, "The central theme of *Naked Lunch* is the strategy of bypassing the new electric environment by becoming an environment oneself."[68] How does one become an environment or a site? By taking drugs, apparently: "Junk," McLuhan elaborates, "is needed to turn the human body itself into an environment that includes the universe."[69] He is undoubtedly thinking of one of the novel's best-known assertions: "The addict regards his body impersonally as an instrument to absorb the medium in which he lives" (*NL*, 57). The Vigilante routine, however, tells a different story that suggests an alternate posthumanism.

When he takes junk, the Vigilante becomes neither an environment nor a cyborg but a cluster of body parts: "sex organs sprout everywhere." Prior to this, though, he simply decomposes like one of the Liquefactionists; his "human lines" are "wash[ed] away" as his flesh dissipates and subsequently transmogrifies. Getting wasted, in this sense, entails becoming like material waste. Just as the objects in his hotel room, the candy boxes and spent cigarettes, have deteriorated from the commodity form into waste matter, so too the Vigilante relinquishes his body to become a mass of "slack tissue." In this version of posthumanism, the human subject and the nonhuman object overcome their division through a mutual decomposition, and as subjects decompose throughout the novel, they figure a distinction between bodies and flesh that parallels the one between commodities and waste. As Burroughs represents it, however, flesh is not simply the soft substance wrapped around the bones of an animal; it is more like what Maurice Merleau-Ponty conceptualized as flesh (*chair*) in his late work. This concept appears in the final chapter, "The Intertwining—The Chiasm," of Merleau-Ponty's unfinished manuscript, which was published as *Le Visible et l'invisible* in 1964. "The Intertwining—The Chiasm" is nothing short of an attempt to overcome the division of subject and object, indeed, to develop a new ontology that can articulate what precedes and underlies that division.[70] "What we are calling flesh, this interiorly worked-over mass," he writes, "has no name in philosophy."[71] By this he means that it "is not matter, is not mind, is not substance," but "the concrete emblem in a general manner of being" and "a sort of incarnate principle that brings a style of being wherever there is a fragment of being."[72] Many scholars have sought to make sense of these definitions. Taylor Carman glosses flesh as "the stuff common to ourselves and the world, what we and it are both made of."[73] Judith Butler defines it as "the web in which one lives."[74] Gilles Deleuze and Félix Guattari understand it as "ideal coincidence," the key to apprehending what they call "the being of sensation."[75]

Yet Merleau-Ponty himself provides the most compelling definition when he writes that flesh is "the formative medium of the subject and the object."[76] Flesh, in this sense, is the medium in which subjects and objects both acquire and lose form, two processes that Burroughs depicts repeatedly throughout *Naked Lunch*. Although the publication of the novel predates that of *Le Visible et l'invisible* by five years, it is something like this medium, this flesh, that Burroughs figures with his copious descriptions of bodily disintegration. These descriptions render a flesh that appears, in a word, "abdicated," a flesh that exceeds what Robert Creeley, the first editor to publish a portion of *Naked Lunch*, named "the explicit package of meat one calls the body."[77] Likewise, Merleau-Ponty conceptualized a flesh that is irreducible to its bodily manifestation—"the sack in which I am enclosed"—in order to apprehend the "element" that is common to the embodied subject and the world.[78] "[M]y body is made of the same flesh as the world," he wrote in a working note dated May 1960; "this flesh of my body is shared with the world, the world *reflects* it, encroaches upon it and it encroaches upon the world."[79] For his part, Burroughs imagines flesh to oscillate between subjective and objective forms, bodily and nonbodily manifestations. On the one hand, there is a character who asserts, "I am always somewhere ... *Inside* this straightjacket of jelly" (*NL*, 185); this image depicts the body as a kind of container, not so much a fleshy form as formed flesh. On the other hand, "bodies disintegrate in green explosions," allowing flesh to assume kaleidoscopic object forms such as "pink convolutions and black blood filters" (*NL*, 84, 185). These explosions make flesh appear to be the "element" common to both bodies and worlds, the "medium" in which they attain and relinquish form.

Naked Lunch, therefore, might be understood to visualize the concept that "The Intertwining—The Chiasm" strives to produce. These two texts obviously deploy very different conventions, yet it seems that both Burroughs and Merleau-Ponty devoted themselves in the 1950s to the project of surpassing the division of subject and object, to fathoming the *something* that both subjects and objects, bodies and worlds, are made of. We can historicize this project by suggesting that both the novelist and the philosopher were responding (from different sites and in different discourses) to the massive changes in the physical object world that occurred in the two decades after World War II. Kristin Ross describes "the almost cargo-cult-like, sudden descent of large appliances into war-torn French households and streets in the wake of the Marshall Plan," arguing that these appliances and other material objects not only transformed everyday life in profound ways but also impacted French intellectual culture. "The coming of objects," she shows, inspired Roland Barthes to pursue, in the occasional pieces collected as *Mythologies*, "the sociohistorical analysis of the object world."[80] Merleau-Ponty's late work registers this coming of objects in its commitment to overcoming the division of subject and object, to conceptualizing their formative medium. Settled in Tangier, Burroughs was not living through the Americanization of France, yet he was thinking about American appliances.

In the "Ordinary Men and Women" routine, an "American Housewife" complains about the "Garbage Disposal Unit snapping at [her]" as she "open[s] a box of Lux" (*NL*, 104). Introduced by General Electric in 1935, the "Disposall" came to symbolize the cleanliness and convenience of the 1950s kitchen, which is why Americans "became so captivated by this mundane household appliance, made it a public health benefit, and turned it into a required accoutrement of the Good Life."[81] What has been described as Burroughs's "radical incorporation of all waste," therefore, might be redescribed as an effort to showcase the contents of the Disposall, to visualize what the aspirants to the American Good Life sought to discard. Portraying one of these aspirants, Burroughs renders a subject that is *literally* constituted by waste: "my intestines is all constipated," the American Housewife grumbles after turning away from the pesky appliance (*NL*, 104). She thus mirrors the malfunctioning object in her failure to eliminate, and this mimetic structure appears throughout *Naked Lunch*. Just as the constipated subject mirrors the broken "Disposal Unit," so too the decomposing subject mirrors the waste object, "dissolving the body's decent skin" to release "globs of rotten ectoplasm" (*NL*, 6, 46).

As such scenes proliferate over the course of the novel, the mutual decomposition of subject and object effects a peculiar impression of sociality—a "larval network and diasporic confederation," it has been called, that looks like a nightmare vision of what Latour has in mind in *Reassembling the Social*.[82] If in Latour's view the social is a network of actors or actants, hybrid entities that manifest the properties of both subject and object, then Burroughs can be read as something like an actor-network-theorist in the extreme, a sociologist high on junk, for *Naked Lunch* conjures a vast network of monstrous hybrids, a "junk world" of actors linked by iridescent flesh and putrid lymph. "Section describing The City and the Meet Café," Burroughs writes, referring to his portrayal of Tangier as a social site, "written in a state of *yagé* intoxication" (*NL*, 91). A great variety of intoxicants were indeed crucial to the creation of the novel, as so many readers have acknowledged, but I have been suggesting that Burroughs was no less interested in that other kind of junk: the material detritus accumulating at the dump. His engagement with the latter was central to his sociological project.

Take, for instance, the one scene in *Naked Lunch* that unfolds at a municipal landfill. "The Island," begins a passage in the key "Interzone" routine,

> was a British Military and Naval station directly opposite the Zone. England holds the Island on a yearly rent-free lease, and every year the Lease and Permit of Residence is formally renewed. The entire population turns out—attendance is compulsory—and gathers at the municipal dump. The President of the Island is required by custom to crawl across the garbage on his stomach and deliver the Permit of Residence and Renewal of the Lease, signed by every citizen of the Island, to the Resident Governor who stands resplendent in dress uniform. (*NL*, 152–53)

As the Governor "takes the permit and shoves it into his coat pocket," his henchmen "sweep mounted machine guns back and forth across the crowd with a slow, searching movement" (*NL*, 153). None of the indigenous people will protest, so the renewal goes off without a hitch, the Governor's "loud metallic laugh ring[ing] out across the dump" as the "prostrate President" lies in a pile of municipal garbage (ibid.).

In this scene, Burroughs's sociology becomes full-fledged social critique: a scathing indictment of Western militarism and imperialism through a searing portrayal of Britain in particular, a nation that he once described as "a fucking blighted dump" (*LG*, 139). Under British rule, democracy is "scrupulously enforced" on the Island, where "[t]here is a Senate and Congress who carry on endless sessions discussing garbage disposal and out-house inspection, the only two questions over which they have any jurisdiction" (NL, 153). Burroughs's none-too-subtle point is that the occupying force controls the local population by equating their social order with their rejectamenta: just as the chief executive is reduced to rubbish when the President "crawl[s] across the garbage on his stomach," so, too, the legislature has no business other than waste management. This scene develops a specific anticolonial critique, therefore, but it relies on a familiar analogy between a given society and its material excrement that appears in much of the art and archaeology devoted to the dump. If you are what you eat, then we are what we throw away—this is not only what DeLillo's garbage archaeologist means to convey when he "take[s] [his] students into garbage dumps and make[s] them understand the civilization they live in" but also what Ukeles argues through her treatment of Fresh Kills, the actual landfill that is so important to *Underworld*. Burroughs's approach to the dump has certain affinities with these projects, both of which belong to an extensive tradition of artistic engagement with waste, yet for him the dump is not just a setting for narrative action (as in DeLillo) but also a site through which to reimagine social form. *Naked Lunch* is, in the end, a more radical endeavor to see the social *as* rather than *in* a dump.

This distinction becomes especially clear when Burroughs is juxtaposed with Ukeles, an artist whose own definition of Fresh Kills as a "social sculpture" aligns her with the garbage archaeologists (both real and imagined) who understand landfills to be among the most significant artifacts of civilization. Ukeles has been the unsalaried artist-in-residence at the New York City Department of Sanitation since the late 1970s. Her work combines feminism, environmentalism, and labor activism with performance, public art, and institutional critique. Along with a handful of other practitioners, including Hans Haacke, Robert Smithson, and Richard Serra, Ukeles was a pioneer of site-specificity, an artist who helped to make specific sites, as well as the category of site, crucial to art after minimalism. She rose to prominence in 1969 when she produced her "Manifesto for Maintenance Art," the same year that Smithson employed dumping as an art-making practice in *Glue Pour*, a performance and earthwork in Vancouver. Unlike most manifesto writers, Ukeles does not call for a revolution but wonders "who's going to pick up the garbage on Monday morning."[83] Her career has been devoted to exploring the ramifications of this question. For example, in "Touch Sanitation," a performance that occurred between July 1979 and June 1980, she shook hands with all 8,500 NYC Department of Sanitation workers, saying to each, "Thank you for keeping New York City alive." A few years earlier—the year after Gordon Matta-Clark shot a film showing the destruction of his truck at Fresh Kills—she had staged two performances at the Wadsworth Atheneum in which she washed the museum grounds on her hands and knees, her objective being to highlight maintenance workers and maintenance work, the undervalued people and processes that allow us to inhabit museums, to keep museums, as it were, "alive."

"To me," Ukeles told the *New York Times* in 1993, "the Sanitation Department [i]s easily among the most essential services in the city, and yet it [i]s perceived in this very repressed manner of being beneath, a displaced service. Even the facilities are always out of sight, out of mind."[84] She therefore aims, above all, to bring these sites and services into view, so her work can be described as both archaeological and revelatory, for it "opens public space," as Helen Molesworth argues, "to the pressures of what it excludes or renders invisible."[85] Moreover, when dealing with dumps in particular, Ukeles seeks what Shannon Jackson calls the "reanimation of a degraded object world," the redemption of the otherwise excluded things that constitute the material substratum of collective life.[86] "My eyes are seeing images of sacred earth mounds, burial grounds in China," Ukeles said to the *Times* reporter as she glanced at Fresh Kills. "How can you not think about that?"[87] Nearly two decades later, she is still thinking about that landfill, the site that received the garbage of the whole city over a fifty-year period: "You think you are standing on Staten Island? You are actually standing on Manhattan, the Bronx, Brooklyn, and Queens. Are you on the ground? What ground? Whose ground? What is this place?"[88]

While such questions animate all her work, they become especially striking in a sculpture titled *The Social Mirror*, which she proposed in 1979 and completed in 1983. *The Social Mirror* is an NYC Department of Sanitation collection truck, measuring twenty-eight feet and weighing twelve tons, whose exterior is wrapped in tempered, reflective glass (figure 2.1). Exhibited many times, it calls attention to a key device of waste management, the vehicle that collects, compacts, and transports our discards. What is a garbage truck? According to Hawkins, it "isn't a site of desecration but an arena for the renegotiation and transformation of value. It's an economy on wheels that reminds us that waste can be commodified." While she suggests that the workings of this economy are signaled by "an everyday acoustic event" with a range of "cultural and affective meanings," she was not the first to make this point.[89] Addressing the Modern Language Association in 1953, Margaret Mead claimed that "the grinding machinery of a garbage truck" is not a "crude sensation" but a complex figure that participates in the "system of tradition" called culture and signifies the elimination of waste, which is why Hawkins can speculate that it prompts "a little moment of satisfaction and well being" as it rumbles down the street.[90] But what happens when this "grinding machinery" is wrapped in reflective glass? Then it becomes less strikingly aural than visual, displaying the likenesses of its spectators, turning them into coproducers of its appearance. Ukeles is mak-

2.1. Mierle Laderman Ukeles, *The Social Mirror*, 1983. Courtesy of Ronald Feldman Fine Arts, New York.

ing an analogical claim: the surface of *The Social Mirror* reflects those who look at it just as waste reflects the society that dumps it.

Burroughs ultimately moves beyond this analogy. Rather than merely seeing society in the dump, he engages this site in a complex effort to re-imagine sociality itself, to portray a social world whose governing logic of decay derives from the landfill. *Naked Lunch* is not only a repository of waste objects and wasted subjects, not only a relentless attempt to reveal everything that resides, soiled and bloodied, in what Burroughs called "America's putrefying unconscious," but also an experiment in site writing whose conversion of spatial into literary form renders the social as a network of monstrous hybrids (*LG*, 18). And yet, while *Naked Lunch* can be understood in Latourian terms, the utter outlandishness of the text finally presents a challenge to any interpretation that draws on Actor-Network-Theory (ANT). "We have seen," writes Graham Harman in his explication of ANT, "that Latour insists on an absolute democracy of objects: a mosquito is just as real as Napoleon, and plastic in a garbage dump is no less an actant than a nuclear warhead."[91] While this claim has been widely influential, it has also provoked controversy: "What kind of world is it," asks one of Latour's detractors, "in which humans are on equal footing with garbage?"[92] Burroughs provides a striking answer to this question, projecting an image of the social that looks like Latour's "association of actants" at its most horrifying—a junk world where no ontological distinctions matter because everything is destined to become a single degraded substance, call it abdicated flesh, rotten ectoplasm, or putrid lymph.[93] In the end, then, *Naked Lunch* suggests how easily hybridization can slide toward homogenization, how the overcoming of artificial divisions can vaporize meaningful distinctions. With this suggestion in mind as a kind of cautionary note, I turn now to the next test site of postwar American fiction, to a site that is also populated by mixed entities, mundane rather than monstrous hybrids of human and machine.

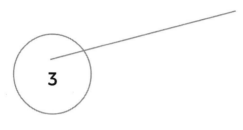

Roads

Although Robert Creeley drove an ambulance in Burma during World War II, his poetry is not especially concerned with roads. His most famous and perplexing lyric, however, is voiced by a melancholic motorist:

As I sd to my
friend, because I am
always talking,—John, I

sd, which was not his
name, the darkness sur-
rounds us, what

can we do against
it, or else, shall we &
why not, buy a goddamn big car,

drive, he sd, for
christ's sake, look
out where yr going.[1]

Written in the mid-1950s, this poem, "I Know a Man," poses a question that captions a certain picture of Cold War America: if "the darkness sur- / rounds us," then "why not, buy a goddamn big car"? Indeed, as Michael

Davidson explains, "Creeley puts in brief what American consumers were being asked to believe—that the postwar economy was prosperous and that further consumption could ameliorate the forces of undifferentiated darkness."[2] But "the darkness sur- / rounds us" can be taken literally as well. Then the poem conjures a scene of late-night driving. You might picture two men huddled in an old jalopy—one babbling in a sort of nervous staccato as he drives; the other silent except when sheer terror motivates an outburst: "for / christ's sake, look / out where yr going." The driver's preoccupation with his existential condition, the metaphorical "darkness," makes him cavalier and even reckless behind the wheel. Does he almost career off the highway while ruminating aloud on the perennial questions of essence and existence? Or is his interlocutor simply fed up with the incessant jabbering? The answer depends on how you hear the tone of the last stanza, on whether "for christ's sake" is read as an expression of panic or of mere frustration. Either way, "I Know a Man" contrasts the power of the car-as-commodity with the altogether different power of the car-as-machine. "[L]ook / out where yr going"—that is not an existential aphorism but a basic tenet of safe motoring shrieked in an emergency.

Or perhaps grumbled out of frustration. The last two lines of the poem are finally ambiguous. This ambiguity and other odd features (abbreviated diction, oblique logic, tortured syntax) make "I Know a Man" one of the strangest and most complicated responses to what has come to be known as American automobility. Adapting Michel Foucault's notion of the *dispositif*, Cotten Seiler conceptualizes automobility as the apparatus of "commodities, bodies of knowledge, laws, techniques, institutions, environments, nodes of capital, sensibilities, and modes of perception" that has coalesced around "the act of driving."[3] His recently issued *Republic of Drivers* provides a cultural history of that act in the United States from 1895 through the 1960s, ending in the period that saw the construction of the Eisenhower Interstate Highway System, an event that, as Louis Menand puts it, "changed the phenomenology of driving."[4] Drawing from these and other scholars, this chapter examines the importance of automobility to postwar American literature. While I consider a broad range of literary texts and cultural artifacts, my emphasis falls on two novels—Jack Kerouac's *On the Road* (1957) and Joan Didion's *Play It as It Lays* (1970)—that imagine what Seiler calls the "habitat and habitus" of driving as a means of reimagining social life.[5] The road appears often as a social site within the English literary tradition, and "it is a rare work," as Mikhail Bakhtin notes, "that does not contain a variation of this motif."[6] What, after all, is Chaucer's ambition in *The Canterbury Tales* if not to imagine social life on the road, to explore what happens when sundry folk representing different social types (a miller, a monk, a wife) enlist as pilgrims in that site-between-sites? Of course, road sociality takes a particular shape in the era of automobility:

hybrid actors, which Tim Dant aptly names "driver-cars," negotiate the network that we call the traffic flow, relying on a refined system of signs and signals to communicate.[7] If Chaucer's succession of narrators reveals what Bruno Latour calls a "collective woven together out of speaking subjects," then the driver-cars in Kerouac and Didion figure "subjects to which poor objects, our inferior brothers, are attached at all points."[8] For both novelists, such attachment was a significant social fact.

On the Road is a semiautobiographical account of Kerouac's road trips in the late 1940s. It is also among the most famous road narratives ever written.[9] Many critics, in dialogue with the pioneering work of Eve Sedgwick, have drawn attention to the homosocial bonds within Kerouac's text, as well as the real-life Beat milieu, and have focused on how specific women, such as Carolyn Cassady and Joyce Johnson, brokered intimacies between men while masking homosexual desire.[10] This chapter suggests that the car plays no less potent a role in facilitating male bonding and in constituting the social world of the novel. To capture the distinctiveness of that world, I contrast it with the representation of two other automotive subcultures—the hot-rodders and the Merry Pranksters—in seminal works by Tom Wolfe that appeared in the wake of On the Road. Then I turn to the writing of Joan Didion, arguing that Play It as It Lays functions as a self-conscious response both to Kerouac's novel and to the mythology of road-tripping that it fostered. For Kerouac's characters, Sal and Dean, going on the road is a way of inhabiting a new social space, whereas for Didion's protagonist, Maria Wyeth, it provides an opportunity to be antisocial, to attain reprieve from a toxic Hollywood that is marked by hollow careerism, lethargic sex, drugs, exploitation, and abuse. Part of Didion's ambition, in painting such a bleak picture of late-1960s Hollywood, is to depict a sort of autophilia, to envisage a compensatory, even redemptive, love between one woman and her car. Despite crucial differences, therefore, both novelists treat the car as a social actor within a particular assemblage of humans and nonhumans: Didion describes Maria and her Corvette as intimate companions, while Kerouac makes various jalopies and hoopties essential to the intimacy of Sal and Dean.

Published thirteen years apart, On the Road and Play It as It Lays appeared on opposite ends of a very rich period in the history of American car culture. Less than four months after Kerouac hammered out the first full draft of On the Road in April 1951, the Museum of Modern Art unveiled Eight Automobiles, the world's first museum exhibition of cars, which the MoMA memorably termed "hollow, rolling sculptures."[11] On September 4, 1957—exactly one day before On the Road was finally published by Viking—Ford introduced the infamous Edsel, a failed design that exemplified the stunning excesses of Detroit styling. The following year, Robert Frank issued The Americans, the groundbreaking collection of photographs that he snapped on the road, for which Kerouac provided the introduction. The year after that, John Chamberlain fabricated his first crushed-car sculpture in the yard outside Larry Rivers's studio in Southampton, New York. Riffing on and revising Frank a few years later, Ed Ruscha generated two collections of photographs—*Twenty-Six Gasoline Stations* (1963) and *Every Building on the Sunset Strip* (1966)—which have been profoundly influential, not least for Lee Friedlander, whose 2010 collection of photographs, *America by Car*, visualizes the American landscape as it appears from the vantage of ordinary rentals, specifically Chevys and Toyotas. The year that Ruscha released his second collection, the Los Angeles County Board of Supervisors tried to prevent Ed Kienholz's *Back Seat Dodge '38* from being exhibited at the Los Angeles County Museum of Art (LACMA), thus making the sculpture, which portrays sexual activity inside an automobile, into an instant classic. The following year, 1967, was something of a banner year for automobility in the visual arts, as both Michael Fried and Robert Smithson were inspired, in vastly different ways, by road travel. In "Art and Objecthood," Fried developed a critical vocabulary for minimalism through an analysis of Tony Smith's account of driving the uncompleted Jersey Turnpike at night, while Smithson, in the midst of feuding vigorously with Fried in the pages of *Artforum*, embarked on a bus trip to New Jersey that formed the basis for his seminal "Tour of the Monuments of Passaic."[12] And all this is to say nothing of how important automobility became to American film during an era that saw the efflorescence of the road movie.[13]

The second decade of the twenty-first century seems an auspicious moment for revisiting this period in the cultural history of automobility, because automobility as we know it may be about to change. "Cars that drive themselves are not far away," wrote designer Donald Norman in 2007, anticipating inventions such as the Google driverless car, which has, amid much hype and some criticism, safely logged thousands of miles since 2010. These cars, as the *New York Times* reports, can exhibit "different driving personalities," from "cautious" to "aggressive," and are therefore programmed to experience something like emotion.[14] Does this mean that they can have road rage? If so, how might they communicate it? The sociologist Jack Katz, in his study of how it feels to become "pissed off" while driving in Los Angeles, has shown that road rage is, for human drivers, a very complex phenomenon involving a wide repertoire of expressive techniques, from tailgating and honking to giving one another "the finger."[15] It is not at all outlandish to imagine a future sociologist studying the expressive techniques of cars themselves, asking them how it feels to become "pissed off" as they idle in traffic.[16] The drivers in this chapter, Dean Moriarty and Maria Wyeth, never put their feelings so crudely. But, then again, they do not hit much traffic.

At around 2:00 AM on Monday, February 23, 1943, Kerouac sat down to write a letter to his childhood friend Sebastian Sampas. He had just returned home from his job as a parking-lot attendant at a nearby hotel garage, a job he liked because it gave him time to read, "despite the fact that [he was] at the beck and call of every customer." It seems the clientele could be demanding. "But parking cars sustains a certain aesthetic satisfaction," he explains, "the subtlety of giving an inch's grace to a sleek fender, and the exhilaration of jamming on the foot brake within certain disaster."[17] Such antics were even more satisfying when they occasioned friendly rivalry. "Today, G. J. the Drunken Sailor was with me," he continues, "and, as usual, I tried to outdo him in virility—I only succeeded in smashing a fender against a garage post while backing up at 30 miles per in the small space that I had to operate in; however, he enjoyed the madness immensely."[18] Charming in its self-deprecation, this letter provides an early example of how Kerouac would go on to portray cars, drivers, and social sites on and around the open road. Such sites were a persistent concern throughout his career, beginning in 1940 with a short story entitled "Where the Road Begins" and ending in the last month of his life with his submission of previously jettisoned material from *On the Road* to his agent Sterling Lord.[19] While the letter to Sampas suggests that he considered good driving to be an aesthetically satisfying act, it is not clear how he understood bad driving. On the one hand, it seems to constitute a spectacle of failed masculinity: instead of proving his virility to the "Drunken Sailor" by showcasing his skills behind the wheel, he embarrasses himself and causes a mess. On the other hand, if "we must admit that there is a certain element of virility in ruining cars," then that mess testifies to his masculine bravura.[20] The fender might be "smashed," but his manhood remains intact.

Either way, Kerouac knew that both good and bad driving could make aesthetically satisfying reading, which is one reason why so many of the best passages in his novels are set on the road. These passages, particularly those starring Dean Moriarty (the fictional Neal Cassady) may be read as compensatory, for Kerouac himself was a terrible driver. "Our last trip to Mexico was marred," he wrote to Cassady on January 10, 1953, "by my not knowing how to take my foot off clutch while stopping and at the same time ponder problems where to park, what to do." Apparently, instead of asking for help, he had led Cassady to believe that he was "d[oing] it on purpose," but in this letter he wanted to come clean: "I didn't do it on purpose, don't know how to drive, just typewrite."[21] This letter and others reveal just how intensely Kerouac thought about masculinity and homosociality when depicting the habitat and habitus of driving. He went on the road, and imagined his experiences there into novelistic form, partly as a way to work out how to be a guy—especially in the presence of other guys.

Many scholars have examined this dynamic. Building on the work of Sedgwick and Adrienne Rich, for instance, Davidson argues that Kerouac's milieu, the milieu of the Beats, was structured by "compulsory homosociality" wherein one finds "a triangulated erotics between two men in which a woman serves as a shared object, a fulcrum of heterosexual legitimacy to mask repressed homosexual desire." As evidence, he points to "the triadic relationship of Neal Cassady, Jack Kerouac, and Carolyn Cassady in which the love between two artistic males was mediated through the wife with whom each shared a sexual relationship."[22] As Kerouac's letters suggest, however, his relationships with other men were also powerfully "mediated" by cars and the material sites of driving. Yes, women did play the role that Davidson describes, but in *On the Road*, I want to propose, the car emerges as the third constituent in the love triangle that includes Sal (the narrator and figure for Kerouac himself) and Dean (the narrator's object of hagiographic attention and affection).

Another way to put this claim would be to say that it is not only the human but also the nonhuman other that helps to facilitate a bond between two men. Kerouac was highly sensitive to otherness, as Rachel Adams has demonstrated in analyzing his treatment of nonwhite subjects.[23] This sensitivity also marks his portrayal of nonhuman objects and environments in his most celebrated novel. Kerouac began brainstorming that novel in the late 1940s. A journal entry dated August 23, 1948, reads, "I have another novel in mind—'On the Road'—which I keep thinking about: about two guys hitch-hiking to California in search of something they don't *really* find, and losing themselves on the road, and coming all the way back hopeful of something *else*."[24] This note anticipates the novel that would emerge after three weeks of manic composition in April 1951.[25] "The most noise you heard while he was typing," recalls poet Philip Whalen, "was the carriage return, slamming back, again and again. The little bell would bing-bang, bing bang! Just incredibly fast, faster than a teletype."[26] Hunkered down in an apartment on West Twentieth Street in Manhattan, and fueled by copious amounts of coffee, not Benzedrine, as is widely presumed, Kerouac typed the now-legendary manuscript as one enormous single-spaced paragraph on eight sheets of tracing paper, which he later taped together into a 120-foot scroll.[27] "I've told all the road now," he wrote to Cassady upon completion, "went fast because road is fast."[28]

He was aware, it seems, that he had pioneered a distinctive literary style by establishing a mimetic relation between the novel and the site—a relation that extends all the way to the material form of the scroll manuscript: "rolled it out on the floor and it looks like a road."[29] The first draft of *On the Road*, much like the first draft of *Naked Lunch*, which I examined in chapter

2, assumed the look and feel of its subject matter. Years later, after the novel had made him a celebrity, Kerouac replicated the conceit in a letter to Allen Ginsberg: "Unbelievable number of events almost impossible to remember, including earlier big Viking Press hotel room with thousands of screaming interviewers and *Road* roll original 100 mile ms. rolled out on carpet."[30] Replacing "foot" with "mile," he underscores the visual analogy, reminding his friend that the object he made, and not just the story he told, is in some sense site specific. Yet he also realized, not long after he had finished, that the story itself was not much of a story: "Plot, if any, is devoted to your development," he wrote to Cassady.[31] A minimal investment in plot was crucial to Kerouac's aesthetic, for it enabled him to focus on other narrative elements, namely, setting ("I've told all the road now") and characterization (the figure of Dean Moriarty).

This is one reason why, as Morris Dickstein puts it, "*On the Road* is somehow a great book without being a good novel."[32] It also accounts for both how and why the text develops such a powerful and original treatment of homosociality. This treatment begins with the very first paragraph:

> I first met Dean not long after my wife and I split up. I had just gotten over a serious illness that I won't bother to talk about, except that it had something to do with the miserably weary split-up and my feeling that everything was dead. With the coming of Dean Moriarty began the part of my life you could call my life on the road. Before that I'd often dreamed of going West to see the country, always vaguely planning and never taking off. Dean is the perfect guy for the road because he actually was born on the road, when his parents were passing through Salt Lake City in 1926, in a jalopy, on their way to Los Angeles. First reports of him came to me through Chad King, who'd shown me a few letters from him written in a New Mexico reform school. I was tremendously interested in the letters because they so naïvely and sweetly asked Chad to teach him all about Nietzsche and all the wonderful intellectual things that Chad knew. At one point Carlo and I talked about the letters and wondered if we would ever meet the strange Dean Moriarty. This is all far back, when Dean was not the way he is today, when he was a young jailkid shrouded in mystery. Then news came that Dean was out of reform school and was coming to New York for the first time; also there was talk that he had just married a girl called Marylou.[33]

This is not the paragraph Kerouac wrote when he began the scroll. That paragraph opens, "I first met met [*sic*] Neal not long after my father died."[34] At some point during the revision process, then, he changed the first line: in the 1957 Viking edition, the narrator-protagonist, Sal, has not lost his father but recently split from his wife. The effect of the revision is to underscore, at the very outset, that Sal is freed from the shackles of heterosexual domesticity and thus fully prepared to begin his life on the road, which is, as the opening foreshadows with its catalog of male proper names, a life lived with other guys. Women will be present, but they will be treated as "minor characters," to borrow Joyce Johnson's apt description. By contrast, Dean, "the perfect guy for the road," is introduced as a kind of messiah ("the coming of Dean Moriarty" invokes the Second Coming) with transformative powers, the ability to change your life.[35] Yet he does not descend from the heavens but emerges from the road itself, the site where he was born and where he was swaddled and nursed in "a jalopy." Kerouac told his publisher Robert Giroux, just after he had completed the scroll, that the "Holy Ghost" had dictated the novel.[36] The effect of the religious overtones, here and elsewhere in the text, is not only to enshroud Dean with the aura of automobility but also to anticipate his godlike power and prowess behind the wheel.

That power and that prowess are his most distinctive features. Although the opening paragraph mentions, almost as an afterthought, that "he had just married a girl called Marylou," his deepest commitment is to cars. Moreover, much of the novel is devoted to convincing us that he is, to put it colloquially, one hell of a driver. Sal feels alternately delighted and terrified by what Dean does behind the wheel, yet even in fear he remains awestruck. Unlike Kerouac himself, Dean is "the most fantastic parking-lot attendant in the world," for "he can back a car forty miles an hour into a tight squeeze and stop at the wall, jump out, race among fenders, leap into another car, circle it fifty miles an hour in a narrow space, back swiftly into tight spot" (*OR*, 6). Indeed, the "drunken sailor" has met his match. When he exits the parking lot, Dean is even more impressive and even more virile: "[H]e hunched over the wheel and gunned her; he was back in his element, everybody could see that ... The white line in the middle of the highway unrolled and hugged our left front tire as if glued to our groove. Dean hunched his muscular neck, T-shirted in the winter night, and blasted the car along" (*OR*, 135). At this moment, Dean's driving is eroticized as an orgy of body, machine, and site: he "hunche[s]" over the car and "gun[s] her," while she (the car) is stroked and embraced by asphalt. At other moments, the tryst is less elegant: "It was a rough trip, and none of us noticed it; the heater was not working and consequently the windshield developed fog and ice; Dean kept reaching out while driving seventy to wipe it with a rag and make a hole to see the road. 'Ah, holy hole!'" (*OR*, 116). Despite the malfunctioning heater, and even though Dean "gestured furiously" as he drove, "the car went straight as an arrow, not for once deviating from the white line in the middle of the road that unwound, kissing our left front tire" (ibid.). Spiritually and erotically connected to cars, in this case a 1949 Hudson, Dean seems to drive by willpower alone.

Yet he also demonstrates technical skill and brute strength: "Dean cut off the gas, threw the clutch, and negotiated every hairpin turn and passed cars and did everything in the books without the benefit of accelerator" (OR, 167–68). Unsurprisingly, he terrifies his passengers from time to time. Just as one of the many hitchhikers in the novel exclaims, "He's a devil with a car," so, too, Sal, right before cowering on the floor of the backseat, labels him an "Angel of Terror," seemingly intent on crashing (OR, 227, 235). The cumulative effect of such scenes—in which Dean's driving renders him frightening and alluring (and alluring because he is frightening)—is not simply to reinforce that "Dean is the perfect guy for the road," although they do that quite convincingly, but to reveal a certain structure of desire: a love triangle. Dean loves cars, perhaps more than anything else: "I have finally taught Dean that he can do anything he wants, become mayor of Denver, marry a millionairess, or become the greatest poet since Rimbaud. But he keeps rushing out to see the midget auto races" (OR, 42–43). And Sal loves Dean not only because Dean loves cars but also because they seem to love him back. While Sal admits that he himself "hated to drive and drove carefully," his exuberant narration celebrates Dean's embodied skills and technical knowledge, his stunning performance behind the wheel, his sexual and spiritual communion with this Cadillac and that jalopy and everything in between (OR, 121). "The novel's dual protagonists," suggests John Leland, "enable Kerouac to address the fissure in himself," and one could argue that his characterization of Dean works to compensate for his own failure (as rendered in his letters and elsewhere) to adopt the risky and rugged masculinity that attracted him to guys like Neal Cassady.[37]

Yet On the Road is not only a story about masculinity but also a study in the way that material sites mediate sociality. The car, often gendered female and portrayed in erotic terms, appears throughout the novel as the third participant in what Davidson calls "a triangulated erotics between two men," but this claim could be stated more generally. "Driving is a way for men to be together," Menand writes, "without the need to answer questions about why they want to be together."[38] The sites of automobility that form settings in the novel—roadhouses, crash pads, street corners, parking lots, bus stations—provide something like the material conditions of possibility for a special mode of male intimacy that, looking back on the Beats, we would call queer: "We're trying to communicate with absolute honesty and absolute completeness everything on our minds. We've had to take benzedrine. We sit on the bed, crosslegged, facing each other" (OR, 41–42). Such moments of male bonding assume (like much else) a sacred quality throughout the novel, which Sal, at his most mystical, tries to explain: "I told Dean that the thing that bound us all together in this world was invisible, and to prove it pointed to long lines of telephone poles that curved off out of sight over the bend of a hundred miles of salt" (*OR*, 211). How does pointing to something visible ("long lines of telephone poles") prove the invisibility of what binds us? It is tempting to say that Sal, in his hurried manner, simply contradicts himself, but Kerouac also seems to be making a subtle, dialectical point about the enigma of the social bond. On the one hand, whatever holds us together is in some sense hidden, mysterious, while on the other hand, it is perfectly visible, for we are literally contained and connected by the sites we inhabit.

JALOPY, HOT ROD, SCHOOL BUS

No matter how one reads Sal at this moment, though, it is clear that Kerouac turned to the open road in order to reimagine sociality. Yet Kerouac's depiction of the car as a social actor is notable for its lack of detail. Although several cars are named—a 1949 Hudson, a 1947 Cadillac limousine, a Buick, a "fag Plymouth"—Sal is noticeably silent on the finer points of automotive design and styling (*OR*, 116, 207, 234, 225). His emphasis falls on Dean's driving. Indeed, many different automobiles are central to the evolving relationship between the two main characters, but none in particular stands out as especially important. They are interchangeable: "Dean rushed out the next moment and stole a car right from the driveway and took a dash to downtown Denver and came back with a newer, better one" (*OR*, 221). Their function within the narrative, irrespective of engineering and design specifications, is to give Dean the opportunity to demonstrate his skills, which are the skills of a hobo—a guy "born on the road" and raised in a "jalopy"—rather than those of an aficionado. Dean's "soul," Sal suggests, "is wrapped up in a fast car," but make and model are unimportant to him, as long as he can speed: "'Hee-hee-hee!' tittered Dean and he passed a car on a narrow bridge and swerved in dust and roared on" (*OR*, 235). For this reason, Dean can be partially aligned with the figure of the "hot-rodder," a custom-car enthusiast frequently caricatured as a speed freak. Hot-rodders garnered much attention in the two decades following World War II. In addition to provoking the ire of safe-driving activists, hot-rodders played an important part in American literary history. They helped to inspire the groundbreaking work of Tom Wolfe, the so-called New Journalism.[39] In Wolfe's 1963 article, often cited as "The Kandy-Kolored Tangerine-Flake Streamline Baby," the car appears as a social actor in what gets called "the hot-rod culture," but its role is strikingly different from what Kerouac imagines.[40]

At the beginning of the narrative, Sal sees "a hot-rod kid" whiz past him "with his scarf flying" (*OR*, 7), but *On the Road* never again mentions the figure of the hot-rodder, defined by David N. Lucsko as "an individual enthusiast who modifies his car for improved performance."[41] Such scant treatment is remarkable given that hot-rodders regularly made headlines during the years when Kerouac was on the road with Cassady. As early as 1949, the *New York Times* was warning of "an outbreak of speed epidemic among youngsters during the vacation period," quoting Thomas W. Ryan, director of the New York State Division of Safety and president of the Automobile Club of New York, as stating that "[p]ossession of a 'hot rod' car is presumptive evidence of an intent to speed. Speed is Public Enemy No. 1 of the highways. It is obvious that a driver of a 'hot rod' car has an irresistible temptation to step on it."[42] A year later, the newly established *American Quarterly* published "The Hot-Rod Culture," the first scholarly study of the phenomenon, by Gene Balsley, an undergraduate at the University of Chicago who had been working with sociologist David Riesman.[43] Balsley anticipated Wolfe's account of hot-rod culture by more than a decade. Contesting "the typical image of the hot rodder . . . as a deliberate and premeditated lawbreaker," Balsley turns attention away from the quest for speed and toward practices of customization and styling. "When the hot rodder rebuilds a Detroit car to his own design," the young sociologist argues, "he is aiming to create a car which is a magical and vibrant thing." Such a thing stands "largely as an engineering protest against Detroit," for "the hot rodder and his circle" are "highly articulate in their objections" to the American automotive industry. "The hot rodder," Balsley reports, "says that this production car is uneconomical, unsafe at modern road speeds, and uglier than it has any right to be."[44]

Without citing Balsley, Wolfe refines many of the themes that appear in "The Hot-Rod Culture," an article that he probably encountered while working toward his PhD in American studies at Yale in the 1950s. Profiling one George Barris, the so-called King of the Kustomizers, Wolfe writes, "Most of the work he was doing then was modifying Detroit cars—chopping and channeling. Chopping is lowering the top of the car, bringing it nearer to the hood line. Channeling is lowering the body itself down between the wheels."[45] These two practices transform commodities into aesthetic objects. "[I]t's like one of these Picasso or Miró rugs," Wolfe asserts, "You don't walk on the damn things. You hang them on the wall. It's the same with Barris' cars. In effect, they're sculpture."[46] But such sculptures do not rest idly in a gallery; they actively help to constitute a vibrant social world, the subculture of hot-rodders and custom-car enthusiasts in and around Los Angeles. For Wolfe, this subculture is best understood as an aesthetic economy: there are showrooms that operate like galleries; "custom-car artist[s]" like Barris who produce gorgeous and expensive objects; event planners who serve as de facto curators; magazine writers and editors who arbitrate questions of taste; and, most important, throngs of "maniacal" kids who not only constitute the

3.1. *Further* or *Furthur*, 1964. Photo © Allen Ginsberg/Corbis.

primary audience for car art but also long to be recognized as significant car artists themselves.[47] Wolfe figures LA car culture, in other words, as what Pierre Bourdieu terms a "field of restricted production" wherein "the producers produce for other producers," and he argues that this field is best understood as a kind of vernacular avant-garde.[48] But while Wolfe shares Kerouac's interest in the role of the car within a specific milieu, the hot-rodders were very different from the Beats, at least insofar as *On the Road* represents them. Dean longs only to drive with his pals—"Come on, man, let's *all* go riding" (*OR*, 222)—yet Barris "create[s] forms" that "will never touch the road." The latter are not "jalopies," acquired in a manic frenzy and discarded on a whim, but works of art: "If Brancusi is any good," Wolfe concludes, "then this thing"—the XPAK-400 Air Car—"belongs on a pedestal, too."[49]

Defining the automobile as an object to behold, this assertion prefigures a key theme of *The Electric Kool-Aid Acid Test* (1968), Wolfe's highly stylized account of the Merry Pranksters' 1964 bus trip and drug bender. Ken Kesey led the group, but Cassady drove the bus, a 1939 International Harvester splattered in psychedelic Day-Glo, named either "Further" or "Furthur," depending on who had completed the most recent paint job (figure 3.1). Although Kesey had achieved success as a novelist—with *One Flew Over the Cuckoo's Nest* (1962) and *Sometimes a Great Notion* (1964)—he got bored with the literary arts, so the bus and the road trip constituted something like his foray into a new mode of artistic production. "Kesey was already talking about how writing was an old-fashioned and artificial form," Wolfe notes, "and pointing out, for all who cared to look . . . the bus."[50] The turn away from literature was for Kesey a turn toward sculpture and performance, and many scholars have argued that the performance (the cross-country road trip) was an effort to upstage Kerouac, and thus to displace the Beats as the major countercultural movement in America.[51] Surely he had Kerouac in mind, yet thanks to Wolfe, the hot-rod culture seems to provide a more relevant context for the Pranksters' enterprise:

> Kesey gave the word and the Pranksters set upon [the bus] one afternoon. They started painting it and wiring it for sound and cutting a hole in the roof and fixing up the top of the bus so you could sit up there in the open air and play music, even a set of drums and electric guitars and electric bass and so forth, or just ride . . . There was going to be no goddamn sound on that whole trip, outside the bus, inside the bus, or inside your own freaking larynx, that you couldn't tune in on and rap off of. The painting job, meanwhile, with everybody pitching in in a frenzy of primary colors, yellows, oranges, blues, reds, was sloppy as hell, except for the parts Roy Seburn did, which were nice manic mandalas. Well, it was sloppy, but one thing you had to say for it; it was freaking lurid.[52]

This collective act of customization produced a stunning new object and lifeworld. Unlike the cars in *On the Road*, however, the bus is figured, here and elsewhere in the book, as what MoMA would call a "hollow, rolling sculpture." The Pranksters, much like the hot-rodders in Wolfe's *Esquire* piece, formed and fashioned themselves as a group through the practice of object making. What distinguishes them, though, is that the bus was a collective project rather than the product of one inspired individual like Barris, so "Further" is perhaps best understood as a kind of totem, which "[b]y expressing the social unit tangibly," as Durkheim puts it in his famous theory of totemism, "makes the unit itself more tangible to all."[53] When the Pranksters eventually did hit the road, moreover, the bus became a control center for social disruption; "it was freaking lurid," after all. Perched atop their totem-vehicle, they engaged in a practice called "tootling the multitudes"—playing music to match the disposition of someone they encountered: "This tootling had gotten to be a thing where you got on top of the bus and *played people* like they were music, the poor comatose world outside. If a guy looked at you fat and pissed off, you played on the flute in dying elephant tones."[54] Transposing facial expressions into sounds, Kesey and his followers transmitted, to paraphrase Georg Simmel, the mental life of the metropolis. They also orchestrated ad hoc social groupings centered on a particular nonhuman actor, the bus like no other.

FREEWAY EXISTENTIALISM

Two years after Wolfe published his book on the Pranksters, with its vivid rendering of social scenes formed in and around a "freaking lurid" bus, Didion published her second novel, *Play It as It Lays*, which is typically considered a finely wrought tale of malaise in Hollywood circa 1970, but also reads, at times, like a love story featuring a woman and a Corvette.[55] Her collection of essays, *Slouching Towards Bethlehem*, had appeared two years earlier, the same year as Wolfe's *Electric Kool-Aid Acid Test*, and showcased her stylistic brio, as well as her ability to combine the techniques of fiction writing and reportage. Along with Wolfe, Hunter S. Thompson, Truman Capote, Norman Mailer, Michael Herr, and others, she would soon come to be associated with both the New Journalism and the nonfiction novel, two subgenres that, as Howard Cunnell points out, have deep roots in *On the Road*, a nonfiction novel *avant la lettre*.[56] But her debt to Kerouac, I want to suggest, is not fully evident in her attempt to trouble the distinction between fact and fiction or between art and life. It is more strikingly revealed in her treatment of the open road, the site that was so important to Kerouac's literary imagination.

This site forms a key setting in Didion's second novel, whose protagonist, Maria Wyeth, spends considerable time driving the freeways of Southern California, partly to escape Hollywood and partly to cope with the loss of her four-year-old daughter, Kate, who has been sent by Carter, Maria's husband and Kate's father, to a hospital for treatment of a vaguely defined mental disorder. "In the first hot month of the fall after the summer she left Carter," the novel begins its first numerical chapter following three prologues, "Maria drove the freeway. She dressed every morning with a greater sense of purpose than she had felt in some time, a cotton skirt, a jersey, sandals she could kick off when she wanted to touch the accelerator."[57] Two of Maria's defining traits are indicated by this passage. First, her relationship to her Corvette is not merely sensuous, but sensual: just as Dean "hunche[s]" over the car and "guns her," Maria enjoys stroking the gas pedal with her bare foot. Second, she imagines and experiences the freeway as a special site. Hurrying to dress, she is invigorated, endowed with an uncommon sense of "purpose," by the anticipation of hitting the road. Of course, the roads that she drives are nothing like those in Kerouac's novel, not least because several of them, such as "the Santa Monica" and "the Santa Ana," form portions of the Interstate Highway System (*P*, 16). *On the Road* was published after the passage of the Federal-Aid Highway Act of

1956, which authorized the construction of the interstates, yet it depicts only local highways and city streets, for it recounts a series of journeys that occurred while the interstates were still just an idea.[58] For Maria, by contrast, they are very much a reality. More than that, though, Didion herself inhabited a car culture, circa 1970, that was very different from what Kerouac was experiencing in the late 1940s.

Play It as It Lays appeared amid widespread condemnation of the American car.[59] "For over half a century," declared Ralph Nader in 1965, "the automobile has brought death, injury, and the most inestimable sorrow and deprivation to millions of people. With Medea-like intensity, this mass trauma began rising sharply four years ago reflecting new and unexpected ravages by the motor vehicle."[60] The auto industry was justifiably alarmed. For its part, General Motors not only sent private detectives to track Nader's moves but also hired prostitutes to tempt him into a scandal (alas, to no avail).[61] A few years later, A. Q. Mowbray lamented "the sterile ooze of steel automata" seeping through American cities, whose "highest function," he proclaimed satirically, "ha[d] become the efficient moving and storage of automobiles." Pointing to the "mounting horror [of] our present orgy of highway building," he recalled Jane Jacobs, who had argued—in a chapter of *The Death and Life of Great American Cities* (1961) bluntly titled "Erosion of Cities or Attrition of Automobiles"—that cities are "casually disemboweled" by cars and their sites.[62] "Traffic arteries," Jacobs writes, "along with parking lots, gas stations, and drive-ins, are powerful and insistent instruments of city destruction."[63] Kenneth R. Schneider, writing the year after Mowbray, put the point even more starkly: "The automobile disperses and isolates the homes and places of interest that together constitute urbanity, while it simultaneously destroys natural openness," which is why "the struggle between man and motor will be revolutionary."[64] In a similar vein, Helen Leavitt attacked "the men and institutions who promote highways," for they "destroy our churches, schools, homes, and parks," while John Jerome was more succinct: "The premise of this book is that the automobile must go."[65] Along with many others, these commentators brought a new kind of attention to American automobility. Concentrating on a set of problems that still plague us, they set a precedent for more recent polemics, while providing a discursive complement to the anti-freeway activism—the so-called freeway revolts—of the period.[66]

Didion entered this conversation, although not to polemicize, with two essays about automobility from the late 1970s that cast an illuminating retrospective light on *Play It as It Lays*. The first, "On the Road," self-consciously recalls and revises Kerouac. It narrates her experience of her first book tour, traveling around the country with her daughter, her frantic schedule crammed with press interviews. "By the time I reached Boston," she writes, "ten days into the tour, I knew that I had never before heard and would possibly never again hear America singing at precisely this pitch: ethereal, speedy, an angel choir on Dexamyl."[67] The allusion to Whitman is meant to interrupt Kerouac. If his America sings, in *On the Road* and elsewhere, like an "angel headed hipster" hopped up on what he liked to call "benny," then hers is addicted to Dexamyl, which is not only a stimulant (like Benzedrine) but also an antidepressant.[68] Like so many of Didion's essays from the 1960s and '70s, especially those in *Slouching Towards Bethlehem*, "On the Road" draws a link between psychological distress and historical malaise. Yet in contrast to those essays, "On the Road" is structured by a series of oppositions to Kerouac that work to make a larger point about the etherealization of America at the dawn of the computer age. Against the image of Sal and Dean cruising intercity highways, Didion depicts herself and her daughter flying from one location to the next: "We spoke not of cities but of airports. If rain fell at Logan we could find sun at Dulles ... We saw air as our element" (*W*, 308–9). Against the thrill of the joyride, she tracks "the peculiar hormonal momentum of business travel" (ibid.). And against what Sal calls the "noble" desire to "*move*," she situates the desire for domestic stasis: "A kind of irritable panic came over us when room service went off, and also when no one answered in the housekeeping department" (ibid.). These oppositions disrupt the gender of travel, dislodging it from the masculine cast set by Kerouac and others, as the essay builds toward its conclusion: "I began to see the country itself as a projection on air, a kind of hologram, an invisible grid of image and opinion and electronic impulse" (*W*, 310).[69]

Thus, before Jean Baudrillard published the theory of simulacra for which he is best known, and before Fredric Jameson popularized the term "postmodern hyperspace," Didion was tracking something like the emergence of the hyperreal: the dispersal, precipitated by various innovations in technology and media, of the real material world into so many images and "electronic impulse[s]."[70] About a year earlier, she wrote an ethnographic and site-specific account of this process entitled "Bureaucrats," a feature that she republished in *The White Album* (1979). Visiting CalTrans, short for the California Department of Transportation, she meets the officials who monitor "The Loop," a forty-two-mile portion of the Southern California freeway system that is regarded "with a special veneration" (*W*, 236). "The Loop has its own mind," she explains, "a Xerox Sigma V computer which prints out, all day and all night, twenty-second readings on what is and is not moving in each of the Loop's eight lanes." These lanes are rendered as images on "the closed-circuit TV on the console," where the eponymous bureaucrats can "verify" an "incident," such as a traffic snarl or a collision. She adds with characteristic irony that "'[v]erifying' the incident does not after all 'prevent' the incident, which lends the enterprise a kind of tranced distance" (*W*, 236–37). Here and throughout the piece, religious language functions less as a nod to Kerouac than as an effort to convey "the state of mechanized rapture" induced by contemplating and especially by driving the roads that she describes:

> To understand what was going on it is perhaps necessary to have participated in the freeway experience, which is the only secular communion Los Angeles has. Mere driving on the freeway is in no way the same as participating in it. Anyone can "drive" on the freeway, and many people with no vocation for it do, hesitating here and resisting there, losing the rhythm of the lane change, thinking about where they came from and where they are going. Actual participants think only about where they are. Actual participation requires a total surrender, a concentration so intense as to seem a kind of narcosis, a rapture-of-the-freeway. The mind goes clean. The rhythm takes over. (*W*, 238–39)

Thinking of passages like this, the conservative critic Joseph Epstein dismissed Didion's project, in a 1984 essay for *Commentary*, as "freeway existentialism."[71] He was being flippant, yet the phrase is more apposite than he realized, especially for *Play It as It Lays*, a novel that draws an axiomatic distinction between two distinct *modes of being* on the road: "[a]ctual participation" versus "mere driving."

Maria Wyeth, Didion's answer to Kerouac's Dean, experiences both yet relishes the former. She was not born on the road but was irrevocably scarred, at a fairly young age, when her "mother ran the car off the highway outside Tonopah," a traumatic event that she learned about while riding "in a taxi one morning" (*P*, 8–9). The first paragraph of the first chapter alludes forcefully to the opening of *On the Road*. Maria's "actual participation" in "the freeway experience" is described just after we learn that she, like Sal, has split from her lover, thus establishing a complicated intertextual link. Like Dean, Maria is a talented driver, for "[s]he could shell and eat a hard-boiled egg at seventy miles an hour." Unlike him, however, she drives alone: hers is not a car full of companions but a solitary space where she can "move across four lanes of traffic . . . without once losing the *beat* on the radio" (*P*, 16; emphasis added). Given Didion's meticulous style, it is telling that "beat" appears as a noun, but not as a *proper* noun, on the second page of the novel. Even at the level of diction, *Play It as It Lays* subtly engages and revamps the precedent set by Kerouac.

Gender plays a role in this process—Maria identifies strongly as a mother; she suffers a botched abortion; "she play[s] a girl who was raped by the members of a motorcycle gang" in her second film with Carter (*P*, 19)— but more important to the story is the experience of loneliness.[72] Maria is often portrayed as an isolated figure. In the first prologue, we meet her, secluded in her room in an inpatient facility, contemplating her life: "Now I lie in the sun and play solitaire and listen to the sea . . . I see no one I used to know, but then I'm not just crazy about a lot of people" (*P*, 10). Carter tells us, a few pages later, "Maria has never understood friendship, conversation, the normal amenities of social exchange. Maria has difficulty talking to people with whom she is not sleeping" (*P*, 13). In fact, she even has difficulty differentiating the latter: "When she was not actually talking to [Les Goodwin] now she found it hard to keep him distinct from everyone else, everyone with whom she had ever slept or almost slept or refused to sleep or wanted to sleep" (*P*, 69). To be fair, her desire for isolation is also a desire for escape from an exhausting social scene: "I'm just very very very tired of listening to you all" (*P*, 85). As Maria experiences it, the social world of late-1960s Hollywood is both vapid ("'You have to come over sometime and use the sauna,' Larry Kulick said when he brushed by the table on his way inside. 'Stereo piped in, beaucoup fantastic'" [*P*, 37]) and brutal ("'Well *go* to sleep, cunt. Go to sleep. Die. Fucking vegetable'" [*P*, 185]). This depiction of sociality dramatizes a theme that Didion develops with less visceral force at other points in her writing. "Not much about California, on its own preferred terms," she argues in *Where I Was From*, "has encouraged its children to see themselves as connected to one another" (*W*, 992). In *Play It as It Lays*, Hollywood forms a microcosm of California, a social-spatial synecdoche that serves to illustrate how geography mediates sociality as well as its failure. Against the backdrop of this failure, however, emerges a redemptive relay between human and nonhuman.

Maria claims she loves her daughter above all: "What I play for here is Kate" (*P*, 4). But she appears most powerfully attached to her car, especially when she is engaged in "[a]ctive participation," to return to the phrase from "Bureaucrats," cruising "an intricate stretch just south of the interchange where successful passage from the Hollywood onto the Harbor require[s] a diagonal move across four lanes of traffic" (*P*, 16).[73] Executing this move, "without once braking or once losing the beat on the radio," leaves her "exhilarated," and when she finally slows, she "feel[s] for the first time the heavy weight of the becalmed car beneath her . . . the organism which absorbed all her reflexes, all her attention" (*P*, 17). Here and throughout the novel, Maria's driving is described in both religious and erotic terms. She inhabits a "state of mechanized rapture" as her full "attention" is "absorbed" during a moment of epiphany with the machine. For its part, the Corvette, which is likened to a living entity, appears postcoital, "becalmed" yet still panting after a major event. Still, even as scenes like this connect Maria to Kerouac's Dean, *Play It as It Lays* offers its own view of social life on the road. Instead of treating the automobile as a lifeworld that facilitates new social bonds, Didion figures it as an animate object, an "organism," that compensates for the failure of the social. Sal hits the road partly to meet new people, and the "greatest ride of [his] life" occurs in the back of a flat-bed truck "with about six or seven boys sprawled out on it" (*OR*, 22). Maria, by contrast, goes there to be alone with the one she loves.

TALKING CARS

The same aspiration, the desire to be alone with her car, animates Erin Hogan's *Spiral Jetta*, a 2008 art travelogue that extends the subgenre of the postwar American road narrative, updating it for the twenty-first century. "[A]s someone undergoing a sort of early midlife crisis," Hogan explains at the outset, "I was . . . interested in testing and challenging myself, breaking out of my nine-to-five routine and trying to find something in myself beyond the ability to answer e-mails, attend meetings, and meet friends for cocktails."[74] Much like Kerouac, she takes to the road in order to interrupt the humdrum of the everyday, but she also has specific destinations in mind, the monumental earthworks of the 1970s and '80s: Robert Smithson's *Spiral Jetty*, Nancy Holt's *Sun Tunnels*, Walter De Maria's *Lightning Field*, James Turrell's *Roden Crater*, Michael Heizer's *Double Negative*, and Donald Judd's exhibition space at Marfa, Texas. As the narrative unfolds, she intertwines lyrical self-reflection in the style of Sal—"I knew it was time to admit that I was a stranger in a strange town, alone out there in the middle of the country"—with extended analyses (drawing on her PhD in art history) of the aesthetic works that she encounters, thereby enacting a broader convergence of verbal and visual art.[75] Although scholarly convention separates the history of literature from that of other artistic disciplines, Hogan reminds us, the road draws them together. Since the dawn of the postwar era, so much of the most important work, within lyric poetry and narrative prose fiction, as well as within photography, sculpture, and performance, has emanated from an encounter with the physical sites of American automobility.

Indeed, minimalism itself might be said to have originated with a road trip. Among its primal scenes is Tony Smith's late-night drive on the unfinished New Jersey Turnpike. "The drive was a revealing experience," he explains. "The road and much of the landscape was artificial, and yet it couldn't be called a work of art. On the other hand, it did something for me that art had never done . . . There's no way you can frame it, you just have to experience it."[76] This quote was made famous by Michael Fried, whose still-controversial "Art and Objecthood" developed the central analytic of minimalism, circa 1967, partly through a reading of Smith. "But," he asks, "what was Smith's experience on the turnpike? Or to put the same question another way, if the turnpike, airstrips, and drill ground are not works of art, what are they—What, indeed, if not empty or 'abandoned' *situations?*" By posing such questions, Fried was arguing that Smith and his cohort (Donald Judd, Robert Morris, Robert Smithson, et al.) were at-tempting to release aesthetic experience from its dependence on an art object: "What replaces the object—what does the same job of distancing or isolating the beholder, of making him a subject, that the object did in the closed room—is above all the endlessness, or objectlessness, of the ap-proach or onrush of perspective."[77] He understood this replacement, exem-plified by Smith's account of being "on the turnpike," as an exercise of "profound hostility to the arts," specifically to the disciplines of painting and sculpture as they had developed through the first half of the twentieth century. This is why "Art and Objecthood" is so often read as a work of mourning for the death of modernism.[78]

But this was not the first time Fried addressed automobility. Earlier in the 1960s, he wrote a series of reviews for *Art International* that included assessments of John Chamberlain, the artist best known for working with trashed car parts.[79] "Within the past few years," Fried effused, "Chamberlain has made himself one of the best sculptors working anywhere in the world."[80] Deeply impressed by *Miss Lucy Pink*—an abstract piece, about the size of a minimalist cube, composed of scratched and dented sheet metal in pink, red, and yellow (figure 3.2)—he argued that the sculptor "articulates a subtle, changing volume that seems almost to breathe," proclaiming "the equilibrium between the curve and the buckle of his materials and the space they enclose [to be] so perfect."[81] Hogan, for her part, sharply dis-agrees; touring the Chamberlain galleries at Judd's Marfa, she declares his sculptures "sloppy and disorderly."[82] She cannot comprehend Judd's ardent support, which appeared as early as 1960 in a review for *Arts* magazine. Discussing Chamberlain's *Swannanoa* (figure 3.3), a 1959 precursor to *Miss Lady Pink*, Judd writes, "It is grandiloquent, proliferating exhaust pipes, rods, and billows of metal, exceedingly keen on remaining junk, and proud to be confused with an ordinary wreck. The verbosity implies the inex-haustible supply of material."[83]

Otherwise stark rivals throughout the 1960s, Judd and Fried could agree about Chamberlain, and their respective reviews are similar in two ways.[84] First, both suggest there is an anthropomorphic quality to his work, which is evoked by its curvy and sumptuous material and by its use of auto bodies to thematize embodiment *as such*. No doubt the artist intended this: speak-ing to Diane Waldman about the decision, made very early in his career, to shift from painting to sculpture, he said, "I was still in art school. I walked past the sculpture studio one time and I saw all these little people"—refer-ring to sculptures on pedestals—"standing on stands."[85] For both Judd and Fried, moreover, this quality is best described as a capacity for speech. On the one hand, as Judd suggests with terms like "grandiloquent" and "verbos-ity," Chamberlain's work can be loud, boisterous; on the other hand, as Fried claims, it can seem "almost to breathe" as it "radiates the kind of qui-

3.2. John Chamberlain, *Miss Lucy Pink*, 1962. Painted and chromium-plated steel, 47 × 42 × 39 inches (119.4 × 106.7 × 99 cm). Private collection. Art © 2014 Fairweather & Fairweather LTD/Artists Rights Society (ARS), New York. Photo credit: David Heald © SRGF, NY.

etness only completely achieved things can afford."[86] Fried's language here is stunning—especially when positioned against "Art and Objecthood," which appeared only three years later. While "Art and Objecthood" attacks the "blatantly anthropomorphic" character of minimalist sculpture, and of Judd's work in particular, Fried's review of Chamberlain imagines the mute aesthetic object as a speaking subject, panting quietly.[87]

Supposing it were to speak, though: What might it say? A sculpture like *Miss Lucy Pink* might apologize. Viewed from a certain vantage, it appears to be opening itself up for a conciliatory embrace. Perhaps on behalf of

3.3. John Chamberlain, *Swannanoa/Swannanoa II*, 1959. Art © 2014 Fairweather & Fairweather LTD/Artists Rights Society (ARS), New York. Photo credit: Whitney Museum of American Art, *Beat Culture and the New America, 1950–1965* (Nov. 9, 1995–Feb. 4, 1996).

every "ordinary wreck," it is asking to be forgiven for causing Nader's trio of "death, injury, and . . . inestimable sorrow." A sculpture like *Swannanoa*, though, might just talk to itself, its constituent parts ("exhaust pipes, rods, and billows of metal") each having their say. Should they start to bicker, they would be acting like the Aramis transportation system as Latour has described it. Conceived in 1970, the year that Didion published *Play It as It Lays*, Aramis was a prototype of personal rapid transit, a hybrid of the automobile and mass transportation that was meant to solve a growing traffic problem in Paris, but the system was never implemented. In Latour's book on the subject, he deploys the literary device of prosopopoeia to give voice to his object of study: "*I glide right over the tracks,*" proclaims the chassis to the computer chip, "*and I actually even let myself be bumped a bit*"; to which the chip retorts, "*Oh, stop pretending you're an automobile!*"[88] At once ludicrous and serious, this scene exemplifies what he defines on the previous page as a *technogram*: "To the *sociogram*," a graphic representation used by social scientists to analyze the structure and pattern of interactions within a group, "you have to add the *technogram*, which charts the interests and attachments of nonhumans."[89] Latour's point, here and throughout his work, is that nonhuman actors, like human ones, have something like needs and desires for collective life, which is why they cannot be understood merely to constitute the passive, mute backdrop for human sociality.

When the literary texts of Kerouac, Didion, and even Wolfe depict life on the road, they become technogrammatic, for they dwell on the "attachments" of a particular nonhuman, treating the car as a dynamic actor in an unfolding drama of social relations. But Chamberlain has been understood to go a step further than his literary contemporaries. His best critics suggest that he grants cars a kind of voice, both "verbos[e]" and "grandiloquent," through his practice of salvage and refabrication, which might be said to render the Latourian technogram in visual and plastic form. And yet, to give voice to the nonhuman is to humanize it, not to see it as a recalcitrant other, which is why his sculptures, as both Fried and Judd intimate, finally point to what Daniel Miller calls "the evident humanity of the car," not only its anthropomorphic quality but also "the degree to which it has become an integral part of the cultural environment within which we see ourselves as human."[90] It is not especially profound to say that this environment is unstable, yet in the era of automobility the road manifests a particular kind of flux—a movement of bodies and machines, of mechanical centaurs, through a space designed specifically for speed. If you visualize the road from the perspective of CalTrans, then you see a striking example of social interaction as an ever-shifting assemblage of humans and nonhumans, a network whose "flows of translation" are constantly remaking the site.[91] Yet what happens to sociality at a site that not only appears static but also seems to exemplify stasis as such, to emblematize ossification, obsolescence, and stalled progress? I explore this question in chapter 4.

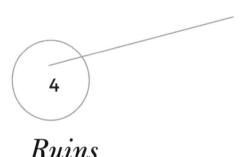

Ruins

President Eisenhower had an epiphany in a traffic snarl. In the spring of 1959, traveling from Washington, DC, to Camp David, he was delayed at a construction site, one of the many such sites that he had authorized three years earlier with his signing of the Federal-Aid Highway Act of 1956. "Your highway taxes at work," asserted the now-familiar green sign that had been planted just at the edge of the city. It turns out that the president, the man behind the largest public works project in history, had not realized until this instant that the interstates would not only *connect* American cities but *cut through* them as well. Somewhat alarmed, Eisenhower sent a "highest priority" directive to General John Stewart Bragdon, assistant for Public Works Planning, that urged him to "[re]examine policies, methods, and standards now in effect," including "intra-metropolitan routing" and "urban planning."[1] We might call this Eisenhower's Jane Jacobs moment—the moment he acknowledged that "[t]raffic arteries," to borrow Jacobs's formulation, "are powerful and insistent instruments of city destruction."[2] After all, the Highway Act not only licensed widespread building and development; it also precipitated large-scale demolition and ruination, the effects of which are still perhaps most palpable in American cities, where "highway taxes" (or, more recently, the funds of the 2009 American Recovery and Reinvestment Act) seem endlessly "at work" on the distressed material infrastructures of American automobility.

Such infrastructures fascinated Robert Smithson. Eight years after Eisenhower's epiphany, the artist saw some version of the same sign ("Your highway taxes at work") while trekking around Passaic, New Jersey. He was on the famous "tour" that would constitute the basis for "The Monuments of Passaic," his well-known travelogue and photo-essay that originally appeared in *Artforum* in 1967. What Smithson called "Site Selection Study"— venturing to specific locales, investigating their geographical, geological, and phenomenological elements, and writing up his findings—was a central component of his artistic practice, and the "Monuments" piece stands among the most influential texts of postwar American art writing. A complex verbal and visual composition, it discloses many of his key concerns, particularly his fascination with ruins. While surveying the landscape, which comes across (especially in the photos) as a drab wasteland, he grows increasingly "perplexed." But then he glimpses the sign, and it "explain[s] everything" to him about the site, including the fact that $2,867,000 from the Federal Highway Trust Fund are, indeed, "at work" there. "That zero panorama," he writes with his characteristic blend of irony and seriousness, "seemed to contain *ruins in reverse*, that is—all the new construction that would eventually be built. This is the opposite of the 'romantic ruin' because the buildings don't *fall* into ruin *after* they are built but rather *rise* into ruin before they are built."[3]

For Smithson, then, such a site not only exemplifies the dialectical entwining of construction and destruction; it also spatializes time as a multidirectional vector. As the highway "*rise*[s] into ruin," it travels both forward and backward in time, developing into the structure it will be while prefiguring its own demolition. Smithson spent much of his career exploring such dynamics, and his engagement with material sites beyond the gallery or museum, especially sites of ruin, often entailed a sophisticated treatment of both temporality and history. For this reason and others, I want to align him with Thomas Pynchon, a novelist whose own treatment of ruins mediates his preoccupation with time, as well as his celebrated critique of conventional historiography.[4] Although Smithson never discussed Pynchon as he did, say, Poe or Ballard, *The Crying of Lot 49* was sitting on a shelf in his library when he died.[5] Both considered key figures in the emergence of postmodernism within their respective disciplines, the artist and the author shared many preoccupations during the 1960s and '70s, such as entropy and the paradox of representation without resemblance.[6] Moreover, while Smithson is best known for his site-specific projects in visual and plastic media, he was also a prolific writer of narrative and essayistic prose, and while Pynchon is most readily appreciated for his experimentation with narrative form, he was (and is) equally interested in material sites, or what he calls "nonverbal reality."[7]

My goal in comparing these two figures, however, is not merely to point out the overlap. Nor is it to dwell on the question of why their respective bodies of work bear a certain similarity to each other, for that question is fairly well answered by the fact that they were almost exact contemporaries (Smithson was born in 1938, Pynchon in 1937) who not only acknowledged many of the same influences, from T. S. Eliot to Norbert Wiener, but also drew inspiration from the paradigm shifts that we now recognize as emergent poststructuralism and the linguistic turn. Rather, the goal of this chapter is to develop a fresh critical vocabulary for apprehending Pynchon's astonishingly strange debut novel, specifically its figuration of Malta as a site of ruin. Since it was first published in 1963, *V.* has alternately mesmerized and bewildered its readers. "Nothing more intricately conceived than Thomas Pynchon's first novel," wrote Richard Poirier in the *New York Review of Books*, "has appeared in American fiction since the work in the thirties by Faulkner, Nathanael West and Djuna Barnes."[8] He was among the earliest critics to note the "cryptographic" quality of a text that, two months earlier, George Plimpton had described in the *New York Times* as "brilliant and turbulent."[9] Analyzing Pynchon's work in relation to Smithson's, I contend, can reorient our sense of that brilliance while helping us to account for the turbulence.

The argument that follows, therefore, begins by tracking the links between the artist and the author through a comparative reading of two texts that appeared less than one year apart: Smithson's 1967 "Monuments" essay and Pynchon's only piece of published journalism, "A Journey into the Mind of Watts," an account of urban ruins and ruination, first published in the *New York Times Magazine* in 1966. Then, adapting Smithson's dialectic of site versus nonsite, I go on to develop an interpretive framework for *V.* Among the most poignant and puzzling scenes in the novel are those that render the massive bombardment of Malta during World War II: "that ongoing, vast—but somehow boring—destruction of an island."[10] Deploying Smithson's terminology, I aim to show that Pynchon did not merely treat Malta, with its "bombed-out buildings" and "buff-colored rubble," as a setting or a mise-en-scène or even a chronotope (*V.*, 423). Rather, he established a complex relay between an aesthetic object (the novel) and a real site (Malta) that can be understood as an instantiation of the nonsite/site dialectic that was so important to the artist. My account of this dialectic ultimately seeks to explain how and why ruins came to matter within what might be called Pynchon's sociological imagination. I argue that the novelist turned to World War II Malta, to a site where a particular society was being systematically ruined, in order to pose a set of interrelated questions about the *limits* of the social. Where does the social end? Where does it begin? Can social relations be understood as diachronic, to extend through a very long stretch of time, such that someone who lived, say, five thousand years ago might be viewed as your associate?

Such questions suggested themselves to Pynchon as he conducted research on Maltese history, geography, and literary culture. The significance of that research is evident in a letter that the novelist sent to his editor, Corlies Smith, on April 30, 1962, as the two were tussling over the title. "No, damnit, I do not want to call it WORLD ON A STRING, not even for a working title." Instead, Pynchon proposed a few other options, including "FOOTSTEPS OF THE GONE, which is taken from a poem by John J. Cremona, a Maltese poet writing in English during the '40s and the basis for Fausto Maijstral," a central character in the Maltese segments of V. To bolster his case, Pynchon goes on to quote the relevant stanza from Cremona:

> The skies are cleft, it seems.
> Beggars walk out of heaven
> to knock at bolted doors,
> and in the distance can be heard
> the din of ancient wars;
> and as forms travel endlessly
> along an endless lawn,
> the footsteps of the coming and
> the footsteps of the gone[11]

What I want to notice about these lines, beyond the fact that they were important enough to Pynchon to inspire a possible title for his debut novel, is the final image that they produce—the "endless lawn" that is peopled by restless "forms." The poem conjures a site of simultaneity or a plane of immanence where the actors of the past ("the gone") meet those of the future ("the coming"); there is movement here but no teleology, infinite extension without development. This is how Pynchon came to understand Malta, a site that functions variously in his experimentation with both historiography and sociology. Making sense of that experimentation will involve following Pynchon through the ruins of the ancient archipelago, but before joining him there, I want to take the full tour of Smithson's Passaic.

PASSAIC AND WATTS

"On Saturday, September 30, 1967," the artist writes, "I went to the Port Authority Building on 41st Street and 8th Avenue. I bought a copy of the *New York Times* and a Signet paperback called *Earthworks* by Brian W. Aldiss. Next I went to ticket booth 21 and purchased a one-way ticket to Passaic" (*CW*, 68). So begins one of the most important road trips in the history of art. This opening gambit already indicates the hyperspecificity of Smithson's description—the exact date, the precise location, the full proper name. He means to register the phenomenological richness of his experience without taking that experience too seriously: "Outside the bus window a

Howard Johnson's Motor Lodge flew by—a symphony in orange and blue" (*CW*, 69). While the irony of his prose is palpable, so is the intensity of his genuine interest in the mundane and the everyday. Like Pynchon, as Jeremy Gilbert-Rolfe and John Johnston point out in their classic essay on *Gravity's Rainbow* and the *Spiral Jetty*, Smithson had "a devout regard for the banal," a quasi-religious ability to appreciate the opacity of the ordinary.[12] Hence, when he finally arrives in Passaic, he will concentrate on what Robert Venturi and his *Learning from Las Vegas* colleagues termed "ugly and ordinary architecture," defining otherwise unremarkable elements in the built environment—a typical bridge, a pumping derrick, a sandbox, a rusty pipe—as "monuments" worthy of scrutiny and contemplation.[13] His aim is to stage the question of what constitutes a monument, to exert pressure on that very category by broadening its application.

Yet "The Monuments of Passaic" amounts to more than a polemic against what the artist called "social structures which confine art" (*CW*, 110). It is also a sustained effort to examine three interconnected problems that he took to be endemic to the site. The first is entropy. This phenomenon, the tendency of any system toward increasing disorder, was immensely important to him throughout his career, and he glimpses it here in the "unitary chaos" of new highway construction near the banks of the Passaic River (*CW*, 71). The second is the homogeneity of postwar suburbia: "The houses mirrored themselves into colorlessness ... Everything about the site remained wrapped in blandness and littered with shiny cars—one after another they extended into a sunny nebulosity" (*CW*, 71, 73). Smithson argued elsewhere that this homogeneity helped to exacerbate the first problem: "The slurbs, urban sprawl, and the infinite number of housing developments of the postwar boom have contributed to the architecture of entropy" (*CW*, 13). But the most important problem in "Monuments" is the problem of temporality.[14] In particular, Smithson seeks to point out how multiple time periods might be understood to coexist within a single space: "Since it was Saturday," he asserts, scanning the construction site, "many machines were not working, and this caused them to resemble prehistoric creatures trapped in the mud, or, better, extinct machines—mechanical dinosaurs stripped of their skin. On the edge of this prehistoric Machine Age were pre- and post–World War II suburban houses" (*CW*, 71).

This conceit, likening the devices of heavy industry to 225-million-year-old beasts, figures Passaic as a palimpsest of distinct epochs, its very distant past made present by the machines that are constructing its future form.[15] "Both past and future," Smithson wrote regarding the work of Donald Judd, Robert Morris, Sol LeWitt, Dan Flavin, and others, "are placed into an objective present," and he seems to be exploring that idea here (*CW*, 11). The trope of the palimpsest is crucial to this exploration, and it appears again a few pages later, just after the artist asks, semiseriously, "Has Passaic replaced Rome as the Eternal City?" He does not provide an answer, exactly, but he does offer a striking image: "If certain cities of the world were placed end to end in a straight line according to size, starting with Rome, where would Passaic be in that impossible progression? Each city would be a three-dimensional mirror that would reflect the next city into existence" (CW, 74). Thus, each city would be a palimpsest of two cities—one manifest, the other latent. "[T]he suburbs," however, are different. While one city contains another future city in Smithson's model, the suburbs hold "an abandoned set of futures," or futures that *will exist* only as what *might have existed* (CW, 74, 72).

Throughout "Monuments," then, Smithson ponders how different sites *materialize* time differently—how cities and suburbs function as distinct "hideouts for time" (CW, 11). This conception of time, as both site specific and material, emerged through his study of geology and crystallography, and it animated his critique of traditional historiography. Indeed, as Jennifer L. Roberts has demonstrated, Smithson's "entire career can be understood as a continuing, and constantly renegotiated, engagement with the practice and philosophy of history"—that is, an effort, in both verbal and visual media, to confront the "profound uncertainty about the shape and meaning of historical time."[16] At his most polemical, Smithson considered history "a facsimile of events held together by flimsy biographical information" (CW, 41). This is where his thinking most closely resembles Pynchon's. The novelist, as several generations of scholars have shown, is not only fascinated by the problem of time but also deeply skeptical of the notion that historical knowledge could be objective and complete, rather than subjective and partial. "People read what news they wanted to," he writes in V., "and each accordingly built his own rathouse of history's rags and straws" (V., 243).[17] In addition, Pynchon often explores his concerns with time and history through an engagement with specific sites, especially Malta but also Watts. The site of a large-scale race riot in August 1965, the Watts neighborhood of Los Angeles caught Pynchon's attention in June 1966.[18] While Watts is very different from Passaic, Pynchon's "Journey into the Mind of Watts" nonetheless bears a certain similarity to Smithson's "Monuments" essay. Both texts deploy the conventions of travel writing and reportage, although "Watts" is more an exposé of urban poverty than an art travelogue. Still, Pynchon's descriptions of the built environment make it seem distinctive for its vernacular monuments: the famous Watts Towers.

Fabricated over the course of thirty-three years by an Italian immigrant named Simon Rodia, the Watts Towers consist of seventeen interconnected structures, two of which stand more than ninety-nine feet tall. They comprise steel pipes and rods, wrapped with wire mesh, coated with mortar, and decorated with found objects—what Pynchon names "a dazzling mosaic of Watts debris," including "busted glass, busted crockery, nails, tin cans, all kinds of scrap and waste."[19] To understand the Towers as monuments is to acknowledge their peculiar temporality. Instead of freezing a moment in time, as most monuments do by commemorating a specific event, they register the processual labor of the sculptor: Rodia's thirty-three-year project of object making. The human subjects at Watts, however, are more conventionally monumental: "Watts," Pynchon writes, "is full of street corners where people stand, as they have been, some of them, for 20 or 30 years" (*J*, 82). For him, these people register a troubling stasis at the site—an extremely poor black neighborhood that was not enjoying the benefits of the booming postwar economy. Hence, adapting C. P. Snow, Pynchon aims to showcase "the co-existence of two very different cultures: one white and one black" within Los Angeles. Both political and ethical, this project involves a two-part rhetorical strategy. Deploying the "you" pronoun, he interpellates his reader as a Watts resident: "So you groove instead down the freeway, maybe wondering when some cop is going to stop you because the old piece of a car you're driving, which you bought for $20 or $30 you picked up somehow, makes a lot of noise and burns some oil" (*J*, 80). The point here is to make "you" see "the poverty of Watts" from the perspective of the impoverished, to cause the reader to inhabit, however imperfectly, the position of the black underclass.[20]

Pynchon also means to vivify the site itself, as Smithson means to vivify Passaic, through hyperspecific descriptions of the banal: "Or, on down the street, vacant lots, still looking charred around the edges, winking with empty Tokay, port and sherry pints, some of the bottles peeking out of paper bags, others busted" (*J*, 78). A year after the riot, then, Watts remains in ruins—"Lots whose buildings were burned off them are still waiting vacant and littered with garbage" (*J*, 80)—even as it sustains a kind of ongoing ruination: "From here," Pynchon continues, "much of the white culture that surrounds Watts ... in a curious way, besieges it" (*J*, 78). Thus, Pynchon defines Watts as an urban ruin in two ways. He not only provides a "panoramic sense" of the material environment as a wasteland but also suggests that this environment is both *anomalous* and *untimely* (*J*, 35). Like other (very different) types of ruins (e.g., the Colosseum in Rome, Machu Picchu), Watts is "surrounded" by a material context, what Pynchon dubs "the L.A. Scene," within and against which it is framed, and its alterity is at least partly an effect of its temporality (*J*, 78). This site has, in some sense, fallen out of time; or, to use Smithson's terms, time is "compressed or stopped" at Watts (*CW*, 17). Pynchon is finally interested in how such stasis ramifies psychologically for the denizens of the neighborhood, which is why the article is pitched as a journey into the *mind* of a locale, a psychogeography. Here again his preoccupations resonate closely with Smithson's, for the artist was consistently engaged by "those aspects of mental experience that somehow coincide with the physical world" (*CW*, 208).

In *V.* the coincidence between mind and matter appears as the correspondence between self and site. "Manhood on Malta," says one character during a moment of acute self-reflection, "thus became increasingly defined in terms of rockhood" (*V.*, 360). Malta is a rocky archipelago that lies approximately 50 miles south of Sicily, 175 miles east of Tunisia, and 207 miles north of Libya. It covers just over 122 square miles, and it is densely populated. First settled in 5200 BCE, it has endured an extensive history of invasion and siege: the Greeks, the Phoenicians, the Romans, the Arabs, the Knights of St. John, Napoleon, and the British Empire have all laid claim to the site.[21] This history, as well as Maltese geography, fascinated Pynchon. Of all the sites that have mattered to him—New York City, Los Angeles, London—Malta, its capital "Valletta" in particular, seems to occupy a privileged position within his literary imagination. Although the biographical details are scant, scholars are fairly certain that, as a member of the US Navy, Pynchon visited Malta between August and November of 1956, exactly when his protagonists in *V.* visit. If the Watts article provides any indication of his approach to site-specific fieldwork, then we can assume his time there involved careful scrutiny of the social and spatial particulars of the archipelago—especially its ruins. This firsthand research, call it Pynchon's journey into the mind of Malta, was complemented by scrupulous reading on Maltese geography, history, politics, and culture.[22] All this attention eventuated in a novel with a very complex relationship to a site that it so stunningly describes.

But Pynchon does not merely describe Malta. He transposes spatial into literary form, thereby establishing a mimetic link between *V.* and the actual archipelago in ruins. This is a way of arguing that, even as Pynchon imagines three distinct Maltese chronotopes[23]—Malta in the midst of World War II, at the height of the Suez Crisis, and during the 1919 uprising known as the Sette Giugno—he also constructs what Smithson calls a "Dialectic of Site and Nonsite" between Malta and *V.* (*CW*, 152–53). Although Smithson defined this dialectic with varying degrees of precision throughout the later part of his career, he achieved some clarity in 1968 with his unpublished "Provisional Theory of Nonsites":

> *The Non-Site (an indoor earthwork)* is a three dimensional logical picture that is *abstract*, yet it *represents* an actual site in N.J. (The Pine Barrens Plains). It is by this three dimensional metaphor that one site can represent another site which does not resemble it—thus *The Non-Site* ... Between the *actual site* in the Pine Barrens and *The Non-Site* itself exists a space of metaphoric significance. It could be that "travel"

in this space is a vast metaphor. Everything between the two sites could become physical metaphorical material devoid of natural meanings and realistic assumptions. (*CW*, 364; italics in the original)

Part of a theory that he said "could be abandoned at any time," this characteristically brilliant and playful passage adumbrates a number of enigmas (indoor earthwork, three-dimensional picture, physical yet metaphorical, abstract yet actual, representation without resemblance) in order to transform dichotomies into dialectics. "The range of convergence between Site and Nonsite," Smithson wrote elsewhere, "consists of a course of hazards, a double path made up of signs, photographs, and maps that belong to both sides of the dialectic at once. Both sides are present and absent at the same time" (*CW*, 153).

He was thinking of an installation such as "A Nonsite, Franklin, New Jersey." First shown in the blockbuster *Earthworks* exhibition at Dwan Gallery in 1968, this installation consists of bins containing limestone from the vicinity of the Franklin Furnace Mines, as well as an aerial map of the site (figure 4.1). An avid student of both geology and crystallography, Smithson carefully examined the limestone that he exhibited. "I chose this site because it has an abundance of broken rock," he wrote. "I needed fragments 2" to 15" thick for the six [*sic*] bins of *The Nonsite*. The most common minerals found on the dump are calcite (physical properties: crystal—hexagonal, cleavage—perfect rhombohedral, fracture—conchoidal, glows red) and willemite (physical properties: crystal—hexagonal, cleavage—basal, fracture—uneven to subconchoidal, glows green)."[24] Assuming "the persona of a geologic agent," Smithson combed the site for these minerals on one of his many "rock hunting trips in New Jersey" (*CW*, 298, 7). Then, in fabricating the installation, he constructed a nonsite, thereby giving aesthetic form to what he called "the physical, raw reality" of the site, the quarry at Franklin (*CW*, 178). Each trapezoidal bin in the gallery contains minerals that correspond to a specific segment of the map on the wall, and the ore is distributed proportionally. In its precisely structured form, therefore, this installation exemplifies how Smithson's nonsites are, as W. J. T. Mitchell puts it, "defined by [their] reference" to a site beyond the exhibition venue.[25]

The artist himself would emphasize that this referential link constitutes a "double path." It is easy enough to see how the nonsite, as a gallery installation, endows the site with a particular aesthetic form, but it is also crucial to recognize that, prior to the scene of exhibition, the site itself has already performed some measure of authorial labor, furnishing source materials (i.e., "the physical, raw reality") as well as a certain *logic* that the artist, as "geologic agent," is excavating and presenting. Nonsites represent sites, but

4.1. Robert Smithson, *A Nonsite (Franklin, New Jersey)*, 1968. Art © Estate of
Robert Smithson/Licensed by VAGA, New York, NY. Collection: Museum of
Contemporary Art Chicago, gift of Susan and Lewis Manilow. Photo credit:
Nathan Keay © Museum of Contemporary Art Chicago.

to a certain degree these representations are, as Miwon Kwon suggests, "formally determined or directed" by their referents.[26] So how does this "double
path," this mutual constitution of site and nonsite, become visible within
the medium of narrative prose fiction? It becomes visible when a given text
(such as Pynchon's debut novel) represents a specific site (such as Malta)
while adopting that site's logic in and as its mode of representation. *V.* represents Malta as a ruin—depicting Valletta in particular as a "[p]oor shat-
tered city" (*V.*, 370)—and in so doing arrogates the logic of the ruin as it has
been defined from Simmel to Stoler.

V. comprises two interrelated and intercalated narratives. The first, whose protagonist is Benny Profane, unfolds mostly in New York City circa 1956, and it is more or less a story about a gang of slackers, the "Whole Sick Crew," hanging around at crash pads and getting into minor trouble. The second narrative, whose protagonist is Herbert Stencil, unfolds between 1898 and 1943 in a series of disparate locales, including New York, Mallorca, Alexandria and Cairo, Paris, Florence, German Southwest Africa (Namibia), and Malta. Fusing the conventions of detective and historical fictions with the experimental techniques of postmodernism, Stencil's narrative is all about obsession. As he hunts relentlessly for his object of desire—the enigmatic V.—his search precipitates the novel's jarring movements through both time and space. While it is Stencil who travels "all over the Western world," Malta is initially mentioned in the opening chapter when Profane and another character, Pappy Hod, are discussing Pappy's estranged wife, Paola (*V.*, 431). "She'd said sixteen" was her age, "but no way of telling because she'd been born just before the war and the building with her records destroyed, like most other buildings on the island of Malta" (*V.*, 6). This passage, which goes on to pinpoint precisely where Pappy first met Paola—"the Metro Bar, on Strait Street. The Gut. Valletta, Malta"—exemplifies how concretely Pynchon means to render this site, whose many "topological deformities" he describes at length (*V.*, 521). Moreover, it depicts Malta as a ruin, a besieged island that has suffered massive architectural damage, thereby anticipating chapter 11, "Confessions of Fausto Maijstral," which details the utter devastation of World War II: "the ruined walls, rubble heaps and holes" (*V.*, 366).

Pynchon's treatment of Malta as a ruin calls to mind a rich theoretical discourse that has sought to define the logic of such sites. Tracking the dialectic between "the will of the spirit and the necessity of nature," Georg Simmel argued in 1911 that ruins reveal "the present form of the past," and Walter Benjamin echoed this point about a decade later, asserting that "[i]n the ruin history has physically merged into the setting."[27] Siegfried Kracauer appreciated how Simmel "reads a deeper symbolic meaning into" the ruin by charting "the impact [it] ha[s] on our feelings," while for Benjamin, he pointed out, "knowledge arises out of ruins."[28] Ernst Bloch understood the ruin along similar lines, but after World War II he sought to draw a sharp contrast between two kinds of ruins and processes of ruination: "How different these sentimentally contrived ruins," he wrote, regarding those found in the Gothic novel, "from the horribly real ones which the American terror-attacks have left behind."[29] These observations have influenced more recent scholarship that cuts across the humanities and interpretive social sciences. Ann Laura Stoler, for example, asserts that ruins "condense alternative senses of history" and "draw on residual pasts to make claims on futures," even as they "create a sense of irretrievability or of futures lost."[30] Likewise, Nick Yablon concentrates on the peculiar temporality of these sites. "To some extent, all ruins exhibit a degree of nonsynchronicity," he claims, "that belies any simple notion of a completed past or a self-contained present." All told, this discourse repeatedly draws attention to what Yablon (following Nietzsche) calls the "untimeliness" of ruins: the way that they spatialize multiple times, as well as multiple *senses* of time, within a single site.[31]

Pynchon visualizes this point at the end of chapter 16, just before Profane disappears into the sea with his new companion, Brenda Wigglesworth: "Later, out in the street, near the sea steps she inexplicably took his hand and began to run. The buildings in this part of Valletta, eleven years after war's end, had not been rebuilt. The street, however, was level and clear" (*V.*, 506). Ambling around Valletta in the autumn of 1956, Profane is surrounded by soldiers preparing for war: "As an indication of the military buildup in Malta since the beginning of the Suez crisis, there overflowed into the street a choppy sea of green Commando berets, laced with the white and blue of naval uniforms . . . Nearby at a newspaper kiosk, red scare headlines proclaimed BRITISH INTEND TO MOVE INTO SUEZ!" (*V.*, 477). Here Profane encounters what Andreas Huyssen terms an "urban palimpsest," wherein the interplay of ruin and repair—bombed-out buildings on a "level and clear" street—dramatizes the friction between one historical epoch and another, disclosing both the passage of time and a kind of temporal stasis, as the buildings appear lodged in 1943, while their environs, from the street to the city to the whole of Malta, have advanced to 1956.[32] Such palimpsests emerge throughout the novel, especially in its eleventh chapter, whose narrator, Fausto Maijstral, depicts the ruination of World War II as he discusses a five-thousand-year-old ruin, a megalith temple complex named Ħaġar Qim. Situating ruins within ruins, then, Fausto's narration deploys the trope of the palimpsest in more ways than one. The manifold use of this trope enables Pynchon to build the logic of the ruin into the formal structure of *V.*

In the strictest sense, "the trope of the palimpsest," as Huyssen puts it, "is inherently literary and tied to writing," for it refers to "a manuscript in which later writing has been superimposed on earlier (effaced) writing." But in a more general sense, a palimpsest is any "multilayered record," including a geographical or geological "structure"—such as a ruin or, as Huyssen suggests, a city like Berlin—"characterized by superimposed features produced at two or more distinct periods."[33] Pynchon conjoins these two meanings of the term in chapter 11. As Fausto confesses his sins, he delineates a "successive rejection of personalities," developing a "multilayered record" of himself (literally: Fausto I, II, III, and IV) while describing Malta in the midst of World War II as a landscape of modern ruins grafted on to ancient ones (*V.*, 335). The narrative form of the chapter, moreover, approx-imates that of a palimpsest. The last page of the previous chapter concludes with Paola giving Fausto's confession to Stencil: "You ought to see this," she says, "[h]anding him a small packet of type-written pages. *Confessions*, the title . . . 'Read,' she said, 'And see'" (*V.*, 331). Thus, when we flip the page to read the confession, our eyes are aligned with Stencil's, a diegetic reader holding a manuscript that not only thematizes effacement and erasure—"a successive rejection of personalities"—but also includes texts embedded within texts, diary entries that Fausto quotes as a means of illustrating his previous selves. These diary entries, literary fragments of extinct Faustos, are situated within and contextualized by the confession, just as the confession itself is embedded within Stencil's scene of reading, which takes place in-side a New York City apartment in 1956. All this layering and contextualiz-ing—of texts within texts, of selves within selves, and of Fausto's scene of writing (World War II Malta) within Stencil's scene of reading (Cold War America)—establishes a formal analogy between this portion of *V.* and the site that it describes. For, as the discourse on ruins since Simmel has sug-gested, the ruin is a site where one historical epoch (and, in some cases, one civilization) is not merely conjoined with but *contextualized by* another that, to a certain extent, shapes it. This is what Simmel meant when he claimed that ruins divulge the present *form* of the past.

Fausto inaugurates his elaborate act of self-contextualization by empha-sizing the physical features of his location. "The room," he explains, refer-ring to his makeshift confessional, "is in a building which had nine such rooms before the war. Now there are three. The building is on an escarp-ment above the Dockyard. The room is stacked atop two others—the other two-thirds of the building were removed by the bombing, sometime during the winter of 1942–43" (*V.*, 334). So begins his lengthy and moving account of how Malta was decimated by the aerial bombing campaigns of World War II. As he cites his diaries and journals, he recalls the crisis of the war— "For a year and a half Malta averaged ten raids per day" (*V.*, 340)—and his depiction of what Stoler terms "processes of ongoing ruination" sets the stage for lyrical and elliptical reflections on time and history.[34] Before com-ing to these reflections, though, he concentrates on the children of Malta, "growing up in the ruin their island was becoming" (*V.*, 367). Quoting from his diary:

> I write this during a night raid, down in the abandoned sewer. It is raining outside. The only light is from phosphorous flares above the city, a few candles in here, bombs. Elena is beside me, holding the child who sleeps drooling against her shoulder. Packed close round us are other Maltese, English servants, a few Indian tradesmen. There's little talk. Children listen, all wide eyes, to bombs above the streets.

For them it is only an amusement. At first they cried on being wak-ened in the middle of the night. But they've grown used to it. Some even stand now near the entrance to our shelter, watching the flares and bombs, chattering, nudging, pointing. It will be a strange gener-ation. What of our own? She sleeps. (*V.*, 340)

A dispatch from an underground shelter, this passage situates Paola, Faus-to's young daughter, among her peers, a generation that has learned to cope with the turmoil of relentless bombardment. "There were children every-where in Valletta today," Fausto continues, "swinging down from the trees, jumping off the ruined ends of jetties into the sea" (*V.*, 369). As they swarm "among the ruins," in other words, they find themselves "drawn by the de-tritus" in "site[s] where things are being visibly worked on."[35] Moreover, as Fausto sees it, "all their dirt, noise and roughnecking" effects yet another, figurative palimpsest: "one metaphor they devised to veil the world that was" (*V.*, 367).

Many actual war diaries develop similar impressions of how the siege was experienced by its youngest victims. "Like other children," writes Mal-tese diarist Laurence Mizzi, "I used to spend hours watching the miners wielding massive picks to dig into the hard stone inch by inch and occa-sionally using dynamite to blast the rock."[36] He is referring to the bomb shelters, hastily carved into the indigenous limestone, where people slept, ate, argued, had sex, and even gave birth (figure 4.2). The siege began on June 11, 1940, and lasted until January 20, 1943; all told, there were 1,409 casualties and 35,000 homes destroyed by both Italian and German bomb-ers.[37] During the most intense period, which began in April 1942, air raids numbered in the double digits on most days, effectively transforming Malta into a subterranean society; as Pynchon himself puts it, "everything civilian and with a soul was underground" (*V.*, 357). People "sheltered themselves in whatever cliffs they could find," explains one historian, and most "inhabi-tants preferred to remain below during this period of heavy bombardment, rarely ever coming up into the daylight."[38] Despite the tremendous strain, though, the Maltese withstood the siege. "The sudden offensive turn-around of Malta," wrote Jack Belden in *Time* on February 15, 1943, "is one of the most dramatic incidents of three and a half years of war."[39] He was among the few American writers to depict this event in any detail, and his account may have influenced Pynchon, whose research for *V.* included stints at the New York Public Library poring over texts on Malta.[40] "Week by week the attack was stepped up," Belden continues, "until Malta was being pounded by an average of 175 bombers a day ... After April 1, except for three days of bad weather, Malta lived constantly underground."[41]

For his part, Fausto depicts a brief lull in the bombardment that gives the children the opportunity to emerge and to gather around "a broken

4.2. Interior view of a Maltese bomb shelter. Photo © 2010 Darrin Zammit Lupi, Reuters/ Corbis.

structure" (*V.*, 379). He himself descends from "the top of a slope of debris" in order to get a better view: "I felt like a spy," he confesses (ibid.). Within a few moments, it becomes clear to him that the children are transfixed by the Bad Priest, a mysterious figure who hails from Sliema on the island's northeast coast. The Priest is the latest victim of an air raid: "[w]edged under a fallen beam," he is "impassive" (ibid.). From a safe distance, Fausto watches the children pick at his clothes and mock him. "Speak to us, Father," they goad, "What is your sermon for today?" (*V.*, 380). Initially, the Priest is taken to be a man, but eventually the children realize that he is . . . something else. They begin an act of disassembly that quickly becomes an act of discovery. First they remove his hat to expose a tangle of long white hair that turns out to be a wig. At this point, they realize that the Priest is female. Then they unlace and remove her shoes, slide off her robes, and forcibly strip off her pants with a stolen commando's bayonet, exposing a nude body that is "surprisingly young" (*V.*, 381). When an artificial foot suddenly pops loose from its slot, one of the children remarks, "She comes apart" (ibid.). The Priest is silent as the boy with the knife cuts into her navel to dislodge a star sapphire, while the others pry a set of false teeth from her jaws and gouge a glass eye from its socket. Fausto wonders how far the children will go: "Surely her arms and breasts could be detached," he surmises, "the skin of her legs be peeled away to reveal some intricate understructure of silver openwork. Perhaps the trunk itself contained other wonders: intestines of parti-colored silk, gay balloon-lungs, a rococo heart" (ibid.). The disassembly ends here, though. Another air-raid siren scatters the children to shelter, leaving Fausto to administer last rites to the dying Priest, while the darkness that surrounds them is sporadically lit by "flares over Valletta, incendiary bombs in the dockyard," their voices "drowned in the explosions or the chattering of the ground artillery" (V., 382).

Here Fausto approaches the denouement of his confession. While it is difficult to make sense of this scene, partly because it is so gripping and so odd, it does seem that Pynchon means to situate an act of disassembly within a context of ruination in order to express particular anxiety about war, while developing the more general theme of blurred boundaries and indistinct limits that appears throughout the novel. As they take apart the Priest, the children are motivated by something like wonder, which turns to cruelty but never to disgust, and Fausto is moved by pity to act when the children depart: "At the time," he declares, "I only knew that a dying human must be prepared. I had no oil to anoint her organs of sense—so mutilated now—and so used her own blood, dipping it from the navel as from a chalice" (V., 382). On the one hand, then, she/he forms a striking composite of human flesh, prosthetic devices, precious stones, and perhaps even an interior made from the materials of arts and crafts and decoration, a rococo latticework of silver and silk. On the other hand, she/he is akin to "a dying human." The ontological status of this figure is therefore uncertain, yet her/his social status is clear: she/he is a casualty of war, a victim of bombardment. "These children knew what was happening: knew that bombs killed," Fausto rues. "But what's a human after all? No different from a church, obelisk, statue. Only one thing matters: it's the bomb that wins" (V., 367). His fundamental point—that bombs impartially pulverize humans, nonhumans, and human–nonhuman hybrids—recasts World War II into a conflict between bombs and everything else: whatever does not fall from the Luftwaffe or the Regia Aeronautica and explode on impact. If you can build a bomb powerful enough, he suggests, then you can destroy cities, islands, archipelagoes, the whole world. Such a scenario might have seemed implausible in 1942–43, but it seemed imminent in 1963, the year V. was first published. Indeed, 1963 sits squarely within a period in American culture, running from the mid-1950s (when Stencil reads the confession) to the mid-1960s, that was, as Paul Boyer puts it, "pervaded by the nuclear theme."[42]

Thus, to borrow Daniel Grausam's terms, this scene conveys "the horror of a fully thermonuclear war," or the fear of what Pynchon himself called "our common nightmare The Bomb," even though nuclear weapons are never "explicitly revealed or named."[43] More generally, though, this scene depicts a ruin—a site that, as Julia Hell and Andreas Schönle have recently argued, "has blurred edges in more ways than one"—while smudging the boundaries of several interrelated distinctions.[44] Is the Priest human or nonhuman, man or woman, holy or wicked? Are the children innocent or culpable? Is Fausto reliable or unreliable? And the war itself, "that ongoing, vast—but somehow boring—destruction of an island," is it a devastating trauma, a thrilling spectacle, a nonevent, or some combination of all three? By staging these questions, without offering explicit answers, Pynchon is not so much breaking down distinctions as he is tracing unstable limits. And given that the ruin, in its untimeliness and its out-of-placeness, poses problems of definition and delimitation, such questions establish another key link between the novel and the site that it conjures through Fausto's confession.[45] This link, which Smithson would understand in terms of the dialectic between site and nonsite, becomes most evident as Fausto turns his attention away from the Maltese children and toward Ħaġar Qim, an ancient ruin within the modern ruinscape.

HAĠAR QIM

Our poets write of nothing now but the rain of bombs from what was once Heaven. We builders practice, as we must, patience and strength but—the curse of knowing English and its emotional nuances!—with it a desperate nervous hatred of this war, an impatience for it to be over. I think our education in the English school and University alloyed what was pure in us. Younger, we talked of love, fear, motherhood; speaking in Maltese as Elena and I do now. But what a language! Have it, or today's Builders, advanced at all since the half-men who built the sanctuaries of Hagiar Kim? We talk as animals might. (V., 338–39)

Written "[i]n the midst of the bombing in 42," this diary entry seems to be most concerned with war, language, and the relation between the two. A poet as well as a diarist, Fausto credits T. S. Eliot and other Anglophone writers as influences, and his wide-ranging interests include the form and function of literary expression. Since the onset of the siege, however, he has also assumed the identity of a "Builder." As such, he understands himself to be practicing a craft—"with pick, shovel and rake we reshape our Maltese earth" (V., 347)—that dates back approximately five thousand years to the Ġgantija phase of Maltese prehistory. Yet the last line of this entry does not exactly indicate that he and his fellow Builders are participating in a long history of architectural labor; it suggests, rather, that no such history exists, because history itself, in the sense of linear progress and evolutionary development, does not exist. What if "today's Builders," Fausto speculates, have not "advanced at all" but remained the same, so that they are no different from the "half-men" who built "Hagiar Kim"? And what if his peers, he goes on to wonder, are "[s]till one with the troglodytes who lived [t]here 400 centuries before Christ's birth?" (*V.*, 339).

Such questions, which defamiliarize conventional notions of time and history, get to the heart of Pynchon's much-studied effort, already evident in his debut novel, to develop an original model for apprehending and narrating the past. I want to suggest that some significant portion of this model, more significant than previous critics have acknowledged, derives from his careful attention to the site of ruins that he names "Hagiar Kim."[46] Fausto mentions this site a second time in his confession, quoting his diary from a particularly grim period in the siege, when "the daily handling of corpses" and other wartime activities were beginning to take a toll on his wife, Elena. "Pain, nostalgia, want mixed in her eyes: so it seemed," he writes (*V.*, 374). He maintains this sentimental tone as he continues:

> But how could I know: with the same positive comfort in knowing the sun grows colder, the Hagiar Kim ruins progress toward dust, as do we, as does my late Hillman Minx which was sent to a garage for old age in 1939 and is now disintegrating quietly under tons of garage-rubble. How could I infer: the only ghost of an excuse being to reason by analogy that the nerves chafed and stabbed by my fingernails were the same as my own, that her pain was mine and by extension that of the jittering leaves all around us. (*V.*, 374)

As Fausto "reason[s] by analogy" in this passage, he draws a composite of ruins that includes the cosmological ("the sun"), the prehistorical ("Hagiar Kim"), and the industrial (his "late Hillman Minx"). This style of reasoning is also evident in the earlier passage dealing with Ħaġar Qim wherein he sets up an analogy between, on the one hand, his fellow "Builders" and himself and, on the other, "the half-men who built" the ancient ruin. Such reasoning has two effects. The first is historiosophical (it mediates a certain philosophy of history) while the second is sociological (it mediates a certain impression of the social).

A little background on Ħaġar Qim may help to clarify the first effect. Constructed between 3600 and 3200 BCE, Ħaġar Qim is an ancient temple complex, a religious site composed of massive limestone megaliths (figure 4.3). Located about a mile south of Qrendi, a small village on Malta's southern coast, it is among the oldest freestanding structures on Earth. Its three temples, which were fabricated from two different types of indigenous limestone, overlook the sudsy Mediterranean. On sunny days, it takes on a yellow hue, assuming the form of what Pynchon calls "buff-colored rubble." How did Pynchon come to know Ħaġar Qim? On the one hand, given that he spent some time on the archipelago, he may have adopted something

4.3. Ħaġar Qim. Courtesy of Susan Silberberg-Pierce/Canyonlights Photography.

like "the persona of a geologic agent" to survey the site as Smithson surveyed quarries and ruins in New Jersey during his rock-hunting trips with Donald Judd and others.[47] On the other hand, owing to the painstaking research of Arnold Cassola, we can be reasonably certain that he learned much about the ruin from one particular source: Themistocles Zammit's *Malta: The Islands and Their History* (1926). With this source, it appears, Pynchon pulled what he calls his "old Baedeker trick," mining the text for "the details" about a given locale.[48] Zammit's *Malta* was a good choice, for it offers a synoptic overview of Maltese geography, culture, and history up through the early twentieth century. And in its early chapters, it devotes significant attention to prehistorical Malta, the ancient temples and their builders in particular.

"There are in Malta a number of highly important megalith monuments," Zammit writes, "which are thought to have been sanctuaries."[49] Indeed, Malta is an archaeological treasure trove with no fewer than eleven megalith temples or temple complexes that were constructed between 5000 and 700 BCE. "The most extensive monument of this type is that known as 'Hagiar Kim,'" Zammit continues, using the spelling that Pynchon would go on to deploy in *V*.[50] Zammit was one of the earliest scholars to become fascinated by a ruin that has befuddled archaeologists since it was first discovered and excavated in 1839. Recently, for instance, Christopher Tilley has pointed to the "bewildering architectural complexity" of Ħaġar Qim, defining it as "a grandiose act of totalization" whose vast range of "references and relationships" renders it "a baroque elaboration of the temple form."[51] Much of this language could be used to describe Pynchon's debut novel, given its encyclopedic scope—"I am the twentieth century," asserts one character, reading from her poetry (*V*., 505)—as well as its disarming intricacy. But there is more to what Fausto would call the "analogy" between Ħaġar Qim and *V*. While "the original puzzling design" of the ruin is "not easily explained," writes archaeologist David Trump, the student of Ħaġar Qim should "[b]e careful of the V-perforation, for tethering and libations, cut into the rock in the front of the door."[52] Pynchon may or may not have seen this perforation firsthand, but in Zammit's book he would have read about the "ruts . . . shaped like the letter V" that constitute prehistorical cart tracks.[53] In addition, he would have read Zammit's account of the confounding temporality at Ħaġar Qim, an account that appears to ramify in Fausto's thinking. The ruin "represents centuries of human activity," Zammit explains, because its various segments were constructed sequentially over many generations.[54] This means that Ħaġar Qim does not simply materialize the prehistorical past; it also spatializes the flow of prehistorical time. Call this the paradox of Ħaġar Qim: time is calcified there, yet not arrested.

Fausto replicates this paradox as he dwells on temporality and history. "It must be an alien passion in Malta," he asserts, "where all history seemed simultaneously present . . . In London were too many distractions. History there was the record of an evolution. One-way and ongoing. Monuments, buildings, plaques were remembrances only; but in Valletta remembrances seemed almost to live" (*V*., 534). While history constitutes a teleological narrative in London, in Malta there is "[n]o history, all history at once," for "Malta itself [i]s alienated from any history in which cause precedes effect" (*V*., 539, 544). Distinguishing between two locales, Fausto contrasts two historical models: one involves the incremental unfolding of events according to a logic of cause and effect; the other denies cause and effect, and the incremental unfolding of events, because it accepts no temporality other than instantaneousness. Both models appear at Ħaġar Qim. As Zammit suggests, and contemporary archaeologists confirm, the ruin makes several centuries "simultaneously present," while revealing a causal, developmental narrative in the form of a sequence of construction. Maltese prehistory manifests on the one hand, then, as a composite of epochs distributed laterally across the ruinscape; on the other hand, as a series of construction episodes, one after another. This tension between *succession* and *simultaneity* structures much of the novel, for *V*. narrates a causal sequence of events, yet also makes distinct epochs seem simultaneous, as in the case of chapter 11, which puts Fausto's descriptions of World War II in the hands of a diegetic reader in Cold War America.

Both succession and simultaneity, moreover, are essential to Pynchon's historiosophy or "theor[y] of history" in general (*V.*, 230). In his 1969 letter to David Hirsch, the letter in which he gives some insight into his research on Malta, he offers his take on the 1904 Herero genocide, the historical event that informs chapter 9 of *V.*[55] "When I wrote *V.*," he explains, "I was thinking of the 1904 campaign as a sort of dress rehearsal for what later happened to the Jews in the '30s and '40s."[56] In this model, one historical atrocity prefigures another. The Holocaust was, Pynchon suggests, latent within the earlier event, which (to extend his metaphor) set the stage for its unfolding years later. These two events, then, can be understood as successive in a particular way, but also in some sense simultaneous, the later embedded in the earlier. A spatial image of Pynchon's theory of history, at least insofar as he defines it here, would look something like Smithson's "straight line" of global cities, from ancient Rome to contemporary Passaic. Just as an older city in Smithson's image constitutes a "three-dimensional mirror" that "reflect[s]" a later city "into existence," so, too, an earlier event in Pynchon's model at once incubates and precipitates what follows. Succession and simultaneity are noncontradictory in this model, and I want to speculate that Pynchon learned to think this way through his literary archaeology of Ħaġar Qim.

SOCIETY IN RUINS

Still, there is another way to understand Pynchon's engagement with this particular ruin. As he ponders Ħaġar Qim, Fausto's "reason[ing] by analogy" not only mediates a certain conception of history but also forms a related image of sociality. When he analogizes his peers and himself to the ancient Maltese architects, to the creators of Ħaġar Qim, Fausto is conjuring a relationship that spans a very long stretch of time: some five thousand years. And yet, his emphasis on simultaneity—"[n]o history, all history at once"—construes the "half-men who built Hagiar Kim" as something other than historical antecedents. Indeed, some significant portion of his unwieldy confession imagines them, along with "the troglodytes who lived [on Malta] 400 centuries before Christ's birth," not as precursors but as live figures, "simultaneously present" with him and his fellow World War II "Builders." At such moments, then, Pynchon is not only questioning the teleological model of historical development, or what Smithson calls "the myth of progress," but also testing the limits and boundaries of the social (*CW*, 15). To ask whether "today's Builders [have] advanced at all since the half-men who built the sanctuaries of Hagiar Kim" is to ask whether one set of social actors, one set of laborers within a given society, can be distinguished from a previous set. And it is to suggest more broadly that, even though the differences are readily apparent between World War II Malta and the Ġgantija phase of Maltese prehistory, there may be no clean lines demarcating the many civilizations—from ancient temple-builders and medieval fortress-dwellers to the Knights of St. John and the British Empire—that have taken root at this site since the time of the troglodytes.

Drawing details from Zammit and other sources, Pynchon refers to these civilizations throughout the novel. "One cannot come to Valletta without knowing about the Knights," remarks one character, Father Avalanche, speaking in 1956 and referring to the Knights of St. John, the main ruling body on Malta from 1530 through 1800 (V., 499). The Knights laid the foundation of the modern archipelago; Valletta, for instance, is named for the grand master, Jean Parisot de la Valette, who oversaw the planning and construction of the capital city circa 1565.[57] Hence the reason Avalanche goes on to assert, "'I still believe'—chuckling —'as I believed then, that [the Knights] roam the streets after sunset. Somewhere'" (V., 499). His point is that their presence is palpable: they are as alive to him as the ancient temple-builders and troglodytes are to Fausto. And although he chuckles at the absurdity of his own contention that the Knights meander about Valletta in the evenings, strolling an urban grid that they themselves laid out, Avalanche cannot deny his intuition, his sense that they still animate the site, somehow, in the mid-twentieth century. Here Pynchon puts a particular spin on the logic of the ruin, incorporating it as a means of dwelling on sociality and social form. If, for much of the novel, a ruined Malta is rendered as what Smithson calls a "junk heap of history" (CW, 293)—a rubble pile of discrete historical epochs—then Avalanche's intuition about the Knights defines this site as something like a junk heap of societies: a palimpsest of distinct civilizations and social formations. By the end of the novel, in other words, Malta appears not only as a zone of siege and ruination but also as a "womb of rock" that has sustained so many civilizations since the Neolithic era, never casting them out, even after they have been technically supplanted by conquest or something else (V., 351). Indeed, while the protagonists of V. visit twentieth-century Malta, earlier societies and cultures register as "simultaneously present," if only through the medium of architecture—from the crumbling megaliths of Ħaġar Qim to the "broken masonry, destroyed churches and auberges" of Valletta (V., 336).

Thus, even as he depicts World War II Malta, a site where a society is being systematically ruined, Pynchon ventures a claim for societal endurance. In fact, his moving account of the Maltese people's resilience in the face of ongoing bombardment forms part of a larger effort to imagine how societies persist. This effort includes a sophisticated meditation on the relationship between sociality and temporality. The figure of the sixteenth-century Knights of St. John "roam[ing] the streets" of twentieth-century Malta dramatizes the afterlife of a society that has been superseded. Even though the Knights no longer rule Valletta, their influence can be felt in and through what Pynchon dubs "the physical shape of the city."[58] They continue to exert some power, however subtle, on the social relations of modern Malta, if only because they did so much to construct the stage, the physical site, on which those relations still unfold. To put this claim in a different register: Pynchon's emphasis on simultaneity and presentness constitutes an argument against synchronic sociality—the notion that all the elements of a given social event occupy a single point in time. Although, in chapters following Fausto's confession, Profane, Stencil, Fausto, Avalanche, and other characters interact on Malta in 1956, their interactions "*overflow*," as Bruno Latour would put it, "with elements which are already in the situation coming from some other *time*."[59] These elements include, most obviously, the sixteenth-century street grid of the capital city, as well as "[t]he buildings in [certain] part[s] of Valletta, eleven years after war's end, [that] ha[ve] not been rebuilt" (*V.*, 506). Because "it is fairly easy to establish some continuous connections," Latour continues, between any interaction and "the dreams and drawings of *someone else*," such as an architect working "at some *other* time," no interaction is ever truly synchronic.[60] So, in this sense, when Avalanche imagines the Knights back to life, he is not merely fantasizing that they form a kind of genius loci, a spirit that haunts and protects the archipelago, but underscoring that their actual "dreams and drawings" continue to exert some agency, some social force, even though they themselves long ago relinquished control of Malta.

Still, it is not Latour but another thinker, one of Latour's key interlocutors, who has developed the most helpful concept for apprehending how *V.* imagines sociality. That thinker is Michel Serres, and that concept is the "quasi-object." The latter, as Serres elaborates in his "Theory of the Quasi-Object," names at once a being and a relation that constitutes both the subject and the collective. His example here is a *furet*: the prop circulated in a familiar French children's game. "The one who is caught with the *furet* has to pay a forfeit," he writes. "The furet points him out. One person is marked with the sign of the furet. Condemned, he goes to the center; he's 'it.'" Thus, on the one hand, the furet "marks or designates" its holder as a subject, for "[h]e who is not discovered with the furet in his hand is anonymous, part of a monotonous chain where he remains undistinguished. He is not an individual." On the other hand, though, the furet, "when being passed, makes the collective ... The moving furet weaves the 'we,' the collective; if it stops, it marks the 'I.'" Hence, Serres concludes, "This quasi-object that is a marker of the subject is an astonishing constructer of intersubjectivity."[61] It is for this reason that Latour, adapting Serres for social and sociological theory, will go on to argue that quasi-objects, rather than human subjects, "are the real center of the social world," for they enable the networks that constitute the collective.[62]

Pynchon's debut novel is finally a story about a quasi-object: the inscrutable V. Although we never learn, exactly, what V. *is*—it could be a person, a thing, a concept, a pathological projection, a cipher for desire, or even nothing at all—the novel is clear on what V. *does*. First and foremost, it forms a subject, Stencil, who is wholly defined by it, or rather by the obsessive and exasperating search to acquire it: "Work, the chase—for it was V. he hunted—far from being a means to glorify God and one's own godliness (as the Puritans believe) was for Stencil grim, joyless; a conscious acceptance of the unpleasant for no other reason than that V. was there to track down" (*V.*, 51). As Stencil pursues his hunt, V. not only gives form and structure to the narrative itself, which, as other critics have noted, takes the shape of the letter "V," but also establishes what Serres calls "a cluster of relations" or what Latour calls a "trail of *associations*" that span both space and time.[63] The novel's eponymous figure is in this sense a quasi-object, "an astonishing constructer of intersubjectivity" that forges an (at times uneasy) alliance between Stencil and Profane while linking Stencil to other social actors in Egypt, Florence, German Southwest Africa, and Malta at earlier moments in the long twentieth century. Thus, even as Pynchon represents a society in ruins, detailing the decimation of Malta, he also explores something like the opposite dynamic throughout the novel: the *emergence* of cliques, collectives, and societies. As Stencil chases his object, he also "trace[s] social connections" through an investigative approach—a "mysterious and Dashiell Hammett–like" following of leads wherever they might take him (*V.*, 133)—that resembles the core method of Actor-Network-Theory (ANT): "trudg[ing] like an ant" through the conduits of interaction that make up any social entity.[64]

But my point, finally, is not to argue that Stencil figures anything like an Actor-Network-Theorist *avant la lettre*. It is, rather, to suggest that Pynchon's sociological imagination—his unusual ability to apprehend what he called "social organization" or "the structure of society"[65]—owes something significant to his engagement with Malta as a ruin, his effort to fabricate what Smithson terms a nonsite, an aesthetic object that would in some sense arrogate the logic of the real, material site to which it refers. While there are many possible definitions for the logic of the ruin, as the discourse from Simmel to Smithson to Stoler has shown, Pynchon seems to have been most interested in the issues of temporality and blurred boundaries that such sites call to mind. Yet he was also deeply attuned to "what it might mean to live in ruins," as Stoler puts it, to the ways that individual subjects, social groups, and whole societies manage to survive, and even to thrive, amid "processes of ongoing ruination."[66] This is his key concern in the Watts article—which concludes with the people of Watts taking a break from their own experience of "siege" to celebrate "the memory of Simon

Rodia" (*J*, 84)—and it appears in a somewhat different way in *V.* Not without conveying the devastation of World War II, for instance, the eleventh chapter underscores the "island-wide sense of communion" that was precipitated by the bombardment of Malta, the social solidarity that took hold inside the rock-cut shelters beneath the cities of Valletta and Vittoriosa (*V.*, 352). As Pynchon brings such a shelter to life ("The rock hears everything"), he renders it as a quasi-object, something that "makes the collective," or re-makes it, in the midst of its unmaking: for the victims of the siege, "it's the rock they come back to" (ibid.). And while this rock, the same *Globigerina* limestone that forms the megaliths of Ħaġar Qim, shields so many individual actors, it also exemplifies how sites sustain sociality, shoring up an entire society against its ruins.

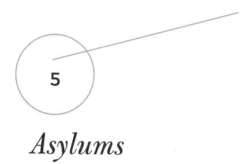

5

Asylums

"Harlem is a ruin," wrote Ralph Ellison in 1948. He was on assignment for *48: The Magazine of the Year*, which had commissioned, but ultimately did not publish, the essay that appears as "Harlem Is Nowhere" in *Shadow and Act* (1964). Trekking around the neighborhood with his friend and collaborator, the photographer Gordon Parks, he was searching for material that would capture both the "Negro personality" and "the psychological character of the scene in which he dwells." Having just returned from Vermont, where a stint at Bea and Francis Steegmuller's cottage had been good for his writing, he found the Harlem scene pretty bleak. "To live in Harlem is to dwell in the very bowels of the city," he declaimed, for its buildings contain "littered area-ways, ill-smelling halls and vermin-invaded rooms," while its streets are "clutter[ed] underfoot with garbage and decay." Such "ordinary aspects" of the neighborhood point to racialized poverty—to what Ellison terms "the Negro's perpetual alienation in the land of his birth." And yet, within this "urban slum," or really *beneath* it, there is a site that offers asylum to the alienated. "One must descend to the basement and move along a confusing mazelike hall to reach it," he tells us. "Twice the passage seems to lead to a blank wall; then at last one enters the brightly lighted auditorium." Here, a bit disoriented, one sees "social workers at the reception desks," as well as "white-jacketed psychiatrists carrying charts" amid a flurry of other activity within "an atmosphere of hurried efficiency." If Harlem is a ruin, then this site is a shelter, providing some reprieve, however fleeting, from what Ann Laura Stoler calls "processes of ongoing ruination."[1] No trash, no vermin, no stench; just a clean, bright space where "concerned faces" are met by "expert workers."[2]

Ellison is describing the LaFargue Psychiatric Clinic, which he helped to establish in 1946 with Richard Wright, psychiatrist Fredric Wertham, and several others. This site was an asylum in two senses. Although it was an outpatient rather than inpatient clinic, it provided psychiatric services, while serving, more generally, as a place of "refuge, shelter, or retreat" for the people of Harlem, as Ellison's description suggests.[3] The clinic was conceived by Wertham and Wright as a partial solution to the growing problem of black juvenile delinquency, but it quickly assumed the more general function of addressing what Wright called "the artificially-made psychological problems of Harlem," by which he meant the mental and emotional distress caused by a racist society.[4] Operating out of two damp rooms below St. Philips Protestant Episcopal Church at 215 West 133rd Street, Wertham and an interracial team of volunteers—including Hilde L. Mosse and, for a brief time, Ed Dalton, the first black psychotherapist in New York City— administered mental health care on Tuesday and Thursday evenings to anyone in need. The clinic stayed open for nearly thirteen years. Wertham and his staff charged twenty-five cents to those who could pay and never discriminated on the basis of race. Before LaFargue, which was the first institution of its kind in Harlem, it was all but impossible for black New Yorkers to obtain psychiatric treatment. "[W]hile in theory," Wright continues, "Negroes have access to psychiatric aid (just as the Negroes of Mississippi, in theory, have access to the vote!), such aid really does not exist owing to the subtle but effective racial discrimination that obtains against Negroes in almost all New York City hospitals and clinics."[5] Checking in to Bellevue was untenable, then, but so was seeing a shrink, since many private practitioners worried that treating black patients would harm their reputations. LaFargue thus provided a much-needed service, and it was roundly celebrated for this reason. "Creation of the new LaFargue Clinic," effused cofounder Dorothy Norman in the *New York Post*, "is living proof that the impossible is still possible."[6]

Although Ellison was not involved in day-to-day operations, he spent considerable time at LaFargue in the 1940s, observing the activity that he describes in "Harlem Is Nowhere" and conversing with Wertham about psychiatry and psychoanalysis. At Wright's behest, he first wrote about the clinic one month after it had opened; in a one-page letter to his friend and mentor, he offered a rationale for psychiatric services in Harlem by focusing on a relationship—the link between the black self ("the total Negro personality") and its social-spatial context ("the urban environment")—that he would go on to examine in many of his published writings, including *Invisible Man* (1952).[7] LaFargue mattered to him, as this letter and other texts indicate, not only as a necessary social intervention, "organized as a result of three men's awareness of the vast nervous and mental disorders found within the urban Negro community," but also as a "scene and symbol" of something more.[8] In this chapter, I argue that it played a decisive role in his lifelong effort to apprehend what he called "the realities of the Negro" within American society (CE, 326). Describing the clinic "as a scientific laboratory" wherein these "realities" could be examined up close, Ellison came to understand asylums as both social microcosms and prisms through which to view broad sociological problems (ibid.). I mean to demonstrate that this understanding of such sites, both psychiatric institutions specifically and zones of refuge in general, suggests a new way of defining his relationship to the discipline of sociology.

The story of this relationship is complicated. It usually begins with Ellison's 1944 review of Gunnar Myrdal's An American Dilemma and places him in a tradition of black writers, including W.E.B. Du Bois, Alain Locke, and James Baldwin, who attacked the discipline's frequently benighted discussion of race.[9] Ellison was at best ambivalent about sociology and at times antipathetic toward it. "Some of the insights are brilliant," he writes in reviewing Myrdal's book, but "[i]t will take a deeper science than Myrdal's, deep as that might be, to analyze what is happening among the masses of Negroes" (CE, 339–40). While Myrdal's study contained several incisive claims, he concluded, it failed to capture the full complexity of Negro humanity (CE, 340). It was therefore the task of the novelist, as Ellison would go on to assert many times throughout his career, to render such complexity and thereby to counteract "the bland assertions of sociologists" (CE, 482). Still, he never completely rejected sociological thought. Although he "tended to highlight the inadequacies of politics and social science when it came to understanding human behavior," as Kenneth Warren explains, he "did not call for a scorched-earth policy against sociology," which is one reason why Invisible Man can be understood in relation to the work of prominent postwar sociologists such as David Riesman, C. Wright Mills, and William H. Whyte.[10]

Ellison's treatment of asylums, however, reveals his affinity with a different sociologist from that era, Erving Goffman, whose own writing on such sites still stands among the most influential. Goffman turned his attention to asylums in the mid-1950s, a few years after Invisible Man was published, when he began a year's fieldwork at St. Elizabeths Hospital in Washington, DC. While he and Ellison were for the most part very different thinkers, writing within obviously nonidentical genres and traditions, their work converges at the asylum, a site they conceptualized in similar ways. In this chapter, I track the overlap in their respective approaches to this site in order to develop a new sense of Ellison's sociological imagination: his attempt to apprehend social reality through an engagement with a particular locale. My argument situates Ellison's writings on the asylum—including unpublished archival documents, as well as "Harlem Is Nowhere" and *Invisible Man*—within an intellectual and cultural history that contains Goffman, and my objects of analysis include the photographs that Parks shot while he and Ellison were working together. The chapter concludes by adapting some of the sociologist's key concepts in an effort to rethink the invisible man's "hole," his distinctive underground lair, itself an asylum and quite possibly the most beguiling site in all of American literature.

What follows, however, is not only an attempt to apprehend Ellison's sociological imagination but also a methodological experiment that seeks to extend site reading beyond the purview of ANT to a broader engagement with sociological thinking. I turn to Goffman in this case because books such as *The Presentation of Self in Everyday Life* and *Asylums* set a key precedent for ANT. He and Bruno Latour both make use of ethnographic methods while deploying the rhetoric of drama and performance (actor, role, player) to describe human behavior within well-defined sites. This rhetoric marks each thinker's sustained engagement with literary theory—for Goffman, the "dramatism" of Kenneth Burke; for Latour, the narratology and semiotics that I discussed in chapter 1—an engagement that, as Heather Love suggests, could inspire new interpretive procedures within literary studies.[11] When Latour himself cites Goffman, he defines his predecessor as an authority on the "thick imbroglio" of social interaction, a thinker who developed an original conceptual idiom for the nuances of self-presentation during scenes of face-to-face encounter.[12] These nuances were no less compelling to Ellison: "I am invisible," the narrator famously proclaims at the beginning of *Invisible Man*, "simply because people refuse to see me."[13] The novelist refined key ideas for that novel, ideas to which he would return throughout his career, as he wrote about the asylum.

THE SICKNESS OF THE SOCIAL ORDER

When Ellison describes the LaFargue Clinic "as a scientific laboratory" in "Harlem Is Nowhere," he is being both literal and figurative. Although Wertham asserted that he and his colleagues were not trying "to make a study of the Negro," the psychiatrist did in fact gather data on the psychological effects of racism.[14] In one experiment, for instance, an interracial group of thirteen children, boys and girls ages nine to sixteen, were bused from Delaware on five separate occasions to be "examined and studied as regular Clinic patients." Like other prominent social scientists working on the eve of *Brown v. Board of Education*, Wertham was interested in how school segregation was influencing child development, and this experiment aimed to probe its "injurious" effects.[15] By describing the clinic as a laboratory, then, Ellison is referring to the practice of conducting research on human beings while administering psychiatric treatment to them. But he also seems to be suggesting something more general about LaFargue. His use of the term "laboratory" is partly metaphorical, figuring the clinic as a special site of access to what he terms "the realities of the Negro," by which he means, above all, "the relation between his problems and his environment" (*CE*, 326–27). Hence, in Ellison's very first piece of writing on the clinic, his letter to Richard Wright on April 4, 1946, he notes that it was created to address "the affect of the urban environment upon the total Negro personality."[16] The published version of "Harlem Is Nowhere" develops this claim into a more fully formed argument, but the process of coming to that argument, it seems, was both difficult and circuitous.

The Ralph Ellison Papers at the Library of Congress include several typewritten pages on the clinic that indicate a restless groping for the right metaphor to convey its "importance" (*CE*, 326). Although undated, these typescripts were probably composed in the spring or summer of 1948: "Two years ago," begins one page, "there was established a psychiatric clinic in Harlem which has assumed an importance seemingly all out of porportion [*sic*] to the small number of patients it is able to treat."[17] In addition to correcting typos and other infelicities, Ellison rephrased this claim several times, until he finally decided on the concise and confident line that appears in the published text: "Certainly [LaFargue] has become in two years one of Harlem's most important institutions" (*CE*, 320). Yet the most fascinating part of his revision process is his experimentation with various metaphors. While "Harlem Is Nowhere" renders the clinic as a "laboratory" and "an underground extension of democracy," his working notes toy with two other possibilities. On the one hand, he likens LaFargue to "a boat with a glass bottom through which, as it moves over the surface of a lake, it is possible to view those objects floating within the depths which would otherwise be obscure." As such, he continues, it "offer[s] insight into the depths of the personality maladjustments / adjustments of Negro Americans [and] it illuminates the connection between ~~these~~ personality problems and environmental factors."[18] On the other hand, though, LaFargue is like a "special type of camera," for its "special arrangement of mirrors and filters . . . split the light rays reflected into it," ultimately "to reproduce a given scene in all its color." This metaphor really takes off, and even gets away from him:

> Let the physical conditions of Harlem stand for one sheet of film; let Negro Americans stand for another; let the color aspects of American democracy stand for the third; and let the clinic stand for the [blank space] in which the three are exposed to the light of understanding / camera that brings the three together to the light of meaning.[19]

In the midst of learning more about photographic technique from Parks, Ellison was exploring how the trope of the camera might explain the importance of the clinic, and this passage would seem to confirm Sara Blair's claim that "photography serves Ellison as a powerful resource for imagining the transformation of lived experience into narrative, of social fact into aesthetic possibility."[20] Nevertheless, the blank space in this note is important, for it anticipates Ellison's ultimate decision to abandon the trope of the camera, as well as that of the "glass bottom" boat, in the final version of "Harlem Is Nowhere." Even though he omitted these tropes, however, he retained their effect. Indeed, the published essay defines LaFargue as a kind of prism, what the typescript calls "a special arrangement of mirrors and filters," through which to view the interrelationship of self, site, and society—the three "sheet[s]" in his photographic conceit of "Negro Americans," "the physical conditions of Harlem," and "American democracy." By shining "the light of understanding" through such a prism, Ellison suggests, this interrelationship attains both "special" clarity and full complexity.

The published essay makes this case through a number of means, above all, its organizational structure, which begins with a striking description of LaFargue, then turns away from it "for a while" before circling back by way of conclusion (CE, 321). When Ellison takes his reader inside the clinic—"One must descend to the basement and move along a confusing maze-like hall to reach it" (CE, 320)—he is not just establishing a mise-en-scène for the essay but is also striving to animate the claims of a very broad argument by looking both *at* and *through* the site. He adopted this approach, it seems, because he had become convinced, by the time he sat down to draft "Harlem Is Nowhere," that LaFargue's "importance" derived not only from its "urgent action," its mission of providing low-cost psychiatric treatment to those in need, but also from what it symbolized. "When [LaFargue] is discusse[d]," he writes in one of his working notes, "subjects ordinarily not associated with psychotherapy arise so frequently that one becomes aware that simply by existing and performing its special task it has come to form a perspective through which many aspects of Harlem reality come into focus."[21] With this last phrase, "come into focus," Ellison again deploys the trope of the camera, but adds something more, defining LaFargue as a site that occasions inquiry into "subjects" that may at first seem unrelated to it. His point, both here and elsewhere, is that these subjects—such as "the total implication of Negro life in the United States" (CE, 320)—are prompted so often because LaFargue is not just a prism but also a kind of social microcosm, "encapsulating in miniature the characteristic qualities or features of something much larger," namely, the psychological and social aspects of Negro experience within American society at this historical moment.[22]

So what are those aspects? In the published text, Ellison forms an answer to this question through an argument that includes but hardly reduces to a set of claims about psychiatry and mental health. His central thesis, which he renders in a few different ways, is that the "American Negro's personality" is shaped by the "three basic social factors" of race, citizenship, and modernization (*CE*, 320). He writes:

> Not quite citizens and yet Americans, full of the tensions of modern man but regarded as primitives, Negro Americans are in desperate search for an identity. Rejecting the second-class status assigned to them, they feel alienated and their whole lives have become a search for answers to the questions: Who am I, What am I, Why am I, and Where? Significantly, in Harlem the reply to the greeting, "How are you?" is often, "Oh, man, I'm *nowhere*"—a phrase revealing an attitude so common that it has been reduced to a gesture, a seemingly trivial word. (*CE*, 322–23)

The main goal of "Harlem Is Nowhere" is to explain why this "attitude" and its attendant "greeting" are in fact nontrivial. "The phrase 'I'm nowhere,'" Ellison continues, "expresses the feeling borne in upon many Negroes that they have no stable recognizable place in society. One's identity drifts in a capricious reality in which even the most commonly held assumptions are questionable. One 'is' literally, but one is nowhere" (*CE*, 325). Hence the urgent need for an asylum such as LaFargue. There, "in the basement, a frustrated science goes to find its true object: the confused of mind who seek reality. Both find the source of their frustrations in the sickness of the social order" (*CE*, 327). The clinic, in this sense, constitutes an asylum for both patients *and* their doctors: Ellison rejects the narrative of black pathology in favor of imagining the two constituencies, those in need of mental health care and their caregivers, as allies in the struggle against both a diseased society and its ramifications within the human psyche.

As he describes it, then, LaFargue is not only a prism and a microcosm but also a site of refuge from the actually existing social order for both patients and staff. To align these two groups, however, is not at all to downplay the patients' psychological distress, which he traces to a "clash" between "urban slum conditions and folk sensibilities" (*CE*, 321). As black Americans migrated north after the Civil War, he contends, they "step[ped] from feudalism into the vortex of industrialism simply by moving across the Mason-Dixon line," and this "vast process of change" accounts for both the peculiar features of Harlem and the existential quest for identity that is so prevalent among its denizens (*CE*, 321–22). "Here a former cotton picker develops the sensitive hands of a surgeon," he notes, "and men whose grandparents still believe in magic prepare optimistically to become atomic scientists" (*CE*, 322). For these people and others, "[l]ife becomes a masquerade" in which "exotic costumes are worn every day," and such "costumes" are readily visible in the "surreal fantasies" that are "acted out upon the streets," as when a man "ducks in and out of traffic shouting and throwing imaginary grenades that actually exploded during World War I," or when "boy gangsters" are seen "wielding homemade pistols" with criminal intent (ibid.). While such images are meant to illustrate Ellison's argument, they are not described in detail, most likely because "Harlem Is Nowhere" was supposed to be accompanied by Parks's photographs, which capture the Harlem streetscape from multiple angles. These photographs, as artist Glenn Ligon points out, have an intimate yet opaque relationship to Ellison's essay and to his other writings from the period, including *Invisible Man*. It can be difficult, for instance, to determine whether Parks means to be documenting Harlem street culture or illustrating scenes from the novel or both.[23] However, there is one photograph in particular, *Untitled, Harlem, New York, 1952*, that appears clearly designed to visualize Ellison's key claim about identity.

Like most of the pictures that Parks took with and for Ellison, *Untitled* renders a streetscape, but it is more like a portrait than a panorama, as it frames a solitary human figure, a black woman, possibly wearing white, carrying something fluffy as she strolls down the sidewalk (figure 5.1). She is in the background, her lines somewhat blurry, in contrast to the neat row of five or six pairs of shoes in the foreground, which are sharply focused, clearly distinguished from the black asphalt. Immediately, a few related questions spring to mind: Whose shoes are these? Why are they here? Was this image staged or captured spontaneously? One way to answer such questions would be to consider *Untitled* as an illustration of the famous eviction scene in *Invisible Man*, when the unnamed narrator "stumble[s] over . . . a lot of junk waiting to be hauled away," as an elderly couple is being tossed from their home in Harlem (*IM*, 267). The link between the photograph and the novel is imperfect, however, not only because Parks omits key elements—such as "pots and pots of green plants" and "the sullen-faced crowd" (*IM*, 271, 267)—but also because there is nothing in the image to specify the site. If this is Harlem, as the title suggests, then Harlem is nowhere. *Untitled* visualizes a generic urban location, a streetscape into which a minimally identified human figure is, literally, blurring. For this reason, it can be understood to dramatize the relationship between identity and environment—the way that, as Ellison puts it, the "physical conditions" of the urban North, not just Harlem in particular, have challenged the "Southern background" of black migrants to prompt existential questions: "Who am I, What am I, Why am I, and Where?" (*CE*, 323). And yet, if the human figure in the background represents a lack or attenuation of identity, then the nonhuman figure in the foreground, the row of shoes, stands for something like the opposite: a set of possibilities for defining oneself on the city street. Urban life is "a masquerade," Ellison writes, so these shoes register as a synecdoche for the "exotic costumes [that] are worn every day" by "Negro Americans . . . in desperate search for an identity" (*CE*, 322).

5.1. *Untitled, Harlem, New York, 1952*. Photograph by Gordon Parks; courtesy of and copyright The Gordon Parks Foundation.

As *Untitled* visualizes such claims, moreover, it also underscores their general rather than specific nature. Ellison frames "Harlem Is Nowhere" as a discussion about a small social microcosm, the LaFargue Clinic, then widens the scope to include all "four hundred thousand Americans" in Harlem, before finally addressing the "sickness" of the entire American "social order" and its "total implication" for the "total being" of the "total Negro" (*CE*, 320, 325, 321). While he begins and ends with LaFargue, in other words, his description of the people there transforms along the way into an argument about the personality and identity formation of the black American as such within a segregated society. He therefore deploys what might be called an inductive method, which moves from "concrete conditions" to abstract concepts and from specific case to generalization (*CE*, 326). This method also structures Erving Goffman's essays on asylums. When, a few years after Ellison, the sociologist turned his attention to St. Elizabeths Psychiatric Hospital, he did not conduct and then write up a conventional ethnography of the site. Rather, he worked his empirical observations into a set of concepts that can be applied broadly to the analysis of everyday life inside all "total institutions," closed worlds such as prisons, army barracks, boarding schools, nursing homes, and monasteries.[24] He deployed many of these concepts, moreover, toward explaining a problem that was central to Ellison: identity formation within a system of social segregation.[25] This system, as Goffman describes it in *Asylums* (1961), is binaristic, like the social order of Jim Crow America, yet not organized by racial difference.[26] Instead, it depends on "a basic split between a large and managed group, conveniently called inmates, and a small supervisory staff" (*A*, 7). Much like Ellison, the sociologist was interested in how members of the subordinated population strive to define themselves, to attain an identity that rejects what the novelist terms "the second-class status assigned them" (*CE*, 322). Although Goffman and Ellison were very different thinkers, in other words, their ideas intersect at the asylum.

SELF AND SITE

This intersection is especially striking because LaFargue and St. Elizabeths were all but antithetical sites. Indeed, it is hard to imagine two psychiatric institutions with less in common. While one was a small, unfunded, ad hoc clinic in a Harlem basement, the other was the nation's first and only federally funded and operated psychiatric hospital, housing 8,000 patients and employing a staff of 4,000 at its peak. LaFargue was both a neighborhood gathering spot and an outpatient facility that focused on talk therapy; as such, it anticipated the community-based approach to mental health care that predominates today, in the wake of the deinstitutionalization movement that began just after World War II and reached its peak in the 1960s and '70s.[27] Under Wertham's leadership, furthermore, the atmosphere of LaFargue was convivial and supportive, for his practice, which he dubbed "social psychiatry," emphasized the link between mental health and the lived environment.[28] St. Elizabeths, by contrast, was an inpatient facility that had earned a reputation of being impersonal, bureaucratic, and prison-like, a site where patients, or what Goffman calls "inmates," were forced to endure a "daily round of petty contingencies," as well as traumatizing experiences such as electroshock therapy (*A*, x). Nevertheless, for all their empirical differences, these two asylums mediated the same fundamental concern for Goffman and for Ellison. Both writers wanted to understand the connection between self and site through an analysis of how subordinated individuals construct and assert their identity.

There are a few ways to account for this overlap. Goffman had a lifelong interest in questions of identity and self-definition, which he explored in *Asylums* and other books, particularly *The Presentation of Self in Everyday Life* (1956, 1959) and *Stigma* (1963). Just as Ellison argues that the search for identity amounts to a kind of frantic costuming within the "masquerade" of the social, so, too, Goffman, in *The Presentation of Self*, emphasizes the performative or "expressive" aspects of social interaction, arguing that clothes, or what he calls "costumes and other parts of personal front," are essential props in "the arts of impression management."[29] We are all role players, in other words, deploying a complex repertoire of techniques to fashion ourselves for one another during any scene of interaction. Goffman developed this idea, which prefigures more recent scholarship on performativity and the self, through a number of means, including ethnographic fieldwork and wide reading in imaginative literature, sociology, and philosophy. Among his key influences was Kenneth Burke, a thinker who was also important to Ellison as the "stimulating source" for many of the ideas in *Shadow and Act* (*CE*, 60).[30] Throughout *The Presentation of Self* and elsewhere, Goffman often cites Burke as a means of clarifying and exemplifying his claims. To underscore the notion that identity is contingent upon the scene of its performance, for instance, the sociologist quotes a passage from *Permanence and Change*: "We are all, in our compartmentalized responses," Burke writes, "like the man who is a tyrant in his office and a weakling among his family, or like the musician who is assertive in his art and self-effacing in his personal relationships."[31] Ellison probably read this passage for the first time in the early 1940s, when he began to use Burke's theories of "symbolic action" and "dramatism" as a framework for analyzing social and political problems. "I propose that we view the whole of American life," Ellison writes in Burke's jargon, "as a drama acted out upon the body of a Negro giant, who, lying trussed up like Gulliver, forms the stage and the scene upon which the action unfolds" (*CE*, 85).

But even more significant as a source of shared influence was Chicago school sociology. Goffman earned his PhD in sociology from Chicago in 1953, and while he would go on to develop an original research program, his work is thoroughly indebted to his doctoral training.[32] Ellison learned some sociology from Wright, who was personally acquainted with members of the Chicago school, and he encountered the work of Chicago school founder Robert E. Park while he was a student at Tuskegee in the 1930s.[33] Prior to teaching at Chicago, Park worked for Booker T. Washington as a kind of public relations executive—"the man," as Ellison puts it, "responsible for inflating Tuskegee into a national symbol" (*CE*, 331). Although Park had departed by the time Ellison arrived, his influence was still palpable in the classroom. Ellison recalls the unsettling moment when he first read

Park and Burgess's *Introduction to the Science of Sociology*, the most prominent textbook in the field. Published in 1921, the *Introduction* includes a number of racist claims that Ellison would go on to challenge. "The Negro," Park writes, "is by disposition, neither an intellectual nor an idealist, like the Jew; nor a brooding introspective, like the East Indian; nor a pioneer and frontiersman, like the Anglo-Saxon. He is primarily an artist loving life for its own sake. His *métier* is expression rather than action. He is, so to speak, the lady among the races."[34] For obvious reasons, Ellison found this claim both "humiliating" and wrong (*CE*, 332). It is not only "pregnant with mixed motives," he argues in his review of *An American Dilemma*, but also pedagogically destructive: "Imagine the effect that such teachings have had upon Negro students alone!" (ibid.). Describing these teachings as part of "that feverish industry dedicated to telling Negroes who and what they are," he claimed that they "deprive both humanity and culture of their complexity" (*CE*, 57). This is why, as Robert O'Meally explains, "Ellison's encounter at Tuskegee with *Introduction to the Science of Sociology* created an accelerated sense of urgency to learn about black American culture and to convert his knowledge into artistic forms."[35]

Still, even as Ellison strived to render the full complexity of that culture, his critique of Park is also a reminder of how strenuously he resisted the notion that identity is fixed by racial or ethnic background—the claim that "Negroes" (or, for that matter, Jews, East Indians, or Anglo-Saxons) "are" something. Had he believed identity was fixed in this manner, he would not have been able to make the argument of "Harlem Is Nowhere," which is devoted to demonstrating how the pressure of a certain environment, the urban North, fuels the "desperate search for identity" among black Americans. Without dwelling on race, Goffman also rejected the notion of fixed identity; the essays that make up *Asylums*, like Ellison's essay on LaFargue, depict a dynamic interplay between self and site, identity and environment. Indeed, the moment an "inmate" enters an asylum, the sociologist argues, "he begins a series of abasements, degradations, humiliations, and profanations of self," precisely because such sites are "forcing houses for changing persons" (*A*, 14, 12). Clearly, this is not the LaFargue Clinic. As Goffman's book unfolds, however, both his method of argumentation and his particular claims begin to approach Ellison's. The fact that they shared intellectual influences, such as Burke and the Chicago school, accounts to some degree for this similarity, but I want to suggest that the site itself did more than anything else to occasion the rhetorical and thematic parallels between "Harlem Is Nowhere" and *Asylums*. For, despite obvious disparities between LaFargue and St. Elizabeths, both were institutions of psychiatric care, not merely set up to treat mental illness but also in the business of remaking the self.

Ellison and Goffman emphasize this point in different ways. The patients at LaFargue are each in the midst of a self-transformation, yet this process actually begins long before they arrive at the clinic. Ellison contends that when the "Southern Negro" encounters the "slum conditions" of the urban North, his "folk personality" sustains an assault that "transform[s] his total being" (*CE*, 325). This transformation is both external ("His speech hardens, his movements are geared to the time clock, his diet changes" [ibid.]) and internal. Although "his sensibilities quicken and his intelligence expands," he nonetheless becomes "confused" and "bewildered" when he feels that "his world and his personality are out of key" (ibid.). Moreover, as he acclimates to life in the new city, he finds himself lacking "certain important supports to his personality"—by which Ellison means "family," "church," and "folk wisdom"—yet he is unable to construct new "bulwarks" against "the constant threat of chaos," for he is "barred from participating in the main institutional life of society" (*CE*, 324). No surprise, then, that he makes his way to LaFargue: "[I]t is precisely the denial of this support through segregation and discrimination," Ellison asserts, "that leaves the most balanced Negro open to anxiety" (*CE*, 325). Given the social conditions of Jim Crow, in other words, the site (Harlem) exerts a certain pressure on the self ("folk personality") that becomes difficult to withstand. "Dr. Wertham and his interracial staff" therefore seek a "modest achievement," which is to make this pressure more tolerable by coaxing a subtle self-transformation in the confused and the distressed. They aim, Ellison concludes, "to reforge the will to endure in a hostile world" by performing a pedagogical function that gives "each bewildered patient" a deeper "insight" into the friction between "his problems and his environment" (*CE*, 327).

This friction is the central theme of *Asylums*. "Without something to belong to," Goffman writes, "we have no stable self, and yet a total commitment and attachment to any social unit implies a kind of selflessness . . . Our status is backed by the solid buildings of the world, while our sense of personal identity often resides in the cracks" (*A*, 320). As soon as the patient or "inmate" arrives at St. Elizabeths, he is expected to make such a "total commitment," for "[h]is self is systematically, if often unintentionally mortified" (*A*, 14). During the "admission procedure," he is "stripped of his possessions" and "disinfected of his identifications," forced to swap his clothes for a "standard issue" uniform that is "clearly marked as really belonging to the institution" (*A*, 19). Unlike the patient at LaFargue, who is treated and released, this patient is at the threshold of an extended stay, so his "civilian self" must be discarded (*A*, 48). At this moment and elsewhere in *Asylums*, however, it is not entirely clear whether Goffman is discussing St. Elizabeths, another psychiatric hospital, or somewhere else entirely, such as an army training camp. This is because *Asylums* does not comprise a series of field reports on St. Elizabeths; instead, it offers a conceptual framework for apprehending social behavior within any "total institution," from the psychiatric hospital to the prison camp to the monastery. Goffman aims, as Pierre Bourdieu explains, "to show that institutions which differ greatly in their declared purposes show striking similarities in their actual functioning."[36] To achieve this aim, he relies on an inductive method, a style of reasoning that is similar to what Ellison deploys in "Harlem Is Nowhere," wherein empirical observations enable the formulation of abstract concepts with broad applicability.[37] What he witnessed at St. Elizabeths, moreover, furnished the evidence for a far-reaching argument partly because of how he understood that site. Just as Ellison imagined LaFargue as a sort of looking glass, "a special arrangement of mirrors and filters," so, too, Goffman considered his "mental hospital" a "thick and faulted prism" through which to view an array of sociological phenomena, above all, the problem of identity formation within a segregated social environment (A, 360).

The "basic split" between inmates and staff has predictably negative consequences. "Each grouping tends to conceive of the other in terms of narrow hostile stereotypes, staff often seeing inmates as bitter, secretive, and untrustworthy, while inmates often see staff as condescending, high-handed, and mean" (A, 7). Given these conditions, Goffman wonders, how does the inmate who has been "stripped" of "his civilian self" nevertheless manage to assert his individuality; or, to use Ellison's terms, how does the "desperate search for identity" appear within the patient population? To ask this question is to take for granted the persistence of individual agency in the face of adverse social strictures—segregation, discrimination, and coercion—a point that Ellison made throughout his career whenever he noted, for instance, the "willful and complexly and compelling human" facts of the Negro both within and against "the divisions of [his] society" (CE, 595). For Goffman, individual agency is fully recognizable in what he calls "secondary adjustments." This term categorizes a range of practices that "provide the inmate with important evidence that he is still his own man, with some control of his environment" (A, 55). In the most interesting cases, "a secondary adjustment becomes almost a kind of lodgement for the self, a *churinga* in which the soul is felt to reside" (ibid.). Goffman provides several examples. Some patients search for a "free place," or a zone of diminished "surveillance and restriction," where they can experience "a feeling of relaxation and self-determination" (A, 230). Other patients turn to scavenging and hoarding. They "ma[k]e the rounds of the refuse dumps" with the goal of finding "food, magazines, newspapers, or other oddments" (A, 213). Such items are then placed in a "stash" or a "personal storage space that is concealed and/or locked" (A, 249). The stash may seem like a meager collection of treats and bric-a-brac, but it represents nothing less than a "repository of selfhood" for the inmate who has been denied other modes of self-expression (A, 248).

Anticipating more recent and familiar work by Jean Baudrillard and Susan Stewart, Goffman draws attention to the mutual constitution of identity and environment that occurs through the act of collecting. "When objects are defined in terms of their use value," Stewart explains, "they serve as extensions of the body into the environment, but when objects are defined by the collection, such an extension is inverted, serving to subsume the environment to a scenario of the personal."[38] Yet Goffman also discusses use value and the laboring body. Along with the free place and the stash, *Asylums* defines another secondary adjustment, the "make-do," which entails "us[ing] available artifacts in a manner and for an end not officially intended" (A, 207).[39] In some instances, "[a] physical reworking of the artifact may be involved," as when a knife is "hammered from a spoon," or when "hospital-issue khaki pants" are "cut and tailored . . . into neat appearing summer shorts" (A, 207, 209). Given that "[t]he personal possessions of an individual are an important part of the materials out of which he builds a self," refabricating an object can be a potent act of self-fashioning (A, 78). Ellison makes his own version of this point in "Harlem Is Nowhere" when he taxonomizes the props and "exotic costumes" of the urban "masquerade" (CE, 322). He suggests that "boy gangsters" fabricate "homemade pistols" not only to "shoot down their young rivals" but also to fashion themselves anew. To the same degree that such pistols once functioned for these boys "in the youth of their origin" as "toy symbols of adolescent yearning for manhood," here in Harlem they materialize the aspiration to attain a new self, to slough off the "folk personality" and don a tough urban identity (ibid.). Both Ellison and Goffman, then, describe object making as a kind of self-fashioning under social conditions that restrict individual agency. The political claim here, which the two writers venture in different ways, is that these conditions should be seen as significant, but not omnipotent.

PATHOGENIC ENVIRONMENTS

This claim becomes a major theme of *Invisible Man*. "Until some gang succeeds in putting the world in a strait jacket," the unnamed narrator asserts in one of the novel's many references to psychiatry, "its definition is possibility" (IM, 576). He is thinking especially of the possibility for creating a unique self: "Whence all this passion toward conformity anyway," he gripes in the epilogue, "diversity is the word. Let man keep his many parts and you'll have no tyrant states" (IM, 577). After enduring the many trials that give *Invisible Man* the plot structure of a bildungsroman, he comes to this conclusion, alone in his underground hideout on the outskirts of Harlem.

But even though he resides in retreat from the urban masquerade, he nevertheless continues to dwell on his identity, enlisting material objects in a practice of self-fashioning. As he fantasizes about inventing two different "gadget[s]"—one to move his coffee to the fire while he lies in bed, the other to warm his shoes—he situates himself "in the great American tradition of tinkers," such as "Ford, Edison, and Franklin," while suggesting that, since he has both "a theory and a concept," he should be considered a "thinker-tinker" (*IM*, 7). His practice of making objects, therefore, distinguishes him as a subject, placing him in a venerable line of American inventors, even as it differentiates him from others, for he is not merely a craftsman, but an intellectual as well. If this understanding of object and subject, fabricated thing and fabricator, resonates with "Harlem Is Nowhere," then it confirms Arnold Rampersad's provocative claim that the essay "should be seen as a kind of apologia for both the substance and style of *Invisible Man*." I want to push this claim a step further. According to Rampersad, drafting "Harlem Is Nowhere" was crucial to Ellison's literary imagination. "No single task," he writes, "honed more sharply Ralph's ability to depict Invisible's experience in Harlem."[40] So, what did Ellison discover while writing about LaFargue that made its way into the novel?

Certainly, the relationship between environment and identity stayed on his mind: "Perhaps to lose a sense of *where* you are," ponders the narrator in the epilogue, "implies the danger of losing a sense of *who* you are" (*IM*, 577). Because this relationship was no less important to Goffman, *Asylums* provides a compelling theoretical framework for interpreting *Invisible Man*, with "Harlem Is Nowhere" serving as a kind of linchpin between the novel and the sociological monograph. Before offering such an interpretation, though, I want to situate both Goffman and Ellison in a wider historical context. One way to account for their shared interest in the problem of self-fashioning within a system of social segregation would be to consider black-white race relations in the United States during the 1940s and '50s. Ellison, of course, was incredibly sensitive to the problem of the color line; this problem is the most obvious referent for phrases such as "the sickness of the social order," which he used when discussing American society in the pre–civil rights era. Goffman did not dwell on this problem as Ellison did, but he was hardly silent on it. *Stigma* often draws evidence from a US context (a 1954 article in *Negro Digest*, for example) to illustrate how race can function as "an attribute that is deeply discrediting" to the individual.[41] Likewise, although race is not a central concern of *Asylums*, it nonetheless appears both explicitly and implicitly throughout the book, as when Goffman examines, for instance, the predicament of black patients in "prize integrated hospitals" by focusing on the racialized division of labor, the fact that "inmate garbage crews . . . tend to be wholly Negro" (*A*, 122). US racial politics, moreover, could be understood to form a subtext of Goffman's remarks on segregation, given that he began his field research in 1954, a few months prior to the *Brown* decision, and published the results in 1961, the year the Freedom Riders took to the interstates. It is not the history and politics of race, however, that provide the most illuminating context for the parallels between Goffman and Ellison, but the history of the site that they engaged.

The asylum has repeatedly posed the question of environmental agency, which captivated both the sociologist and the novelist: To what extent can a site transform the mind and remake the self? One answer emerged with the rise of the asylum in the nineteenth century. In 1840, there were 18 mental hospitals in the United States; that number had increased to 139 by 1880 and close to 300 by the start of the twentieth century.[42] St. Elizabeths, where Goffman conducted his fieldwork, opened its doors in 1855, largely thanks to the efforts of social reformer Dorothea Dix, who was part of the "moral treatment" movement, a utopian enterprise that had been initiated across the Atlantic by figures such as William Tuke and Philippe Pinel. Advocates of moral treatment, including the asylum superintendents who were the nation's first psychiatrists, argued that mental illness was best treated in a peaceful environment, away from the urban center, where pa-tients could lead highly regimented lives under paternalistic supervision. They also believed in a strong form of environmental determinism, which held that well-designed buildings on verdant grounds could actually *heal* the afflicted.[43] "[T]he treatment of the insane," one doctor put it, "is con-ducted not only *in*, but *by*, the asylum."[44] No one took this notion further than Thomas Story Kirkbride, an asylum superintendent in Pennsylvania and a founder of the Association of Medical Superintendents of American Institutions for the Insane (the precursor to the American Psychiatric Asso-ciation). Kirkbride was both professionally and personally involved with his patients—he was shot in the head by one, prosecuted in a circuslike trial by another, and married a third late in life—but he was best known for his architectural theory.[45] When he outlined his principles in an 1854 treatise, he set the standard for asylum construction through the 1880s, and many of the magnificent buildings that he inspired now lie in ruins across the country.[46] "The land chosen should be of good quality and easily tilled," he urged; "the surrounding scenery should be of a varied and attractive kind, and the neighborhood should possess numerous objects of an agreeable and interesting character." The building itself, moreover, "should be in good taste," and "everything repulsive and prison-like should be avoided."[47] These suggestions were not merely cosmetic. Like others associated with moral treatment, Kirkbride emphasized the curative effects of the lived environ-ment. He saw a causal relation between site and psyche.[48]

Had he lived long enough to read Goffman's book, therefore, he would have been scandalized by the many "prison-like" aspects of the twentieth-century asylum. Yet he would not have objected to the reasoning behind the claim that "the environment itself may be the pathogenic agent" (*A*, 334). This is really to say that, although Goffman professed "no great respect for the discipline of psychiatry," he nonetheless agreed with Kirkbride, one of that discipline's founders, that the material and social facts of the asylum play a decisive role in mental health, that their agency cannot be discounted (*A*, x). What the sociologist means to suggest, often through wrenchingly deadpan descriptions of "especially threatening or unpleasant aspects of the environment," is that the asylum was doing more harm than good, which is why his book is so often read (alongside works by R. D. Laing, Thomas Szasz, and Michel Foucault) as a seminal work of antipsychiatric literature that helped to grease the wheels of deinstitutionalization (*A*, 316). It is true that *Asylums* brought new attention to the plight of mental patients, but by the time Goffman began his research, exactly one hundred years after the initial publication of Kirkbride's treatise, the foundation for deinstitution-alization had already been built. Mary Jane Ward published *The Snake Pit* in 1946, a semiautobiographical account of the harsh conditions inside an insane asylum called Juniper Hill, where, for instance, "the food [i]s somewhat reminiscent of real food."[49] Ward's book sold well enough to be adapted into a film, which not only won an Oscar in 1948 but also spurred state hospital reform across the country.[50] The same year *The Snake Pit* appeared, Albert Q. Maisel published "Bedlam," a photo-essay in the May 6 issue of *Life*, which revealed the wretched conditions of mental hospitals in Ohio and Pennsylvania. "Through neglect and legislative penny-pinching," Maisel asserts, "state after state has allowed its institutions for the care and cure of the mentally sick to degenerate into little more than concentration camps."[51] This assertion was echoed two years later by Albert Deutsch, a documentarian in the tradition of Jacob Riis, whose *Shame of the States* (1948) disclosed "appalling state[s] of disorientation and disrepair," as well as widespread neglect. "Automobiles," he wrote, "get better attention than most mental patients today."[52]

Such harsh assessments appeared just prior to the rise of psychopharma-cology. The first antipsychotic, chlorpromazine, was discovered in 1952; the first antidepressant, imipramine, in 1957. The advent of new drugs, along with rising antipathy toward institutionalization, set the stage for the community-based mental health care model that predominates today. This model was anticipated and promoted by Goffman—who suggested, two years prior to the Community Mental Health Act of 1963, that "pursuing medicine at the community level" might be preferable to locking patients inside a "pathogenic" asylum (*A*, 344)—but it began to take shape just after World War II. The LaFargue Clinic admitted its first patients in 1946, the year *The Snake Pit* appeared, and another groundbreaking community mental health center, Fountain House, opened its doors in New York in 1948.[53]

Wertham, the leading physician at LaFargue, was generally interested in the link between the troubled mind and the lived environment, but his particular emphasis fell on what could be named, adapting Goffman, the pathogenic agency of an individual's social and material context. Instead of seeking an internal cause of mental illness, in either the unconscious mind or the damaged brain, he looked to external realities, such as racial discrimination and poverty. In *The Circle of Guilt*, for instance, the psychiatrist developed a profile of Frank Santana, a Puerto Rican immigrant and youth gang member who had been convicted of murder, which suggested that "the ruthlessly hostile environment" of Santana's upbringing was as much to blame as anything else for his psychological distress and criminal behavior.[54] Wertham held the same view toward his patients at LaFargue: "'What else could one expect?' he asked," wrote one journalist in profiling the psychiatrist. "Harlem's people were packed—1600 to the acre—into filthy, decaying tenements."[55] Ellison picked up on this idea, arguing in "Harlem Is Nowhere" that the "slum scenes of filth, disorder, and crumbling masonry" were severely "damaging to Negro personality" (*CE*, 324). Harlem was not just a ruin, in other words, but also a pathogenic agent. It was this understanding of the lived environment that Ellison meant to explore and finally to resist as he sat down to work on *Invisible Man*.

THE INVISIBLE ASYLUM

"I reached Men's House in a sweat," Ellison's narrator exclaims, moments after his arrival in New York. "I would have to take Harlem a little at a time" (*IM*, 161). He is relieved to have some respite from what he calls "the jungle" after a slightly harrowing walk from the subway (*IM*, 5). "I had never seen so many black people," he asserts, "moving along with so much tension and noise that I wasn't sure whether they were about to celebrate a holiday or join a street fight" (*IM*, 159). His ambivalence foreshadows both the reverie and the violence that he will experience soon enough—"It was as though a riot would break any minute" (*IM*, 160)—while marking Harlem as a thrilling and volatile environment, one that is "so fluid and shifting," as Ellison puts it in the LaFargue essay, "that often within the mind the real and the unreal merge, and the marvelous beckons from behind the same sordid reality that denies its existence" (*CE*, 322). In the mind of the invisible man, this merger includes the fusion of memory and experience, recollection and lived reality:

> Sure I had heard of it, but this was *real*. My courage returned. This really was Harlem, and now all the stories which I had heard of the city-within-a-city leaped alive in my mind. The vet had been right: For me this was not a city of realities, but of dreams; perhaps because

I had always thought of my life as being confined to the South. And now as I struggled through the lines of people a new world of possibility suggested itself to me faintly, like a small voice that was barely audible in the roar of city sounds. I moved wide-eyed, trying to take the bombardment of impressions. (*IM*, 159)

This is Ellison's version of the classically modernist scene of encounter (a scene that appears in Dreiser, Dos Passos, and Wright, and in James, Larsen, and Hemingway) wherein the perceiving subject first meets the metropolis. As the invisible man registers the overwhelming flux of "impressions," along with a "sensation of shock and fear," he toggles between the thoughts "leap[ing] alive in [his] mind" and the "bombardment" of external stimuli. It is difficult, especially toward the end of this passage, not to hear in Ellison's prose an echo of Georg Simmel's famous account of mental life in the city—his description of how human consciousness tries to manage "the unexpectedness of onrushing impressions" from the urban mise-en-scène.[56] Having just arrived from the South, and only familiar with what Simmel calls "rural life," the invisible man is simultaneously jolted and frayed by the walk to Men's House. His sweat is a physiological sign of what Ellison termed, in his working notes on LaFargue, "the affect of the urban environment upon the total Negro personality."

If Ellison did in fact have Simmel in mind when he wrote this passage, then he and Goffman shared another key influence. Ellison would have encountered Simmel's teachings in Park and Burgess's *Introduction to the Science of Sociology*, the textbook that he used at Tuskegee. Park was not merely Simmel's student; he stated that his "only formal instruction in sociology" came from listening to Simmel lecture in Berlin.[57] After Park founded the Chicago school, he passed along Simmel's ideas to Everett C. Hughes, Goffman's most important teacher, and when it was time for Goffman himself to defend his methodology in *The Presentation of Self*, he explained that "the justification for [his] approach [is] the justification for Simmel's also."[58] In addition, this passage of *Invisible Man* also mediates a site-specific connection between Ellison and Goffman. When the narrator recalls "[t]he vet," he is referring to a mental patient who is on his way to St. Elizabeths (*IM*, 153). A black war veteran and skilled physician, the vet is initially institutionalized, for dubious reasons, in the "insane asylum" near the narrator's college (*IM*, 35). He is then transferred to St. Elizabeths after the chaotic scene at the Golden Day, the bar and brothel that literally becomes a "house of madness" when a group of mental patients, on leave from the local asylum, attack their attendant: a "huge black giant" who "threaten[s] the men with a strait jacket" (*IM*, 151, 110, 35, 82). This scene includes only a small number of the novel's many references to madness, psychiatric treatment, and the asylum itself, a site that is figured variously throughout.

The main asylum in the novel, however, is neither the institution adjacent to the college nor St. Elizabeths but the site from which the narrative voice emanates—the invisible man's hole—his retreat from a Harlem that becomes increasingly hostile and dangerous as the narrative progresses. Of course, the hole is not a psychiatric institution, although it is, like LaFargue, a place of refuge within an abandoned basement. It is also, surely, one of the strangest sites in all of American literature, in part because Ellison leaves so much up to the reader's imagination, but Goffman's sociology can help us understand it in a new way. While the sociologist devoted his attention to a very different type of asylum—to the total institution that claims the vet—*Asylums* nonetheless provides a compelling set of terms for apprehending the invisible man's peculiar little hideout.

"So I took to the cellar; I hibernated. I got away from it all," Ellison's narrator states matter-of-factly in the epilogue (*IM*, 573). He means to justify his choice to hide underground after so many trials, conflicts, and unfortunate events, not the least of which is his experience of electroshock therapy (EST). "I was pounded between crushing electrical pressures," he exclaims, "pumped between live electrodes like an accordion between a player's hands" (*IM*, 232). He finds himself here, at the mercy of a quack doctor in the "factory hospital," after the boiler at Liberty Paints explodes and knocks him unconscious (*IM*, 245). "My lungs were compressed like a bellows," he goes on to describe, "and each time my breath returned I yelled, punctuating the rhythmical action of the nodes" (*IM*, 232). As the electrical current courses through the invisible man's body, this scene vivifies Goffman's (characteristically understated) claim that "shock therapy" causes its recipients "to feel that they are in an environment that does not guarantee their physical integrity" (*A*, 21). While the shocks continue, the doctors argue about what else to do with their patient, the leader explaining that his "little gadget," the EST machine, "will produce the results of a prefrontal lobotomy without the negative effects of the knife," by which he means a "complete change in personality" (*IM*, 236). The procedure works, more or less, precipitating a sort of identity crisis for the invisible man: "I realized that I no longer knew my own name" (*IM*, 239). He discovers that the trauma of EST has left him with an "alien personality," as well as an "obsession with [his] identity" (*IM*, 249, 259). Upon leaving the hospital, he remains, literally, marked by the site—"I can smell that hospital smell on you," Mary Rambo says to him (*IM*, 254)—yet otherwise liberated from the sites and scenes that have defined him so far: "Certainly," he asserts, "I couldn't help being different from when I left the campus" (*IM*, 259). So, from this point forward, he redoubles his effort to fashion himself, and as he assumes and abandons various roles in the Brotherhood both in and beyond Harlem, *Invisible Man* dramatizes the friction between identity and environment that comprises the central theme of "Harlem Is Nowhere."

Mary encapsulates this friction: "I'm in New York," she advises, "but New York ain't in me, understand what I mean? Don't git corrupted" (*IM*, 255).

The narrator's subjection to EST therefore constitutes a pivotal narrative moment, aligning *Invisible Man* with a range of other postwar American novels that render psychiatric hospitals as what Goffman calls "forcing houses for changing persons" (*A*, 12). Ellison set an important precedent for Ken Kesey's *One Flew Over the Cuckoo's Nest* (1962), probably the most famous asylum novel of all.[59] Kesey alludes to Ellison in several ways, not least in his portrayal of "shock and lobotomy" as extremely cruel psychiatric procedures. What Kesey dubs "The Shock Shop" leaves "the victim" in a state of disorientation—"You are unable to think coherently. You can't recall things"—which the invisible man experiences in his post-EST haze. "Enough of these treatments," Kesey's novel argues, "and a man could turn . . . into a mindless organism."[60] Moreover, both Kesey and Ellison, in referring to lobotomy and emphasizing personality transformation, recall a slightly earlier novel, Robert Penn Warren's *All the King's Men* (1946), with its visceral depiction of "electrocautery," the burning and cutting of brain tissue. "After the little pieces of brain [are] cut out," Warren writes, "the gaunt individual [i]s sealed back up and left to think up an entirely new personality."[61] There is nothing quite this gruesome in Sylvia Plath's *The Bell Jar* (1963), which was inspired by its author's own experience at McLean Hospital in Massachusetts, but it too focuses on how psychiatric procedures aim to change the self: "I decided to practice my new, normal personality on this man," asserts Esther Greenwood, Plath's protagonist, after enduring electroshock therapy and other treatments. Like Kesey, Plath was not only critical of EST, and of psychiatric medicine in general, but also interested in the mental hospital as a lived environment. She dwells, for example, on the architectural details of the site where Esther receives her first round of shocks, describing the "yellow clapboard walls of the large house, with its encircling veranda, gleam[ing] in the sun."[62] It is evident that Esther's doctor has bought into Kirkbride's basic claim that a bucolic site is good for the troubled mind, which allies him with the architects behind Worcester State Hospital (a Kirkbride-style building) as E. L. Doctorow portrays them in *The Book of Daniel* (1971). "The old hospital was put up around the turn of the century," he writes. "It was designed with the idea that madness might be soothed in a setting of architectural beauty."[63]

These novels by Warren, Ellison, Kesey, Plath, and Doctorow form but a small portion of the postwar American literary response to the asylum, a site that was no less crucial to the poetry and poetics of the period. Two months before LaFargue opened its doors, Charles Olson began visiting Ezra Pound at St. Elizabeths, taking notes on the condition of his elder ("his eyes seemed inside his stomach") cooped up behind the "high penitentiary wall."[64] Three years after *Invisible Man* appeared, Allen Ginsberg composed "Howl," with its famous imagery of "Pilgrim State's Rockland's and Greystone's foetid / halls" and other "invincible mad / houses."[65] And this is to say nothing of how important the asylum became for other literary genres (from feminist science fiction to Southern regionalism) and for other media, especially photography and film.[66] Ellison himself continued to care about asylums as he worked on the second novel that he never finished; "Cadillac Flambé," the short story that he published from the longer manuscript in 1973, concludes with its main character getting "lashed into a straightjacket" and taken away.[67] Still, *Invisible Man*, a text that stands out among all the other responses to this site in postwar American culture, constitutes his most profound treatment of the asylum. It is neither its depiction of EST nor its references to hospitals like St. Elizabeths, however, that distinguishes *Invisible Man* as an asylum novel but the way that it imagines the physical space from which it is voiced: the asylum that the narrator calls home.

"My hole is warm and full of light," he states in the novel's famous prologue. "Yes, full of light. I doubt if there is a brighter spot in all New York than this hole of mine, and I do not exclude Broadway" (*IM*, 6). His voice emanates—like "one long, loud rant, howl and laugh" (*CE*, 111)—from this subterranean sanctum that he describes by itemizing a few key details: 1,369 lightbulbs, a bed, a coffee pot, a chair, perhaps a few gadgets, and one radio-phonograph, animating the "acoustical deadness" with the blues of Louis Armstrong (*IM*, 8). Down here, somewhere underneath the border of Harlem, the invisible man sits alone, sweating under the lights that cover "every inch" of the ceiling, as he treats himself to ice cream and sloe gin (*IM*, 7). He revels in his theft of electricity from Monopolated Light and Power. He composes his memoir and broods over the events that he describes. He tinkers with objects and fantasizes about acquiring more. While it is difficult (if also irresistible) to visualize him in situ, photographers have tried. In 1952, Gordon Parks created a picture, *Invisible Man Retreat, Harlem*, for a photo-essay in *Life* that was inspired by the novel. Establishing a key precedent for Jeff Wall's more recent photograph, *After "Invisible Man" by Ralph Ellison, the Prologue*, Parks renders Ellison's protagonist with his legs crossed in a chair, adjusting his radio-phonograph with his left hand and clutching a bottle of booze with his right (figure 5.2). Behind him, a wall of lightbulbs contributes to what Ellison calls, in one of his working notes for Parks, "a chiaroscuro effect," a patterning of light and dark that permeates the whole composition.[68] Glowing like lightbulbs themselves, the invisible man's eyes match the wall behind him, a detail that complicates the novel's theme of invisibility by suggesting that it is the narrator himself who is blind or un-

5.2. *Invisible Man, Retreat, Harlem, New York, 1952*. Photograph by Gordon Parks; courtesy of and copyright The Gordon Parks Foundation.

reliable, incapable of seeing clearly from this vantage. "To take this symbolic picture," *Life* explains, "Parks built a special room and wired it for lights. Then he superimposed the picture of the room on a picture of New York at night."[69] The result is composition that not only illustrates and complicates the novel but also points back to Ellison's LaFargue essay. This hole, which appears to subtend what the invisible man calls "all New York," is nowhere because it is everywhere.

5.3. Jeff Wall, *After "Invisible Man" by Ralph Ellison, the Prologue*, 1999–2001, transparency in light box, 174.0 × 250.5 cm. Courtesy of the artist.

Fifty years after Parks, Wall constructed his own version of this site. His *After "Invisible Man"* situates Ellison's narrator inside a bright, messy interior whose ceiling is covered in lightbulbs, some illuminated, others sparkling with a reflected glimmer (figure 5.3). Like Parks, Wall fabricated an elaborate stage for his picture, "a special room" that is a work of art in its own right, a kind of installation that calls to mind the environmental assemblages of artists such as Tara Donovan and Sarah Sze.[70] The photographer filled this site with an array of artifacts—clothes, dishes, buckets, manuscript pages, little gadgets, assorted knickknacks, and objects from the narrative—using his imagination to compensate for the fact that, as he himself puts it, "the novel does not go into great descriptive detail."[71] Michael Fried underscores this point, arguing that "Wall's picture goes far beyond Ellison's prologue in seeking to recreate the *world* of the invisible man."[72] While Fried uses the term "world" within a thorough Heideggerian interpretation of the photograph, I want to point out that Wall is stressing a fundamental yet easily overlooked narrative detail: the invisible man's hole is a site of everyday life—a home—where one person does his dishes and dries his laundry and drafts his manuscript. This is a *lived* environment whose occupant is, as Goffman might put it, just trying to get by. Here, the invisible man retreats from the pathogenic Harlem that Ellison describes in both the LaFargue essay and the final chapters of the novel, when the neighborhood erupts into a riot. It is tempting to think of this character as a recluse, hiding from society, not least because he himself suggests that his "greatest social crime" has been his "hibernation," his abdication of "social responsibility," but this understanding would be inaccurate (*IM*, 581). Although the invisible man has little human contact, he still manages to see "a junk man," who supplies him "with wire and sockets" for his lightbulbs, and his theft of electricity is "an act of sabotage" that, however tenuously but also literally, keeps him connected to others (*IM*, 7). By tapping into the electrical grid, in other words, he forms part of the wider network of humans and nonhumans that Bruno Latour would define as the social, even as he confirms the claim from Ellison's own sociology textbook that "[a]bsolute isolation of the person from the members of his group is unthinkable."[73]

So, if the invisible man's hole is not exactly a zone of reclusion from society, then what is it? I propose that we understand it as what Goffman calls a secondary adjustment. This understanding is imperfect but, I hope, still illuminating. Discussing the inmate population of a total institution, the subordinated group within a system of social segregation, Goffman defines the secondary adjustment as any indirect challenge to the social order that allows the individual to claim an identity by taking some measure of control over the lived environment. "Secondary adjustments," he writes, "represent ways in which the individual stands apart from the role and the self that were taken for granted for him by the institution" (*A*, 189). By the end of his tale, the invisible man is fed up with the Brotherhood and every other institution that has sought to conscript him—"So after years of trying to adopt the opinions of others I finally rebelled" (*IM*, 573)—which is why he "take[s] up residence underground," inhabiting a site where he can, literally, "stand apart" from any socially prescribed role (*IM*, 571). His hole comprises three types of secondary adjustment in one. It is not only a "free place," a site of "relaxation and self[-]determination" that enables him to "be [his] own man" but also a "stash" or "personal storage space" that adds up to a physical "extension of the self" (*A*, 230, 248–49). What has been called Wall's "aesthetic of accumulation" emphasizes this point, imagining Ellison's protagonist as both a scavenger and a hoarder, one who acquires some material objects (from the junk man, for instance) and saves others, such as the calfskin briefcase, the chain link, and the rabbit's foot, all of which are significant in the narrative and visible in the photograph. Moreover, an abandoned basement repurposed as a home and writing studio, the hole exemplifies what Goffman calls a "make-do," a third type of secondary adjustment that involves reworking the material environment "for an end not officially intended" (*A*, 207). In this sense, finally, the hole recalls the other basement, the LaFargue Clinic, which was so important to Ellison's literary and sociological imagination. Both register as secondary adjustments, local efforts to cope with a national problem, the system of constitutionally sanctioned segregation that Ellison termed the sickness of the social order. Longing for a cure, the novelist was drawn to subterranean sites of diminished suffering.

AFTERWORD: SITE UNSEEN

There can be no asylum in Cormac McCarthy's postapocalypse. In a desolate land stalked by ruthless cannibals, every site poses a threat, so we expect the worst as the unnamed protagonist of *The Road* (2006) descends into a "bunker" beneath the "charred ruins" and "cauterized terrain" of a "wasted country."[1] What awaits him, however, is not certain death. "Oh my God," he whispers to his boy as he looks around. "Come down. Oh my God. Come down" (*TR*, 138). The two characters, father and son, behold a marvelous anachronism, "[t]he richness of a vanished world" (*TR*, 139). Just below the "gullied and eroded and barren" terrain, the only terrain that the boy has ever known, they discover "a tiny paradise," stocked to the hilt with "[c]rate upon crate of canned goods. Tomatoes, peaches, beans, apricots. Canned hams. Corned beef. Hundreds of gallons of water in ten gallon plastic jerry jugs. Paper towels, toiletpaper, paper plates. Plastic trashbags stuffed with blankets . . . Chile, corn, stew, soup, spaghetti sauce" (*TR*, 150, 138). This site provides some respite for the beleaguered pair, a brief hiatus from the deprivation and depravity of the road, where they are perennially starving, cold, and terrified. But it also presents both a practical problem (they can be readily discovered and trapped) and an existential dilemma—"He'd been ready to die and now he wasn't going to and he had to think about that" (*TR*, 144)—that the father never fully resolves. His few nights in the bunker are restless:

> When he woke again he thought the rain had stopped. But that wasn't what woke him. He'd been visited in a dream by creatures of a kind he'd never seen before. They did not speak. He thought that they'd been crouching by the side of his cot as he slept and then had skulked away on his awakening. He turned and looked at the boy. Maybe he understood for the first time that to the boy he was himself an alien. A being from a planet that no longer existed. The tales of which were

suspect. He could not construct for the child's pleasure the world he'd lost without constructing the loss as well and he thought perhaps the child had known this better than he. He tried to remember the dream but he could not. All that was left was the feeling of it. He thought perhaps they'd come to warn him. Of what? That he could not enkindle in the heart of the child what was ashes in his own. Even now some part of him wished they'd never found this refuge. Some part of him always wished it to be over. (*TR*, 154)

To perform a site reading of this passage is to ask how the bunker, an utterly anomalous site within the universe of the novel, mediates sociality. What happens, here in this tiny paradise, to social form?

Most obviously, the two main characters inhabit the fantasy of a preapocalyptic ordinary. Their interactions bespeak a kind of subdued pleasure. Instead of scavenging for edible scraps in the barren woods, they eat "a sumptuous meal by candlelight" and "drink Coca Cola out of plastic mugs" (*TR*, 152, 148). They sleep for a full day. They bathe and use the toilet. The father cuts his son's hair, then his own. They play checkers. "I wish we could live here," the boy rues. "I know," responds his father (*TR*, 151). But the boy, who was born *after* the unspecified apocalyptic event—the full-scale thermonuclear war or the asteroid strike or whatever it was that obliterated civilization and scorched the earth—has his doubts, or so his father suspects. "The boy was sitting quietly on the bunk, still wrapped in the blanket, watching. The man thought he had probably not fully committed himself to any of this. You could wake in the dark wet woods at any time" (*TR*, 141). Even as the bunker facilitates their intimacy, then, it heightens their alterity by spatializing asymmetrical experiences of time travel. When the father descends through the bunker's hatch, he returns to "the world he'd lost," encountering the material objects of this environment, the crates and cans and Coca Cola, as concrete manifestations of figures in memory. The boy has no such encounter. For him, drinking "the rich sweet syrup" from a can of pears, there is no relay of "pleasure" and "loss," no recollection of a vanished plenitude, but only what his father calls "the feeling of it" (*TR*, 141).

That feeling is powerful, however, not just because he has not eaten anything "in a long time," and not simply because the relative strangeness of this site piques his interest, but also because the bunker reveals itself to him as a repository of souvenirs from an earlier historical time (or from a time prior to the catastrophic end of history) that his father must explicate (*TR*, 141). "What is all this stuff, Papa?" the boy asks. "It's food," his father responds. "Can you read it?" (*TR*, 139). Susan Stewart has argued that the souvenir performs a "double function," which "is to authenticate a past or otherwise remote experience and, at the same time, to discredit the present.

The present is either too impersonal, too looming, or too alienating compared to the intimate and direct experience of contact which the souvenir has as its referent."[2] But this function fails in a novel where "all stores of food ha[ve] given out and murder [i]s everywhere upon the land" (*TR*, 181). The hostility of *this* present overwhelms the nostalgic force of the souvenir, which is why the father, even after a few restorative moments with his boy, still "wish[es] they'd never found this refuge" and still longs for the end of their ordeal. By this point in the novel, then, it is unclear why they keep struggling to survive, why they decide to trudge southward toward the coast instead of remaining in the bunker, which is to say, instead of giving up. One answer is that the bunker itself propels them forward, for it reminds them of their social mandate by spotlighting an otherwise dim connection to the members of their tribe.

"Why is this here," the boy asks upon entering the site: "Is it real?" (*TR*, 139). "Oh yes," his father assures him, it is real and good and in some sense meant for them:

> Is it okay for us to take it?
> Yes. It is. They would want us to. Just like we would want them to.
> They were the good guys?
> Yes. They were.
> Like us.
> Like us. Yes.
> So it's okay.
> Yes. It's okay.

This dialogue, clipped yet expressive, typifies how they communicate. To reassure his son, a Christ figure always seeking the ethical good, the father relies on two rhetorical devices, repetition and simile, that appear throughout the novel. "Okay" is their cant; the term signifies rightness and assent, while functioning as a sort of phatic gesture, indicating presence, nearness, and mutual understanding as they repeat it to each other. In a similar way, the use of simile in this dialogue (also repetitive: "They were. Like us. Like us. Yes.") forms part of a larger rhetorical pattern that the novel establishes in its opening paragraph. McCarthy employs dozens of similes, often choosing "Like" to begin a sentence fragment: "Nights dark beyond darkness and the days more gray each one than what had gone before. Like the onset of some cold glaucoma dimming away the world ... Their light playing over the wet flowstone walls. Like pilgrims in a fable swallowed up and lost among the inward parts of some granitic beast" (*TR*, 3). In general, this rhetoric lays bare a certain grammar of sense-making: the analogical reasoning that aims to define the postapocalyptic world—a world that comprises "One vast sepulchre. Senseless. Senseless" (*TR*, 222)—in terms of the world that preceded it. "They plodded on, thin and filthy as street addicts" (*TR*, 177).

In the bunker dialogue, specifically, this rhetoric not only links worlds but also establishes a social bond that connects the father and the boy to the unnamed survivalists, "the good guys," who built the site. The bunker, in this sense, achieves materially what the similes achieve rhetorically, functioning as a hinge between social actors past and present. As the father surveys the "stores" of food and supplies, he imputes an intention to the bunker makers that contains an imperative for him and his son: "It's here," he asserts, "because someone thought it might be needed" (*TR*, 149, 139). This assertion implies that the site is not merely a serendipitous find but an intentional object that was left for them by an earlier group of good guys, which is why they must utilize it: "They would want us to. Just like we would want them to." To do so, therefore, is not just to survive a little longer; it is to fulfill the wish of the bunker makers and to extend the lineage of good guys into the postapocalyptic present, to keep "carrying the fire" of civilization, amid and against the barbarism of "the bad guys" (*TR*, 83, 77).

Given that their world is "mostly burned," however, "fire" represents civilization with no small degree of irony (*TR*, 12). Although *The Road* ends ambiguously—the father dies, his son lives—it offers scant evidence to suggest a happy future for the good guys; "the agony of the novel," writes Jennifer Egan, "is that things are getting worse, not better."[3] For this reason, it is hard to accept the critical consensus, voiced most eloquently by Susan Mizruchi, that the bunker scene is "the one notable instance of recuperation" in the novel.[4] Indeed, even for a novelist with a special talent for making *setting* meaningful, this scene stands out for its *site specification*, but what constitutes "recuperation" in a world "populated by men who would eat your children in front of your eyes" (*TR*, 181)?[5] In such a world, the bunker can provide only false recuperation, until the potentially redemptive moment of the Rapture, as the scene's final simile suggests by likening its "faintly lit hatchway" to "a grave yawning at judgment day in some old apocalyptic painting" (*TR*, 155) (figure A.1).

While this simile sets the novel in relation to a long painterly tradition, it also figures an image that conjures the recent photography of Richard Ross, who shot dozens of underground bunkers, including several that resemble a "tiny paradise," for a project called *Waiting for the End of the World* (2003). Ross's goal, as he himself puts it, "was to make what is hidden, visible—by changing the status of these structures from covert to overt."[6] A fuller analysis of McCarthy's bunker, a longer site reading than I will offer here, would follow up on the reference to painting by tracking the novel's connection to visual representations of such sites. How do painting, photography, film, television, and other media convey what Paul Virilio calls "the poetry of the bunker"?[7] This question is intimately linked to my initial

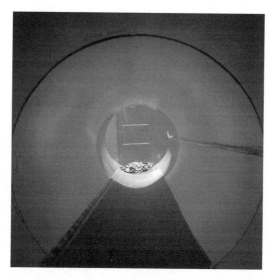

A.1. Richard Ross, *Family Shelter, Salt Lake City, Utah*, 2003. Entrance view. Photo courtesy of and © Richard Ross, www.richardross.net.

question of how the bunker mediates sociality. For Ross, such sites constitute "the architecture of failure—the failure of moderation, politics, communication, diplomacy, and sustaining humanity." To build a bunker, and to stock it with "everything" that would embody the "richness of a vanished world" (*TR*, 139), is to oscillate between what Ross calls "the ultimate in optimism and belief in individual survival and paradoxically the ultimate in pessimism."[8]

His photographs render this oscillation with a sort of droll precision. Inside this backyard family shelter in Utah, for instance, a single shelf holds raisins and bullets, soap and a radiation detection kit (figure A.2). Partially obstructed, the wall text appears to read, "In war, maintain at least 8 inches between personnel and shelter walls at all times."[9] The oscillation is not only emotional but also practical: on the one hand, this site envisages the type of domestic normalcy that McCarthy's characters experience as they eat and sleep and bathe, whereas, on the other hand, it reminds its occupants that total thermonuclear war would put all survivors of the initial attack on the front line, thus casting them as "personnel." Although Ross's photograph dates to 2003, then, it documents the continuity of this site with its Cold War antecedents, including the family fallout shelter (built circa 1955) that currently resides at the Smithsonian (figure A.3).[10] Facing "the possibilities of nuclear war in the missile age," President Kennedy "pledged a new start on Civil Defense" in 1961 by calling for a na-

A.2. Richard Ross, *Family Shelter, Salt Lake City, Utah*, 2003. Interior view. Photo courtesy of and © Richard Ross, www.richardross.net.

tional program that would "identify and mark space in existing structures—public and private—that could be used for fallout shelters in case of attack." It would be a dismal "failure of responsibility," he argued, to deny that "every family" has a "need for this kind of protection."[11] While the national fallout shelter program was short-lived, its structure of feeling—the relay between optimism and pessimism—was well documented. Four months after *Life* published a lavishly illustrated cover story detailing all the "big things to do" in light of Kennedy's speech, and three months after *Time* proclaimed that "survival stores" in Los Angeles were "doing a boom business selling shelter supplies," *Life* ran a sobering editorial on the "limit of shelters."[12]

So how does *The Road* negotiate this relay? While the bunker episode includes fleeting instances of something like pleasure, it offers no radical

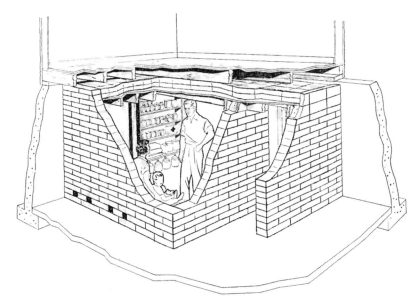

A.3. *The Family Fallout Shelter*, Office of Civil Defense Mobilization, June 1959.

break from what Andrew Hoberek calls the "unremitting affect of exhaustion" that structures the entire novel.[13] McCarthy has outdone his own proclivity for bleakness, depicting a setting where even "recuperation" skews pessimistic: "Maybe he understood for the first time that to the boy he was himself an alien. A being from a planet that no longer existed." Site reading reveals the social and political claim that inheres in this depiction of setting. If the term "site," as I suggested in the introduction, implies human activity and sociality, then McCarthy has imagined his own version of a "nonsite," a realm of starkly inhuman activity and radical antisociality. Here, in this realm, the bunker would seem to be antithetical, to be "sustaining humanity" against barbarism, but it provides no permanent asylum, no sustainable home for the good guys, which is why McCarthy, tellingly, never calls it a "shelter." Rather, the bunker constitutes the architecture of failure, a would-be grave, in a novel that ultimately registers as a telegraph from a site, indeed a planet, that we do not want but seem disastrously committed to producing. Does it even matter what caused the apocalypse? McCarthy himself has said it "could be anything ... It is not really important. The whole thing now is, what do you do?"[14] It's a good question, but the nightmare setting of the novel impels us just as forcefully to ask whether we are doing enough now, in the era of nuclear danger and climate crisis, to protect the only social site we have.[15]

To perform a site reading of *The Road*, then, is to appreciate how the text functions as a novel of purpose that aims to vivify the planet as what Latour would call a "matter of concern."[16] Still, *The Road* reads less as a critique of contemporary social problems (nuclear weapons, greenhouse gases, over-consumption) than as a "thought-experiment," a sort of literary climate model, forecasting a chillingly plausible correlation between a ruined site and a grisly social order.[17] By imagining this correlation through narrative form, McCarthy offers his own striking contribution to environmental and sociological thought, a contribution that starts to become apparent the moment we ask how his setting functions as an *actant*, both in the novel itself and beyond. This question has animated the foregoing analyses, and it will continue to be worth asking as we confront the increasingly complex challenges of collective life on a fragile site.

ACKNOWLEDGMENTS

Writing a book about social life has been a social endeavor. I am grateful for the ongoing support of friends and colleagues in the Department of English and in the Program in History and Literature at Harvard University. Over the past three years, Louis Menand has been a constant source of inspiration and support, and his keen advice has improved every aspect of this book. John Stauffer, commenting thoroughly on the entire manuscript, inhabited the argument with unabashed reverie as he helped me to refine the methodological and conceptual stakes of the enterprise. The critical light of Amanda Claybaugh, one of my most discerning readers, allowed me to see problems and possibilities that otherwise would have remained obscure. Nicholas Watson, in a detailed reading of the manuscript that came at a crucial moment, showed me how to make the argument more convincing and compelling. Werner Sollors attended to this project with breathtaking care, pointing me toward new ventures while making me feel at home. Lawrence Buell asks the right question every time, and he is patient when the answer proves elusive until further reflection. James Simpson brought his critical acumen and intellectual exuberance to my work, and his comments steered me away from numerous potholes. Leah Price, a generous font of advice and support, asked questions that helped me recast the argument in more capacious and ambitious terms. And Peter Sacks, in his typically generous manner, gave me a new sense of Robert Smithson and aesthetic theory.

Both within and beyond Harvard, many discussions have had a positive impact on this project. For these, I thank Homi Bhabha, Stephen Burt, Glenda Carpio, Nicholas Dames, Elizabeth Maddock Dillon, Nicholas Donofrio, Daniel Donoghue, James Engell, Jennifer Fleissner, Jeanne Follansbee, Marjorie Garber, Stephen Greenblatt, Gordon Hutner, Shannon Jackson, Jill Lepore, Heather Love, Deidre Shauna Lynch, William J. Maxwell, Timothy McCarthy, Elisa New, Samuel Otter, Joseph Rezek, Jennifer

Roberts, Kathryn Roberts, Elaine Scarry, Diana Sorensen, Gordon Teskey, Helen Vendler, Andrew Warren, Leah Whittington, and Sarah Williams.

This book began as a doctoral dissertation, completed in the Department of English at the University of Chicago. My first readers were thus my advisors, teachers, colleagues, and friends in graduate school. Every conversation with Bill Brown was a genuine inspiration; he responded, patiently and thoroughly, to many drafts, and his incisive, energetic comments not only kept me on track but also demanded the very best thinking I could muster. Our ongoing dialogue remains a special source of intellectual joy. Deborah Nelson guided me through every iteration of this project, and her wisdom and advice are reflected on every page. Kenneth Warren, a deeply engaged third reader, offered the perfect balance of criticism and encouragement, and his analytical insight improved all facets of my argument.

Other teachers were crucial as well. For an early reading of my work that pulled no punches, and for subsequent conversations that helped me find my claims, I am immensely grateful to W.J.T. Mitchell. In addition, conversations with James Chandler, Darby English, Mark B. N. Hansen, Jacqueline Goldsby, Elaine Hadley, Leela Gandhi, Heather Keenleyside, and Marshall Sahlins turned into eye-opening interventions that expanded my sense of what I was doing. Several friends at Chicago, especially Michael Sauvé, Daniel Harris, and James Hodge, were no less eye-opening in their responses to early drafts and inchoate ideas. Many of these ideas were first hatched in the Social Science Research Council's Dissertation Proposal Development Fellowship (DPDF) Program, where I had the good fortune of working with Elizabeth Lunbeck and Emily Martin, two scholars who facilitated my thinking across and between disciplines. In the years before graduate school, well before I even considered writing a dissertation, my teachers at New York University introduced me to a world of scholarship. I am particularly grateful to John Guillory, Ross Posnock, Lytle Shaw, Richard Sieburth, G. Gabrielle Starr, and Philip Brian Harper for treating me like I had something valuable to say.

As I worked on the manuscript, I received important feedback from journals and audiences. An earlier version of chapter 1 appeared as "Supermarket Sociology" in the special issue of *New Literary History* devoted to "New Sociologies of Literature." My editors, Rita Felski and James F. English, provided a remarkably astute report on the essay that transformed my thinking in ways that continue to influence all my work. A portion of chapter 4 was published as "Pynchon's Malta" in *Post45: Peer Reviewed*; the readers at this journal were equally incisive, so I am grateful to them and to the other members of the Post45 Collective—especially Amy Hungerford, Deak Nabers, Sean McCann, J. D. Connor, Michael Szalay, and Florence Dore—whose collective critical intelligence has improved this project over the years. Audiences asked challenging and helpful questions at the Social

Science Research Council, the University of Chicago, New York University, the University of Utah, the Futures of American Studies Institute at Dartmouth College, Harvard University, the Modern Language Association Annual Convention, the Modernist Studies Association Conference, the American Comparative Literature Association Conference, the International Conference on Narrative, and the Post45 Conference. Presenting at the Mahindra Humanities Center New Faculty Lunch was especially illuminating, as I worked to transform the dissertation into a book, so I thank Homi Bhabha for convening a rigorous, searching discussion about literature and social theory.

This book could not have been completed without financial support from several sources. A Century Fellowship from the University of Chicago funded the initial research, while a Mellon Foundation/University of Chicago Dissertation Completion Fellowship gave me time to write the first draft. A Dissertation Proposal Development Fellowship from the Social Science Research Council facilitated research in Malta and introduced me to a new community of scholars and friends. I owe special thanks to Marco and Vanessa Frazier for letting me into their Maltese bomb shelter and for showing me warm hospitality. More recently, a Mayers Fellowship from the Huntington Library enabled archival research for chapter 4, while financial support from the Division of Arts and Humanities at Harvard allowed me to complete the last round of revisions. I am grateful to deans Diana Sorensen and Heather Lantz for their belief in this project.

Working with Princeton University Press has been a pleasure. I am grateful to Alison MacKeen for her early enthusiasm and to Anne Savarese, Ellen Foos, and Juliana Fidler for shepherding this book into print. Two anonymous readers for the press produced stunningly detailed, cogent, and persuasive reports that prompted many early mornings and late nights of revision. After I submitted the final manuscript, the meticulous copy editing of Cathy Slovensky and the superb proofreading of Miranda Kaplan made everything better.

Over the past two years, as I worked, Maggie Gram helped me see around the dark corners. Adam Day talked me through the ups and downs of this work, as he has done for many years, bringing a poet's ear to the sounds of prose. My parents, Jane and Steve Menta and Dave Alworth, always believed I could do it, and my brother, Ryan Alworth, kept me smiling as I tried. My grandmother, Marie Realmuto, did not live to hold this book in her hands, but early discussions with her about literature and art set me on the path toward writing it. My greatest debt is to Colleen Ammerman, whose faith in this project has underwritten my own.

NOTES

INTRODUCTION: THE SITE OF THE SOCIAL

1. Erving Goffman, "The Interaction Order," *American Sociological Review* 48 (1983): 1–17.

2. Rob Nixon, *Slow Violence and the Environmentalism of the Poor* (Cambridge, MA: Harvard University Press, 2011); Ursula Heise, *Sense of Place and Sense of Planet: The Environmental Imagination of the Global* (Oxford: Oxford University Press, 2008), 10.

3. Bill Brown, "Thing Theory," *Critical Inquiry* 28.1 (2001): 1–22; Graham Harman, *Tool-Being: Heidegger and the Metaphysics of Objects* (Peru, IL: Open Court, 2002), ch. 3; Walter Benjamin, "Dream Kitsch" (1927), trans. Howard Eiland, *Selected Writings*, trans. Rodney Livingstone et al., ed. Michael Jennings, Eiland, and Gary Smith, 4 vols. (Cambridge, MA: Harvard University Press, 1999), 2:4; Martin Heidegger, *Poetry, Language, Thought*, trans. Albert Hofstadter (New York: Harper Perennial Classics, 2001), 112; Georg Lukács, *History and Class Consciousness*, trans. Rodney Livingstone (Cambridge, MA: Harvard University Press, 1972), 92.

4. Lawrence Buell, *The Future of Environmental Criticism* (Malden, MA: Blackwell, 2005), 33.

5. Seymour Chatman, *Story and Discourse: Narrative Structure in Fiction and Film* (Ithaca, NY: Cornell University Press, 1978), 264; "setting, n.1," *OED Online*, June 2014, Oxford University Press. Another way to put this point would be to say that we do not have a study of setting that is comparable in scope and orientation to those on character (e.g., Alex Woloch's *The One vs. The Many*) or on plot (e.g., Peter Brooks's *Reading for the Plot*) partly because, as Marie Laure-Ryan has observed, narrative theory often emphasizes temporal rather than spatial aspects of narrative (while acknowledging the interconnection of time and space) and partly because, as Ursula Heise notes, environmental criticism "has achieved its greatest successes at what one might broadly call the thematic level" (Ursula Heise, "Comparative Literature and the Environmental Humanities," 2014–15 *State of the Discipline Report*, http://stateofthediscipline.acla.org/entry/comparative-literature-and-environmental-humanities). Still, several narrative theorists have produced incisive work on narrative setting; for an overview that defines the many "laminations of narrative space," see Marie Laure-Ryan, "Space," in Peter Hühn et al., eds., *The Living Handbook of Narratology* (Hamburg: Hamburg University Press, 2012), http://wikis.sub.uni-hamburg.de/lhn/index.php/Space.

6. Latour uses both *actant* and *actor* throughout his writings to define anything human or nonhuman that "modif[ies] a state of affairs by making a difference" (Bruno Latour, *Reas-

sembling the Social: An Introduction to Actor-Network-Theory [Oxford: Oxford University Press, 2005], 71). As I explain in detail in chapter 1, he borrows the term *actant* from narratology and semiotics, typically employing it to designate a generic rather than specific constituent of a social network, a usage I adopt. For a thorough account of the term *actant* in literary theory, see David Herman, "Existentialist Roots of Narrative Actants," *Studies in Twentieth Century Literature* 24.2 (2000): 257–70.

7. Buell, *The Future*, 4; Elaine Freedgood, *The Ideas in Things: Fugitive Meaning in the Victorian Novel* (Chicago: University of Chicago Press, 2006). For a concise overview of a heterogeneous subfield, see Bill Brown, "Introduction: Textual Materialism," *PMLA* 125.1 (2010): 24–28.

8. Franco Moretti, *Atlas of the European Novel, 1800–1900* (New York: Verso, 1999), 5.

9. James F. English, "Everywhere and Nowhere: The Sociology of Literature After 'the Sociology of Literature,'" *New Literary History* 41.2 (2010): xii; Stephen Best and Sharon Marcus, "Surface Reading: An Introduction," *Representations* 108.1 (2009): 1, 2. I am also thinking of Moretti's concept of "distant reading" (Franco Moretti, *Distant Reading* [New York: Verso, 2013]); Felski's polemic against contextualization (Rita Felski, "Context Stinks!," *New Literary History* 42.4 [2011]: 573–91); Love's method of "close but not deep reading" (Heather Love, "Close but not Deep: Literary Ethics and the Descriptive Turn," *New Literary History* 41.2 [2010]: 371–91); Posnock's definition of "receptive reading" (Ross Posnock, "'Don't think, but look!': W. G. Sebald, Wittgenstein, and Cosmopolitan Poverty," *Representations* [2010]: 110–39); and Price's account of "not reading" and "rejection history" (Leah Price, *How to Do Things with Books in Victorian Britain* [Princeton, NJ: Princeton University Press, 2012], 1–18).

10. English, "Everywhere and Nowhere," xii.

11. Although this claim echoes a famous statement of Margaret Thatcher's, as Latour himself acknowledges, it is obviously not meant as an endorsement of Thatcherism: "With some provocation," he explains, his sociology "could use as its slogan what Mrs. Thatcher famously exclaimed (but for very different reasons!): 'There is no such thing as a society'" (Latour, *Reassembling the Social*, 5).

12. Felski, "Context Stinks!," 578.

13. Latour, *Reassembling the Social*, 1.

14. Émile Durkheim, *The Elementary Forms of Religious Life*, trans. Karen E. Fields (New York: Free Press, 1995), 443.

15. Best and Marcus, "Surface Reading: An Introduction," 3. On Jameson's method of historicism, as well as its reception within literary studies, also see James Chandler, *England in 1819: The Politics of Literary Culture and the Case of Romantic Historicism* (Chicago: University of Chicago Press, 1998), ch. 1.

16. Fredric Jameson, *The Political Unconscious: Narrative as a Socially Symbolic Act* (Ithaca, NY: Cornell University Press, 1981), 48.

17. Although I emphasize Latour's thinking about the social, he is perhaps most widely known within literary studies for his effort to develop an alternative to critique. See, for instance, Bruno Latour, "Why Has Critique Run Out of Steam? From Matters of Fact to Matters of Concern," *Critical Inquiry* 30 (2004): 225–48.

18. In addition to the essay cited in the note directly above, also see Bruno Latour, "From Realpolitik to Dingpolitik, or How to Make Things Public," in *Making Things Public: Atmospheres of Democracy* (Cambridge, MA: MIT Press, 2005), 4–31.

19. Emma Donoghue, *Room* (New York: Little, Brown, 2010), 3; hereafter cited parenthetically in the text as *R*.

20. Aimee Bender, "Separation Anxiety," *New York Times*, September 16, 2010.

21. Gérard Genette, *Narrative Discourse: An Essay in Method*, trans. Jane E. Lewin (Ithaca, NY: Cornell University Press, 1980), ch. 4.

22. Chatman, *Story and Discourse*, 139.
23. Erving Goffman, *The Presentation of Self in Everyday Life* (New York: Anchor, 1959), 25. Goffman takes this point from Kenneth Burke, *A Grammar of Motives* (New York: Prentice-Hall, 1945), 6–9.
24. Emily Landau, "Living Room," *Walrus Blog*, October 25, 2010, http://walrusmagazine.com/blogs/2010/10/25/living-room.
25. Emma Donoghue, "On *Room*," *Economist*, November 17, 2010.
26. Daniel Defoe, *Robinson Crusoe* (New York: Penguin, 2001), 40; hereafter cited parenthetically in the text as *RC*.
27. Susan Stewart, *On Longing: Narratives of the Miniature, the Gigantic, the Souvenir, the Collection* (Durham, NC: Duke University Press, 1993), 5.
28. Ian Watt, *The Rise of the Novel: Studies in Defoe, Richardson, and Fielding* (Berkeley: University of California Press, 1957), 92. My brief remarks hardly do justice to the complexity of how *Robinson Crusoe* figures society and social interaction, particularly through its treatment of nonhuman animals, but see Heather Keenleyside, "Animals and Other People in Eighteenth-Century Literature," PhD diss., University of Chicago, 2008, ch. 2.
29. Roland Barthes, "The Reality Effect" (1968), in *The Rustle of Language*, trans. Richard Howard (Berkeley: University of California Press, 1989), 141.
30. Ibid., 148; Freedgood, *Ideas in Things*, 9.
31. Georg Lukács, "Narrate or Describe? A Preliminary Discussion of Naturalism and Formalism" (1936), in *Writer and Critic and Other Essays*, trans. Arthur D. Kahn (New York: Merlin Press, 1970), 135–36.
32. Watt, *Rise of the Novel*, 26. Cynthia Wall reiterates Watt's point about "solidity" when she asserts that "Defoe's fiction (1719–24) depends heavily on things," yet she also demonstrates that the emergence of setting as a "fully visualized" zone of action and interaction (i.e., setting as we typically understand it today) was a process that unfolded over the course of the eighteenth century (Cynthia Wall, *The Prose of Things: Transformations of Description in the Eighteenth Century* [Chicago: University of Chicago Press, 2006], 110).
33. Mary Poovey has shown that "by the late 1720s, social had come to seem like one attribute of an objectified abstraction—human nature—viewed as given to all individuals by God," as in William Wolloston's claim from 1722 that "man is a Social creature" (Mary Poovey, "The Liberal Civil Subject and the Social in Eighteenth-Century British Moral Philosophy," *Public Culture* 14.1 [2002]: 127–28). *Robinson Crusoe* was published in 1719.
34. Lukács, "Narrate or Describe?," 115. In his own discussion of Flaubert, Allen Tate asserts that "one of the amazing paradoxes of the modern novel" is that, even though its "great subject is man alone in society or even against society, almost never with society," it nonetheless "put[s] man wholly into his physical setting" in order to render social interaction "in terms of situation and scene" (Allen Tate, "Techniques of Fiction" [1944], in *Essays of Four Decades* [Chicago: Swallow Press, 1968], 138–39).
35. Lukács, "Narrate or Describe?"; Gustave Flaubert, *Madame Bovary* (New York: W. W. Norton, 2005), 120, 108, 112.
36. "Flaubert the sociologist," Bourdieu writes, "gives us a sociological insight on Flaubert the man" (Pierre Bourdieu, *The Field of Cultural Production* [New York: Columbia University Press, 1993], 145); Wolf Lepenies, *Between Literature and Science: The Rise of Sociology*, trans. R. J. Hollingdale (Cambridge: Cambridge University Press, 1988), 6. On the reception of Bourdieu's sociology within the discipline of literary studies, see John Guillory, "Bourdieu's Refusal," *Modern Language Quarterly* 58.4 (December 1997): 367–98.
37. The American literary tradition includes a particularly rich and sophisticated treatment of setting, as Philip Fisher has shown in *Hard Facts: Setting and Form in the American Novel* (Oxford: Oxford University Press, 1985).
38. Mikhail Bakhtin, *The Dialogic Imagination: Four Essays*, trans. Caryl Emerson and Michael

Holquist (Austin: University of Texas Press, 1981), 84, 263. For a particularly influential answer to this question, an answer that adapts Bakhtin for cultural theory, see James Clifford, *The Predicament of Culture: Twentieth-Century Ethnography, Literature, and Art* (Cambridge, MA: Harvard University Press, 1988), ch. 1.

39. Henri Lefebvre, *The Production of Space*, trans. Donald Nicholson-Smith (Malden, MA: Blackwell, 1991), 404.

40. Latour, *Reassembling the Social*, 39.

41. Tony Bennett, "Sociology, Aesthetics, Expertise," *New Literary History* 41.2 (2010): 253.

42. English, "Everywhere and Nowhere," viii.

43. Latour discusses the opposition between Tarde and Durkheim in *Reassembling the Social*, as well as in Bruno Latour, "Gabriel Tarde and the End of the Social," in Joyce, ed., *The Social in Question*, 117–33.

44. Latour, *Reassembling the Social*, 2.

45. Poovey, "Liberal Civil Subject," 125.

46. Raymond Williams, *Keywords: A Vocabulary of Culture and Society* (London: Flamingo, 1986), 291. As Williams also notes, this conception of society was "remarkably extended" in the late nineteenth century by Durkheim and Max Weber, an extension that Latour seeks to reverse. On the emergence of sociology as an academic discipline and society as its object of analysis, see Peter Wagner, "'An Entirely New Object of Consciousness, of Volition, of Thought': The Coming into Being and (Almost) Passing Away of 'Society' as a Scientific Object," in Lorraine Daston, ed., *Biographies of Scientific Objects* (Chicago: University of Chicago Press, 2000), 132–57.

47. Latour, *Reassembling the Social*, x.

48. Ibid., 82.

49. Ibid., 55, 82. Latour's commitment to the arts was also evident in his work as cocurator for two exhibitions at the Zentrum für Kunst und Medientechnologie in Karlsruhe: *Making Things Public: Atmospheres of Democracy* (2005) and *Iconoclash: Beyond the Image Wars in Science, Religion and Art* (2002).

50. On the link between Latour and Goffman, see Love, "Close but not Deep."

51. Latour, *Reassembling the Social*, 21.

52. Ibid.

53. C. Wright Mills, *The Sociological Imagination* (Oxford: Oxford University Press, 2000), 14. "In the past," Mills wrote in 1959, "literary men as critics and historians made notes on England and on journeys to America. They tried to characterize societies as wholes, and to discern their moral meanings. Were Tocqueville and Taine alive today would they not be sociologists?" (17). This question "haunts the practice of literary study in a deep and unacknowledged way," as John Guillory suggests, because it emphasizes the historical and formal propinquity (and thus de-emphasizes the distinctiveness) of literary and sociological writing; see John Guillory, "The Sokal Affair and the History of Criticism," *Critical Inquiry* 28 (2002): 483. Avery Gordon expands the definition of the sociological imagination in *Ghostly Matters: Haunting and the Sociological Imagination* (Minneapolis: University of Minnesota Press, 2008). "Literature," she writes to her colleagues in the social sciences, "often teaches us, through imaginative design, what we need to know but cannot quite get access to without our given rules of method and modes of apprehension" (25).

54. Latour, *Reassembling the Social*, 7. Woolgar, it should be noted, invited Latour to give the Clarendon Lectures in Management Studies at Oxford, which formed the basis for *Reassembling the Social*.

55. On the reception of *Laboratory Life*, see Ian Hacking, *The Social Construction of What?* (Cambridge, MA: Harvard University Press, 1999), ch. 3.

56. Bruno Latour and Steve Woolgar, *Laboratory Life: The Construction of Scientific Facts* (Princeton, NJ: Princeton University Press, 1986), 274, 18, 27. Also see Bruno Latour, *Sci-*

ence in Action: How to Follow Scientists and Engineers through Society (Cambridge, MA: Harvard University Press, 1987).

57. Latour and Woolgar, *Laboratory Life*, 105.

58. Ibid., 27, 64–65.

59. Eudora Welty, *Stories, Essays & Memoir* (New York: Library of America, 1998), 781.

60. Virginia Woolf, "Modern Fiction," in *The Common Reader* (London: L. & V. Woolf at the Hogarth Press, 1929), 190; Don Gifford and Robert J. Seidman, eds., *Ulysses Annotated: Notes for James Joyce's "Ulysses"* (Berkeley: University of California Press, 1988), xv.

61. Woolf, "Modern Fiction," 189.

62. James Joyce, *Ulysses* (New York: Vintage, 1986), 58; hereafter cited parenthetically in the text as *U*.

63. Hugh Kenner, *The Pound Era* (Berkeley: University of California Press, 1971), 46.

64. Ibid., 272.

65. Latour, *Reassembling the Social*, 46.

66. Joseph Frank, "Spatial Form in Modern Literature," *Sewanee Review* 53.2 (1945): 233.

67. Chatman, *Story and Discourse*, 138–39.

68. "It makes no sense," Chatman argues, "to treat crowds of walk-ons or extras as characters" (139). But by analyzing what he calls "character-space," a compound noun whose hyphen alone indicates the porous boundary between character and setting, Alex Woloch offers a different and fuller account of such figures in *The One vs. The Many: Minor Characters and the Space of the Protagonist in the Novel* (Princeton, NJ: Princeton University Press, 2003).

69. Chatman, *Story and Discourse*, 141.

70. Edgar Allan Poe, *Poetry and Tales* (New York: Library of America, 1984), 388; hereafter cited parenthetically in the text as *PT*.

71. Walter Benjamin, "The Paris of the Second Empire in Baudelaire," trans. Harry Zohn, in Michael W. Jennings, ed., *The Writer of Modern Life: Essays on Charles Baudelaire* (Cambridge, MA: Belknap Press of Harvard University Press, 2006), 79.

72. Lukács, "Narrate or Describe?," 137.

73. See Charlton Lewis and Charles Short, *A Latin Dictionary* (Oxford: Clarendon Press, 1879); and *The Oxford Latin Dictionary* (Oxford: Oxford University Press, 2012). I am grateful to Leah Whittington for these references.

74. See "site, n. 2," *OED Online*, June 2014, Oxford University Press.

75. For an overview of the space/place dialectic as it pertains to literature, art, and visual culture, see W.J.T. Mitchell, ed., *Landscape and Power*, 2nd ed. (Chicago: University of Chicago Press, 2002). The global environmental crisis is a key context for the work of Buell, Heise, and Nixon; also see Latour, *Politics of Nature: How to Bring the Sciences into Democracy* (Cambridge, MA: Harvard University Press, 2004).

76. Bruno Latour, *We Have Never Been Modern*, trans. Catherine Porter (Cambridge, MA: Harvard University Press, 1993), 10–11. For Latour's fullest account of these twinned forces, see *An Inquiry into Modes of Existence: An Anthropology of the Moderns*, trans. Catherine Porter (Cambridge, MA: Harvard University Press, 2013).

77. Erving Goffman, *Asylums* (New York: Anchor Books, 1961), xiii.

78. Mark Seltzer, "The Official World," *Critical Inquiry* 37.4 (2011): 727. Seltzer would argue that the "scene of the crime" is the key site of the social in "America's wound culture" and in "the pathological public sphere" more generally. See the essay cited above, as well as Mark Seltzer, *Serial Killers: Death and Life in America's Wound Culture* (New York: Routledge, 1998).

79. Latour, *Reassembling the Social*, 46. John Law, another prominent Actor-Network-Theorist, discusses ANT's debt to Goffman in "Notes on the Theory of the Actor-Network: Ordering, Strategy, and Heterogeneity," *Systems Practice* 5 (1992): 379–93.

80. Burke, *Grammar*, 489.

81. On Goffman's use of Melville, see David J. Alworth, "Melville in the Asylum: Literature, Sociology, Reading," *American Literary History* 26.2 (2014): 234–61.

82. I am thinking specifically of Catherine Jurca, *White Diaspora: The Suburb and the Twentieth-Century American Novel* (Princeton, NJ: Princeton University Press, 2001); Madhu Dubey, *Signs and Cities: Black Literary Postmodernism* (Chicago: University of Chicago Press, 2003); and Rachel Adams, *Continental Divides: Remapping the Cultures of North America* (Chicago: University of Chicago Press, 2009). In addition to the books listed above, also see Mark McGurl, *The Program Era: Postwar Fiction and the Rise of Creative Writing* (Cambridge, MA: Harvard University Press, 2009), which argues for the centrality of a certain social site, the classroom, to the production of postwar American literature. For a site-specific analysis of literary culture in a slightly earlier period (the American 1930s), see Jani Scandura, *Down in the Dumps: Place, Modernity, American Depression* (Durham, NC: Duke University Press, 2008).

83. Fredric Jameson, *Postmodernism, or The Cultural Logic of Late Capitalism* (Durham, NC: Duke University Press, 1991), 361.

84. Michel Foucault, "Of Other Spaces," trans. Jay Miskowiec, *Diacritics* 16.1 (1986): 23; Robert Smithson, *The Collected Writings*, ed. Jack Flam (Berkeley: University of California Press, 1996), 60.

85. Hal Foster, *The Return of the Real: The Avant-Garde at the End of the Century* (Cambridge, MA: MIT Press, 1996), ch. 2.

86. Miwon Kwon, *One Place after Another: Site-Specific Art and Locational Identity* (Cambridge, MA: MIT Press, 2002), 24. Lytle Shaw provides an insightful critique of Kwon's argument and a capacious history of site-specific poetry in *Fieldworks: From Place to Site in Postwar Poetics* (Tuscaloosa: University of Alabama Press, 2013).

87. Smithson, *Collected Writings*, 110, 154.

88. Shannon Jackson provides an incisive account of the "social turn" in recent visual and performing art in *Social Works: Performing Art, Supporting Publics* (New York: Routledge, 2011). The second quotation in this sentence comes from Nicolas Bourriaud, *Relational Aesthetics*, trans. Simon Pleasance et al. (Paris: Les presses du reel, 2002), 113.

89. Many examples of such scholarship could be cited here, but I am thinking specifically of Moretti's *Distant Reading*.

1: SUPERMARKET SOCIOLOGY

1. Victoria de Grazia, *Irresistible Empire: America's Advance through Twentieth-Century Europe* (Cambridge, MA: Belknap Press of Harvard University Press, 2005), 376–416.

2. Rachel Bowlby, *Carried Away: The Invention of Modern Shopping* (New York: Columbia University Press, 2001), 157.

3. Ibid., 160–63.

4. Bruno Latour, *Reassembling the Social: An Introduction to Actor-Network-Theory* (Oxford: Oxford University Press, 2005), 65; hereafter cited parenthetically in the text as *RS*.

5. See, for instance, Bill Brown, ed., *Things* (Chicago: University of Chicago Press, 2004); N. Katherine Hayles, *How We Became Posthuman: Virtual Bodies in Cybernetics, Literature, and Informatics* (Chicago: University of Chicago Press, 1999); Cary Wolfe, *What Is Posthumanism?* (Minneapolis: University of Minnesota Press, 2009); Jane Bennett, *Vibrant Matter: A Political Ecology of Things* (Durham, NC: Duke University Press, 2010); Graham Harman, *Towards a Speculative Realism: Essays and Lectures* (Ropley, UK: Zero Books, 2010); Ian Bogost, *Alien Phenomenology, or What It's Like to Be a Thing* (Minneapolis: University of Minnesota Press, 2012); and Timothy Morton, *Hyperobjects: Philosophy and Ecology after the End of the World* (Minneapolis: University of Minnesota Press, 2013).

6. Many critics have drawn insights from Baudrillard, Debord, Beck, and other theorists in

demonstrating how *White Noise* addresses the problems of postmodern culture. Tom Le-Clair set an important precedent in 1987 when he suggested that DeLillo is a writer who "internalizes fully his cultural context" (Tom LeClair, *In the Loop: Don DeLillo and the Systems Novel* [Urbana: University of Illinois Press, 1987], xii). Joseph Dewey echoes this claim, arguing that DeLillo is "[e]ver the cultural anatomist" (Joseph Dewey, *Beyond Grief and Nothing: A Reading of Don DeLillo* [Columbia: University of South Carolina Press, 2006], 83). While LeClair reads *White Noise* as a "systems novel," other critics have focused on its treatment of image, spectacle, and the commodity form. See, for example, John N. Duvall, "The (Super)Marketplace of Images: Television as Unmediated Mediation in DeLillo's *White Noise*," in Mark Osteen, ed., *White Noise: Text and Criticism* (New York: Penguin, 1998), 432–56; Frank Lentricchia, "Tales of the Electronic Tribe," in *New Essays on White Noise*, ed. Frank Lentricchia (Cambridge: Cambridge University Press, 1991), 87–113; and N. H. Reeve and Richard Kerridge, "Toxic Events: Postmodernism and Don DeLillo's *White Noise*," *Cambridge Quarterly* 23 (1994): 303–23. On DeLillo's relationship to risk society and risk theory, see Ursula Heise, *Sense of Place and Sense of Planet* (Oxford: Oxford University Press, 2008), 162–69; and Susan Mizruchi, "Risk Theory and the Contemporary American Novel," *American Literary History* 22.1 (2010): 109–35. Finally, for a reading of *White Noise* that makes use of Michel Serres's work, see David Cowart, *Don DeLillo: The Physics of Language* (Athens: University of Georgia Press, 2002), ch. 5.

7. For a thorough account of this critical paradigm, see James F. English, "Everywhere and Nowhere: The Sociology of Literature after 'the Sociology of Literature,'" *New Literary History* 41.2 (2010): v–xxiii.

8. Pierre Bourdieu, *The Field of Cultural Production*, ed. Randal Johnson (New York: Columbia University Press, 1993), 161.

9. On the problem of contextualization, see Rita Felski, "Context Stinks!" *New Literary History* 42.4 (2011): 573–91.

10. Wolf Lepenies, *Between Literature and Science: The Rise of Sociology*, trans. R. J. Hollingdale (Cambridge: Cambridge University Press, 1988 [1985]), 1.

11. Susan L. Mizruchi, *The Science of Sacrifice: American Literature and Modern Social Theory* (Princeton, NJ: Princeton University Press, 1998), 10.

12. Durkheim was committed to distinguishing sociology from other disciplines, especially psychology, by stressing the peculiarity of its object of study. For an overview of his position, see Steven Lukes, *Émile Durkheim: His Life and Work* (New York: Penguin, 1973), 1–36.

13. Émile Durkheim, *Sociology and Philosophy*, trans. D. F. Pocock (New York: Free Press, 1974), xxi.

14. A. J. Greimas and J. Courtés, *Semiotics and Language: An Analytical Dictionary* (Bloomington: Indiana University Press, 1982), 5. For a thorough explication of the term "actant" within narrative theory, see David Herman, "Existentialist Roots of Narrative Actants," *Studies in Twentieth-Century Literature* 24.2 (Summer 2000): 257–71. Although Latour does not mention Vladimir Propp, Herman shows that Propp's *Morphology of the Folktale* (1928) "provided the basis for structuralist accounts of actants," like the one represented by Greimas (259).

15. Greimas and Courtés, *Semiotics and Language*, 7.

16. Bennett, *Vibrant Matter*; Alfred Gell, *Art and Agency: An Anthropological Theory* (Oxford: Oxford University Press, 1998); Mark B. N. Hansen, "Engineering Pre-individual Potentiality: Technics, Transindividuation, and 21st-Century Media," *SubStance* 129.41.3 (2012): 32–59. The notion of "distributed agency" is closely related to the notion of "distributed cognition" as it has been defined by thinkers such as Edwin Hutchins (*Cognition in the Wild* [Cambridge, MA: MIT Press, 1995]) and Andy Clark (*Natural-Born Cyborgs: Minds, Technologies, and the Future of Human Intelligence* [Oxford: Oxford University Press, 2003]).

17. Don DeLillo, *White Noise* (New York: Penguin, 1985), 167; hereafter cited parenthetically in the text as *WN*.

18. Avery Gordon, *Ghostly Matters: Haunting and the Sociological Imagination* (Minneapolis: University of Minnesota Press, 2008), 14.

19. Thomas DePietro, ed., *Conversations with Don DeLillo* (Jackson: University Press of Mississippi, 2005), 70.

20. Ira Levin, *The Stepford Wives* (HarperCollins Perennial, 2002), 120; Philip K. Dick, *Time Out of Joint* (New York: Vintage, 2002), 184.

21. Paul Auster, *The New York Trilogy* (New York: Penguin, 1987), 258.

22. Joan Didion, *Play It as It Lays* (New York: Farrar, Straus and Giroux, 1970), 122.

23. Spalding Gray, *Swimming to Cambodia* (New York: Theatre Communications Group, 1985), 123.

24. Honoré de Balzac, *The Wild Ass's Skin*, trans. Herbert J. Hunt (New York: Penguin, 1977), 34; Émile Zola, *The Ladies' Paradise*, trans. Brian Nelson (Oxford: Oxford University Press, 2008), 4.

25. Theodore Dreiser, *Sister Carrie*, ed. Donald Pizer (New York: W. W. Norton, 2006), 16; James Joyce, *Dubliners*, ed. Margot Norris (New York: W. W. Norton, 2006), 23.

26. Charles Dickens, *A Christmas Carol and Other Writings* (New York: Penguin Classics, 2003), 76.

27. Alain Robbe-Grillet, *For a New Novel*, trans. Richard Howard (Evanston, IL: Northwestern University Press, 1989), 19.

28. Allen Ginsberg, *Howl and Other Poems* (San Francisco: City Lights, 1956), 29–30.

29. Bennett, *Vibrant Matter*, xi. DeLillo's effort to find "radiance in dailiness" can also be understood as a religious or mystical project, part of what Amy Hungerford defines as a broader attempt within his novels to "translate religious structures into literary ones without an intervening secularism" (Amy Hungerford, *Postmodern Belief: American Literature and Religion since 1960* [Princeton, NJ: Princeton University Press, 2010], 53).

30. Juan A. Suárez, *Pop Modernism: Noise and the Reinvention of the Everyday* (Urbana: University of Illinois Press, 2007), 147.

31. André Breton, *Nadja*, trans. Richard Howard (New York: Grove Press, 1960), 52.

32. See, for example, the flea market scene in *Mad Love*, trans. Mary Ann Caws (Lincoln: University of Nebraska Press, 1987), 25–34. Also see *Manifestoes of Surrealism*, trans. Richard Seaver and Helen R. Lane (Ann Arbor: University of Michigan Press, 1969).

33. Bruno Latour, *We Have Never Been Modern*, trans. Catherine Porter (Cambridge, MA: Harvard University Press, 1993), 10–11.

34. Donna J. Haraway, *Simians, Cyborgs, and Women: The Reinvention of Nature* (New York: Routledge, 1991), 154.

35. There is some controversy over which company opened the *first* supermarket. I follow the Smithsonian Institution in giving credit to King Kullen; see David Merrefield, "Supermarkets Reach a Milestone: The 75th Anniversary," *Supermarket News*, August 29, 2005. On the origin of the supermarket, see Bowlby, *Carried Away*, ch. 7; and Tracey Deutsch, *Building a Housewife's Paradise: Gender, Politics, and American Grocery Stores in the Twentieth Century* (Chapel Hill: University of North Carolina Press, 2010).

36. "Bread & Circuses," *Time*, June 8, 1959, 92.

37. "As marketing advanced in the postwar era," writes Lizabeth Cohen, "scholars rather than marketing executives defined and refined the field ... The budding scholarly field of sociology in particular became the provider of a major body of research and a steady supplier of researchers" (Cohen, *Consumers' Republic*, 299).

38. Vance Packard, *The Hidden Persuaders* (New York: David McKay, 1957), 3.

39. Ibid., 108, 106.

40. William D. Zabel, "The Easy Chair: What's in the Package?," *Harper's*, August 1963, 12. Za-

bel's treatment of gender is obviously problematic, not least because it elides what Deutsch terms "the long history of women's reputation as difficult and demanding shoppers" (2). See Deutsch's study for an incisive account of the gendered dynamics of food retailing in the supermarket and elsewhere.

41. Randall Jarrell, *A Sad Heart at the Supermarket* (London: Eyre and Spottiswoode, 1965), 15, 58–77.
42. Leslie Fiedler, *Waiting for the End* (New York: Stein and Day, 1964), 249.
43. See Dwight Macdonald, "Masscult and Midcult," *Partisan Review* 17.2–3 (1960): 203–33, 589–631.
44. Ibid., 609.
45. Ibid., 618.
46. Grazia, *Irresistible Empire*, 376–416.
47. "La Méthod Américaine," *Time*, November 16, 1959, 105.
48. "The Supermarket Gains Ground," *Japan Quarterly* 10.3 (1963): 290.
49. "The Yankee Marketeers," *Time*, April 23, 1965, 97.
50. Ibid.
51. "More Class," *Time*, December 31, 1965, 36.
52. Terry Eagleton, *Against the Grain: Essays, 1975–1985* (London: Verso, 1986), 70.
53. Robert Venturi et al., *Learning from Las Vegas* (Cambridge, MA: MIT Press, 1972), xi, 90.
54. Ibid., 9.
55. Ibid., 13.
56. M. M. Zimmerman, *The Super Market: A Revolution in Distribution* (New York: McGraw Hill, 1955).
57. Among retail professionals, as Bowlby notes, the commodity package is known as the "silent salesman," an anthropomorphism that marks the transfer of agency from human to nonhuman (30–48).
58. W. F. Haug, *Critique of Commodity Aesthetics: Appearance, Sexuality, and Advertising in Capitalist Society*, trans. Robert Bock (Minneapolis: University of Minnesota Press, 1986), 8, 10.
59. John Updike, *Pigeon Feathers and Other Stories* (New York: Alfred A. Knopf, 1962), 187.
60. Ibid.
61. Ibid., 190.
62. Peter Boxall also suggests a link between DeLillo and Warhol, but he argues that this scene deals primarily with the problem of death in avant-garde art; see Peter Boxall, *Don DeLillo: The Possibility of Fiction* (New York: Routledge, 2006), ch. 4.
63. DePietro, ed., *Conversations*, 118.
64. Andy Warhol and Pat Hackett, *The Andy Warhol Diaries* (New York: Hachette, 2009), 626.
65. Andy Warhol, *The Philosophy of Andy Warhol: From A to B and Back Again* (New York: Harcourt, 1975), 79.
66. Alan Gillmor, "Interview with John Cage," *Contact* 14 (Autumn 1976): 21.
67. Suárez, *Pop Modernism*, 297.
68. Arthur Danto, "The Artworld," *Journal of Philosophy* 61.19 (1964): 580.
69. Martha Buskirk, *The Contingent Object of Contemporary Art* (Cambridge, MA: MIT Press, 2003), 78.
70. Thomas Crow, *Modern Art in the Common Culture* (New Haven, CT: Yale University Press, 1996), 60.
71. Rachel Carson, *Silent Spring* (New York: Mariner / Houghton Mifflin, 2002), 127, 174.
72. Bennett, *Vibrant Matter*, xviii; italics in the original.
73. Ibid., 25.
74. Bruno Latour, *Pandora's Hope: Essays on the Reality of Science Studies* (Cambridge, MA: Harvard University Press, 1999), 189.
75. Ibid., 204; Latour, *Reassembling the Social*, 75–76.

76. Felski, "Context Stinks!," 575.

77. John A. Kouwenhoven, "Waste Not, Have Not: A Clue to American Prosperity," *Harper's* (March 1959): 72.

2: DUMPS (WILLIAM S. BURROUGHS, MIERLE LADERMAN UKELES)

1. Quoted in Mira Engler, *Designing America's Waste Landscapes* (Baltimore, MD: Johns Hopkins University Press, 2004), 99.

2. Quoted in Aleksandra Wagner and Carin Kuoni, eds., *Considering Forgiveness* (New York: Vera List Center for Art and Politics, New School, 2009), 178. The Fresh Kills Landfill was closed in March 2001 only to be reopened six months later as the main sorting and dumping site for the remains of the 9/11 attacks. For an incisive discussion of the reopening, see Marita Sturken, *Tourists of History: Memory, Kitsch, and Consumerism from Oklahoma City to Ground Zero* (Durham, NC: Duke University Press, 2007), ch. 4.

3. Don DeLillo, *Underworld* (New York: Scribner, 1997), 287; hereafter cited parenthetically in the text as *UW*.

4. William Rathje and Cullen Murphy, *Rubbish! The Archaeology of Garbage* (New York: HarperCollins, 1992), 11.

5. Ibid., 112; W. L. Rathje et al., "The Archaeology of Contemporary Landfills," *American Antiquity* 57.3 (1992): 442, 444. On sanitary landfills and other waste-disposal technologies pioneered after World War II, see Martin V. Melosi, *Garbage in the Cities: Refuse Reform and the Environment* (Pittsburgh, PA: University of Pittsburgh Press, 2004), 168–227.

6. Lawrence Buell, *The Dream of the Great American Novel* (Cambridge, MA: Harvard University Press, 2014), 3.

7. William S. Burroughs, *Naked Lunch: The Restored Text*, ed. James Grauerholz and Barry Miles (New York: Grove Press, 2001 [1959]), 125, 203; hereafter cited parenthetically in the text as *NL*.

8. Bruno Latour, *We Have Never Been Modern*, trans. Catherine Porter (Cambridge, MA: Harvard University Press, 1993), 10–11.

9. *Big Table, Inc. v. Carl A. Schroeder, United States Postmaster for Chicago*, 186 F. Supp. 254 (1960), http://web.lexis-nexis.com/universe/.

10. Rathje and Murphy, *Rubbish!*, 88, 122.

11. Ibid., 59, 10.

12. Two important biographies of Burroughs give extended accounts of his life in Tangier during the 1950s: Barry Miles, *William Burroughs: El Hombre Invisible* (London: Virgin Books, 2002); and Ted Morgan, *Literary Outlaw: The Life and Times of William S. Burroughs* (New York: Henry Holt, 1988).

13. On the "consumers' republic," see Lizabeth Cohen, *A Consumers' Republic: The Politics of Mass Consumption in Postwar America* (New York: Vintage, 2003); on the "throwaway society," see Susan Strasser, *Waste and Want: A Social History of Trash* (New York: Metropolitan Books, 1999), 5–21. For more focused histories of sanitation and waste management during the period, see Suellen Hoy, *Chasing Dirt: The American Pursuit of Cleanliness* (Oxford: Oxford University Press, 1955), ch. 6; and Melosi, *Garbage in the Cities*, 168–227.

14. William Burroughs, *Letters to Allen Ginsberg, 1953–1957* (New York: Full Court Press, 1982), 162; hereafter cited parenthetically in the text as *LG*.

15. Iain Finlayson, *Tangier: City of the Dream* (New York: HarperCollins, 1992), 73.

16. Ibid., 4, 215.

17. Ansen is quoted in Jennie Skerl and Robin Lydenberg, *William S. Burroughs at the Front: Critical Reception, 1959–1989* (Carbondale: Southern Illinois University Press, 1991), 27; Bowles is quoted in Miles, *El Hombre Invisible*, 82.

18. Rathje et al., "Archaeology of Contemporary Landfills," 444.

19. Diana Fuss, *The Sense of an Interior: Four Writers and the Rooms that Shaped Them* (London: Routledge, 2004), 215.

20. On that episode, see, for example, Oliver Harris, *William Burroughs and the Secret Fascination* (Carbondale: Southern Illinois University Press, 2003), ch. 6.

21. Fuss, *Sense of an Interior*, 1.

22. Burroughs writes in *Naked Lunch*, "And now I will unlock my Word Hoard" (97). He speaks at length about "verbal garbage" in Sylvère Lotringer, ed., *Burroughs Live: The Collected Interviews of William S. Burroughs, 1960–1997* (Los Angeles: Semiotext(e), 2001), 36.

23. *Attorney General v. A Book Named "Naked Lunch,"* 351 Mass. 298. (1966), http://web.lexis-nexis.com/universe/.

24. When Charles Rembar, the well-known First Amendment rights lawyer, defended John Cleland's *Fanny Hill* before the United States Supreme Court in 1966, he argued, "Obscenity is worthless trash. That is its definition constitutionally" (Charles Rembar, *The End of Obscenity: The Trials of "Lady Chatterley's Lover," "Tropic of Cancer," and "Fanny Hill"* [New York: Harper & Row, 1986], 467). For the full case history of *Naked Lunch*, see Michael Barry Goodman, *Contemporary Literary Censorship: The Case History of Burroughs' Naked Lunch* (Metuchen, NJ: Scarecrow Press, 1981). And for a wider study of literary obscenity, see Elisabeth Ladenson, *Dirt for Art's Sake: Books on Trial from "Madame Bovary" to "Lolita"* (Ithaca, NY: Cornell University Press, 2007).

25. *Big Table, Inc. v. Carl A. Schroeder, United States Postmaster for Chicago*, 186 F. Supp. 254 (1960), http://web.lexis-nexis.com/universe/.

26. Quoted in Kevin J. Hayes, ed., *Conversations with Jack Kerouac* (Jackson: University Press of Mississippi, 2005), 60.

27. Quoted in Skerl and Lydenberg, *William S. Burroughs at the Front*, 41.

28. Ibid.

29. Donald Malcolm, "The Heroin of Our Times," *New Yorker* (February 2, 1963): 117, 114.

30. Quoted in Miles, *El Hombre Invisible*, 87. I should note here that Miles claims that this quote exemplifies "typical Girodias exaggeration," arguing that the manuscript was "a bit tatty," but still readable (87–88).

31. Carol Loranger, "'This Book Spill Off the Page in All Directions': What Is the Text of *Naked Lunch*?," *Postmodern Culture* 10.1 (September 1999), http://pmc.iath.virginia.edu/text-only/issue.999/10.1loranger.txt.

32. Hudson is quoted in Goodman, *Contemporary Literary Censorship*, 235.

33. Frederick Whiting, "Monstrosity on Trial: The Case of *Naked Lunch*," *Twentieth-Century Literature* 52.2 (2006): 158.

34. John Scanlan, *On Garbage* (London: Reaktion, 2005), 14.

35. Elaine Tyler May, *Homeward Bound: American Families in the Cold War Era* (New York: Basic Books, 1989), 153.

36. Michael Shanks, David Platt, and William L. Rathje, "The Perfume of Garbage: Modernity and the Archaeological," *Modernism/modernity* 11.1 (2004): 69.

37. Ibid., 71.

38. John Dos Passos, *The Garbage Man: A Parade with Shouting* (New York: Harper and Brothers, 1926), 123–24. Burroughs knew and admired Dos Passos's work. He remarked that the "Camera Eye" sequences in the *U.S.A. Trilogy* were "a major revelation" because they seemed to set a precedent for the "cut-up" method that he developed with the visual artist Brion Gysin (Lotringer, ed., *Burroughs Live*, 66).

39. For an insightful discussion of Chris Ofili, see W.J.T. Mitchell, *What Do Pictures Want? The Lives and Loves of Images* (Chicago: University of Chicago Press, 2005), ch. 6.

40. Brian T. Edwards, *Morocco Bound: Disorienting America's Maghreb from Casablanca to the Marrakech Express* (Durham, NC: Duke University Press, 2005), 165.

41. Mary Douglas, *Purity and Danger* (London: Routledge, 2003 [1966]), 41; Gay Hawkins, *The Ethics of Waste: How We Relate to Rubbish* (Lanham, MD: Rowman & Littlefield, 2006), vii, 2.

42. The technical definitions of "garbage" and "trash," as well as all the other technical definitions in this paragraph and the next, come from Rathje, *Rubbish!*, 9.

43. For an understanding of "junk" as both the discarded and the reclaimed, see Miles Orvell, *The Real Thing: Imitation and Authenticity in American Culture, 1880–1940* (Chapel Hill: University of North Carolina Press, 1989), 287–301.

44. Oliver Harris and Ian MacFadyen, *Naked Lunch @ 50: Anniversary Essays* (Carbondale: Southern Illinois University Press, 2009), xi.

45. Upton Sinclair, *The Jungle* (New York: Oxford University Press, 2010), 125.

46. James Joyce, *Ulysses*, ed. Hans Walter Gabler (New York: Random House, 1986), 50, 590.

47. Samuel Beckett, *Stories and Texts for Nothing* (New York: Grove Press, 1967), 118.

48. Joyce, *Ulysses*, 37.

49. Victor Bockris, *With William Burroughs: A Report from the Bunker* (New York: St. Martin's Press, 1996), 209.

50. T. S. Eliot, *The Waste Land: Authoritative Texts, Contexts, Criticism*, ed. Michael North (New York: Norton, 2001), 11, 15, 5, 14; Maud Ellmann, *The Poetics of Impersonality: Eliot and Pound* (Brighton: Harvester, 1987), 93. On abjection in general, see Julia Kristeva, *Powers of Horror: An Essay on Abjection* (New York: Columbia University Press, 1981).

51. Quoted in Eliot, *Waste Land*, 141.

52. Wallace Stevens, *The Collected Poems* (New York: Vintage, 1990), 201.

53. A. R. Ammons, *Garbage* (New York: Norton, 1993), 8, 89.

54. Georges Bataille, *Visions of Excess: Selected Writings, 1927–1939*, trans. Alan Stoekl with Carl R. Lovitt and Donald M. Leslie Jr. (Minneapolis: University of Minnesota Press, 1985), 142.

55. Ibid., 91–105, 16.

56. Yve-Alain Bois and Rosalind E. Krauss, *Formless: A User's Guide* (New York: Zone Books, 1997), 18.

57. Mary McCarthy, *The Writing on the Wall and Other Literary Essays* (Orlando, FL: Harcourt Brace Jovanovich, 1970), 48; Klaus Theweleit, *Male Fantasies*, vol. 1, *Women, Floods, Bodies, History* (Minneapolis: University of Minnesota Press, 1987).

58. Thomas Heinrich and Bob Batchelor, *Kotex, Kleenex, Huggies: Kimberly-Clark and the Consumer Revolution in American Business* (Columbus: Ohio State University Press, 2004), 2.

59. Ibid., 111.

60. Melosi, *Garbage in the Cities*, 217.

61. On the "garbage crisis," see Melosi, *Garbage in the Cities*, ch. 8; on the "litter problem," see Hoy, *Chasing Dirt*, ch. 6.

62. President Lyndon B. Johnson, "Special Message to the Congress on Conservation and Restoration of Natural Beauty," February 8, 1965, Lyndon Baines Johnson Library and Museum, www.lbjlib.utexas.edu/johnson/archives.hom/speeches.hom/650208.asp.

63. Carson's *Silent Spring* alerted readers to the dangers of pesticides and other industrial pollutants, while Packard's *The Waste Makers* targeted the consumer packaged goods industry, among others, as well as the strategy of "planned obsolescence."

64. Marianne DeKoven, *Utopia Limited: The Sixties and the Emergence of the Postmodern* (Durham, NC: Duke University Press, 2004), 176. Also see N. Katherine Hayles, *How We Became Posthuman: Virtual Bodies in Cybernetics, Literature, and Informatics* (Chicago: University of Chicago Press, 1999), 42–43.

65. Leslie Fiedler, *A New Leslie Fiedler Reader* (Amherst, NY: Prometheus Books, 1999), 202.

66. Ibid., 192.

67. Quoted in Skerl and Lydenberg, *William S. Burroughs at the Front*, 69.

68. Ibid., 70.

69. Ibid.
70. For more on the ontological turn in Merleau-Ponty's late work, see Taylor Carman, *Merleau-Ponty* (London: Routledge, 2008), 120–32.
71. Maurice Merleau-Ponty, *The Visible and the Invisible* (Evanston, IL: Northwestern University Press, 1968), 147.
72. Merleau-Ponty, *The Visible*, 139, 147.
73. Carman, *Merleau-Ponty*, 124.
74. Judith Butler, "Merleau-Ponty and the Touch of Malebranche," *The Cambridge Companion to Maurice Merleau-Ponty*, ed. Taylor Carman and Mark B. N. Hansen (Cambridge: Cambridge University Press, 2005), 181.
75. Gilles Deleuze and Félix Guattari, *What Is Philosophy?*, trans. Hugh Tomlinson and Graham Burchell (New York: Columbia University Press, 1994), 178.
76. Merleau-Ponty, *The Visible*, 147.
77. Robert Creeley, *The Collected Essays of Robert Creeley* (Berkeley: University of California Press, 1989), 539.
78. Merleau-Ponty, *The Visible*, 134, 139.
79. Ibid., 248.
80. Kristin Ross, *Fast Cars, Clean Bodies: Decolonization and the Reordering of French Culture* (Cambridge, MA: MIT Press, 1995), 4, 5, 182. For a broader history of the modernization and Americanization of Europe in the wake of the Marshall Plan, see Victoria de Grazia, *Irresistible Empire: America's Advance through 20th-Century Europe* (Cambridge, MA: Harvard University Press, 2005).
81. Hoy, *Chasing Dirt*, 170.
82. Edwards, *Morocco Bound*, 161.
83. The entire manifesto is available from Ronald Feldman Fine Arts: http://www.feldmangallery.com/pages/home_frame.html.
84. James Barron, "Art Work Is (Yes, Really) Garbage," *New York Times*, June 10, 1993, B5.
85. Helen Molesworth, "House Work and Art Work," *October* 92 (2000): 82.
86. Shannon Jackson, *Social Works: Performing Art, Supporting Publics* (London: Routledge, 2011), 81.
87. James Barron, "Art Work," B5.
88. Quoted in Aleksandra Wagner and Carin Kuoni, *Considering Forgiveness*, 177–78.
89. Hawkins, *Ethics of Waste*, 93–94.
90. Margaret Mead, "Cultural Bases for Understanding Literature," *PMLA* 68.2 (1953): 13; Hawkins, *Ethics of Waste*, 93–94.
91. Graham Harman, *Prince of Networks: Bruno Latour and Metaphysics* (Melbourne, Australia: re.press, 2009), 34.
92. Alexander R. Galloway, "The Poverty of Philosophy: Realism and Post-Fordism," *Critical Inquiry* 39.2 (2013): 364. Galloway is challenging Latour as well as several other philosophers, including Graham Harman, Quentin Meillassoux, and Alain Badiou, in a broad critique of what he calls "recent realist philosophy" (348).
93. Bruno Latour, *Pandora's Hope: Essays on the Reality of Science Studies* (Cambridge, MA: Harvard University Press, 1999), 182.

3: ROADS (JACK KEROUAC, JOAN DIDION, JOHN CHAMBERLAIN)

1. Robert Creeley, *For Love: Poems, 1950–1960* (New York: Charles Scribner's Sons, 1962), 38.
2. Michael Davidson, *Guys Like Us: Citing Masculinity in Cold War Poetics* (Chicago: University of Chicago Press, 2004), 132.

3. Cotten Seiler, *Republic of Drivers: A Cultural History of Automobility in America* (Chicago: University of Chicago Press, 2008), 5–6. Also see the special issue of *Theory, Culture & Society* (2004) that is devoted to the topic of automobility.

4. Louis Menand, "Drive, He Wrote: What the Beats Were About," *New Yorker*, October 1, 2007, 91.

5. Seiler, *Republic of Drivers*, 9.

6. Mikhail Bakhtin, *The Dialogic Imagination*, trans. Caryl Emerson and Michael Holquist (Austin: University of Texas Press, 1981), 98. Bakhtin argues that "the chronotope of *the road*" enables "random encounters" that are typically precluded "by social and spatial distance" and thereby reveals "the *sociohistorical heterogeneity* of one's own country" (243–45). Although my emphasis falls on the social interactions between humans and nonhumans, this chapter nonetheless seeks to extend Bakhtin's key insight that the figure of the road performs an important sociological function within literary discourse.

7. Tim Dant, "The Driver-Car," *Theory, Culture & Society* (2004): 61–79.

8. Bruno Latour, *Aramis, or The Love of Technology*, trans. Catherine Porter (Cambridge, MA: Harvard University Press, 1996), viii.

9. The road narrative, like the road movie, flourished in postwar United States. On this genre, see Kris Lackey, *Road Frames: The American Highway Narrative* (Lincoln: University of Nebraska Press, 1999); and Ronald Primeau, *Romance of the Road: The Literature of the American Highway* (Bowling Green, OH: Bowling Green State University Popular Press, 1996). Primeau points to the tremendous influence of Kerouac: "Whatever else might be conjectured about his place in contemporary fiction, *On the Road* became the prototypical road narrative from which others have drawn and with which they have had to contend" (37).

10. For example, see Davidson, *Guys Like Us*, 16–17. For a firsthand account of being a woman in the Beat milieu, see Johnson's *Minor Characters: A Beat Memoir* (New York: Penguin, 1999).

11. "Hollow Rolling Sculpture," *Time*, September 10, 1951, 74.

12. Michael Fried, *Art and Objecthood* (Chicago: University of Chicago Press, 1998), 148–73; Robert Smithson, *Robert Smithson: The Collected Writings*, ed. Jack Flam (Berkeley: University of California Press, 1996), 68–74.

13. There are several engaging studies of the road movie. Among the best is Devin Orgeron, *Road Movies: From Muybridge and Méliès to Lynch and Kiarostami* (New York: Palgrave Macmillan, 2008). Also see Steven Cohan and Ina Rae Hark, eds., *The Road Movie Book* (New York: Routledge, 1997); David Laderman, *Driving Visions: Exploring the Road Movie* (Austin: University of Texas Press, 2002); Katie Mills, *The Road Story and the Rebel: Moving through Film, Fiction, and Television* (Carbondale: Southern Illinois University Press, 2006); and Edward Dimendberg, *Film Noir and the Spaces of Modernity* (Cambridge, MA: Harvard University Press, 2004), ch. 4.

14. Donald A. Norman, *The Design of Future Things* (New York: Basic Books, 2007), 157; John Markoff, "Google Cars Drive Themselves, in Traffic," *New York Times*, October 9, 2010. On nonhuman emotion, see Donald A. Norman's other book, *Emotional Design: Why We Love (or Hate) Everyday Things* (New York: Basic Books, 2004), ch. 6.

15. Jack Katz, *How Emotions Work* (Chicago: University of Chicago Press, 1999), ch. 1.

16. On traffic, see Tom Vanderbilt, *Traffic: Why We Drive the Way We Do (and What It Says About Us)* (New York: Knopf, 2008).

17. Jack Kerouac, *Selected Letters, Volume 1: 1940–1956* (New York: Viking Press, 1995), 38.

18. Ibid.

19. See Jack Kerouac, *On the Road: The Original Scroll*, ed. Howard Cunnell (New York: Viking Press, 2007), 7–8.

20. Kerouac, *Selected Letters*, 38.

21. Ibid., 396.

22. Davidson, *Guys Like Us*, 16. Davidson is drawing from Eve Kosofsky Sedgwick, *Between Men: English Literature and Male Homosocial Desire* (New York: Columbia University Press, 1985) and from Adrienne Rich, "Compulsory Heterosexuality and Lesbian Existence," in *Adrienne Rich's Poetry and Prose*, ed. Barbara Charlesworth Gelpi and Albert Gelpi (New York: Norton, 1993). Sedgwick developed her theory of homosociality by queering the triangular structure of desire in René Girard, *Deceit, Desire, and the Novel: Self and Other in Literary Structure*, trans. Yvonne Freccero (Baltimore, MD: Johns Hopkins University Press, 1965).

23. Rachel Adams, *Continental Divides: Remapping the Cultures of North America* (Chicago: University of Chicago Press, 2009), 160. Adams addresses the complex problem of race on the American road; this problem, especially as it pertains to African American car culture, has been examined closely by Paul Gilroy, *Darker than Blue: On the Moral Economies of Black Atlantic Culture* (Cambridge, MA: Harvard University Press, 2010), ch. 1. Also see Seiler's excellent discussion of black travel guides, such as *The Negro Motorist Green Book*, in ch. 4 of *Republic of Drivers*. For an analysis of how race on the road achieved literary form, see Lackey, *Road Frames*, ch. 4.

24. Douglas Brinkley, ed., *Windblown World: The Journals of Jack Kerouac, 1947–1954* (New York: Viking Press, 2004).

25. Kerouac's real-life trips with Cassady have been usefully documented in Paul Maher Jr., *Jack Kerouac's American Journey: The Real-Life Odyssey of "On the Road"* (Cambridge, MA: Thunder's Mouth Press, 2007).

26. Kerouac, *Original Scroll*, 23.

27. On the composition history of the novel, see Howard Cunnell's meticulous introduction to *On the Road: The Original Scroll*, 1–53.

28. Ann Charters, ed., *The Portable Jack Kerouac* (New York: Viking Press, 1995), 606.

29. Ibid.

30. Ibid., 612.

31. Ibid., 606.

32. Morris Dickstein, *Leopards in the Temple: The Transformation of American Fiction, 1945–1970* (Cambridge, MA: Harvard University Press, 2002), 100.

33. Jack Kerouac, *On the Road* (New York: Penguin Books, 1976), 1; hereafter cited parenthetically in the text as *OR*.

34. Kerouac, *Original Scroll*, 109.

35. Dean is, in other words, "the daemon who presides over the road" (Dickstein, *Leopards*, 96).

36. Cunnell, *Original Scroll*, 32.

37. John Leland, *Why Kerouac Matters: The Lessons of "On the Road" (They're Not What You Think)* (New York: Viking Press, 2007), 33.

38. Menand, "Drive, He Wrote," 92.

39. On the history of the New Journalism, see Marc Weingarten, *The Gang that Wouldn't Write Straight: Wolfe, Thompson, Didion, Capote, and the New Journalism Revolution* (New York: Three Rivers Press, 2005). For an insightful analysis of Wolfe's writing style in particular, see Marianne DeKoven, *Utopia Limited: The Sixties and the Emergence of the Postmodern* (Durham, NC: Duke University Press, 2004), ch. 3.

40. Originally published in *Esquire*, the version of the article that I cite appears in Tom Wolfe, *The Kandy-Kolored Tangerine-Flake Streamline Baby* (New York: Bantam Books, 1999).

41. David N. Lucsko, *The Business of Speed: The Hot Rod Industry in America, 1915–1990* (Baltimore, MD: Johns Hopkins University Press, 2008), 10.

42. Bert Pierce, "Teen-Agers' Ego Held Road Peril," *New York Times*, June 19, 1949, 39.

43. Gene M. Balsley, "The Hot-Rod Culture," *American Quarterly* 2.4 (1950): 353–58.

44. Ibid., 353, 355, 357.

45. Wolfe, *Kandy-Kolored*, 87. Barris refers to himself as "King of the Kustomizers" on his personal website: www.barris.com.

46. Ibid., 82.

47. Ibid., 93, 77.

48. Pierre Bourdieu, *The Field of Cultural Production* (New York: Columbia University Press, 1993), 39.

49. Wolfe, *Kandy-Kolored*, 81–82.

50. Tom Wolfe, *The Electric Kool-Aid Acid Test* (New York: Picador, 2008 [1968]), 103. For an account of the Pranksters' trip that is not mediated by Wolfe, see Paul Perry, *On the Bus: The Complete Guide to the Legendary Trip of Ken Kesey and the Merry Pranksters and the Birth of the Counterculture* (New York: Thunder's Mouth Press, 1990).

51. See, for example, Rachel Adams, "Hipsters and *jipitecas*: Literary Countercultures on Both Sides of the Border," *American Literary History* 16.1 (Spring 2004): 58–84. Echoing Adams, Mark McGurl writes, "Most important to Kesey, no doubt, was the precedent of the car in Jack Kerouac's transcontinental Beat narrative, *On the Road* (1957)" (McGurl, *The Program Era: Postwar Fiction and the Rise of Creative Writing* [Cambridge, MA: Harvard University Press, 2009], 200).

52. Wolfe, *Kool-Aid Acid Test*, 68.

53. Émile Durkheim, *The Elementary Forms of Religious Life*, trans. Karen E. Fields (New York: Free Press, 1995), 231.

54. Wolfe, *Kool-Aid Acid Test*, 101; italics in the original.

55. On *Play It as It Lays* as a Hollywood novel and as a "Lacanian tragedy," see Chip Rhodes, *Politics, Desire, and the Hollywood Novel* (Iowa City: University of Iowa Press, 2008), ch. 4. Mark Winchell also examines "the nightmare vision of her Hollywood novel," but provides a more thorough analysis of its irony: "At one level, Maria's story is one of genuine suffering and despair. Yet, at another level, Didion seems to be writing a parody of the novel of despair" (Mark Winchell, *Joan Didion* [Boston: Twayne, 1980], 99, 100). Also useful are two edited collections: Sharon Felton, ed., *The Critical Response to Joan Didion* (Westport, CT: Greenwood Press, 1994); and Ellen G. Friedman, ed., *Joan Didion: Essays and Conversations* (Ontario, Canada: Ontario Review Press, 1984).

56. Cunnell makes this point in his introduction to Kerouac, *Original Scroll*, 26.

57. Joan Didion, *Play It as It Lays* (New York: Farrar, Straus and Giroux, 2005 [1970]), 15; hereafter cited parenthetically in the text as *P*.

58. On the history of the interstates, see Mark H. Rose, *Interstate: Express Highway Politics, 1939–1989* (Nashville: University of Tennessee Press, 1990); and Tom Lewis, *Divided Highways: Building the Interstate Highways, Transforming American Life* (New York: Penguin Books, 1999).

59. Brian Ladd calls this moment "the golden age of car bashing in the U.S. and Europe" (Ladd, *Autophobia: Love and Hate in the Automotive Age* [Chicago: University of Chicago Press, 2008], 4).

60. Ralph Nader, *Unsafe at Any Speed: The Designed-In Dangers of the American Automobile* (New York: Grossman, 1965), vii.

61. For the seamy details, see James Ridgeway, "The Dick," *New Republic* 154.11 (March 12, 1966): 11–13; and James Ridgeway and David Sanford, "The Nader Affair," *New Republic* 156.7 (February 18, 1967).

62. A. Q. Mowbray, *Road to Ruin* (Philadelphia, PA: J. B. Lippincott, 1969), 9–10; Jane Jacobs, *The Death and Life of Great American Cities* (New York: Modern Library, 1993 [1961]), 440.

63. Jacobs, *Death and Life*, 440.

64. Kenneth R. Schneider, *Autokind vs. Mankind: An Analysis of Tyranny; A Proposal for Rebellion; A Plan for Reconstruction* (New York: W. W. Norton, 1971), 23.

65. John R. Jerome, *The Death of the Automobile: The Fatal Effect of the Golden Era, 1955–1970*

(New York: W. W. Norton, 1972), 10; Helen Leavitt, *Superhighway—Superhoax* (New York: Doubleday, 1970), 20.

66. Among the best of these recent polemics is Catherine Lutz and Anne Lutz Fernandez, *Carjacked: The Culture of the Automobile and Its Effect on Our Lives* (New York: Palgrave Macmillan, 2010). On anti-freeway activism, see Raymond A. Mohl, "Stop the Road: Freeway Revolts in American Cities," *Journal of Urban History* 30.5 (2004): 674–706.

67. Joan Didion, *We Tell Ourselves Stories in Order to Live: Collected Nonfiction* (New York: Everyman's Library / Alfred A. Knopf, 2006), 307; hereafter cited parenthetically in the text as *W*.

68. Allen Ginsberg famously used the term "angelheaded hipsters" in his own Whitmanian text, "Howl" (Allen Ginsberg, *Howl and Other Poems* [San Francisco: City Lights Books, 1956], 9). Kerouac often uses the term "benny"; see, for example, Kerouac, *Original Scroll*, 24.

69. Many scholars have examined the gender of travel as it pertains to literature. Two books are especially relevant here: Deborah Clarke, *Driving Women: Fiction and Automobile Culture in Twentieth-Century America* (Baltimore, MD: Johns Hopkins University Press, 2007); and Sidonie Smith, *Moving Lives: Twentieth-Century Women's Travel Writing* (Minneapolis: University of Minnesota Press, 2001).

70. Jean Baudrillard, *Simulacres et simulation* (Paris: Éditions Galilée, 1981); Fredric Jameson, *Postmodernism, or The Cultural Logic of Late Capitalism* (Durham, NC: Duke University Press, 1991), 44.

71. Joseph Epstein, *Plausible Prejudices: Essays on American Writing* (New York: W. W. Norton, 1985), 247.

72. I agree with Katherine Henderson, who argues that Maria drives the freeways partly to "avoid emotional closeness and the mutual responsibility it implies" (Katherine Henderson, *Joan Didion* [New York: Ungar, 1981], 32). I would add, however, that she attains a new closeness to her Corvette as a consequence.

73. Deborah Clarke offers a different interpretation, echoing others in claiming that "Maria's strongest tie is to her daughter," but that her "anchor in the arid Hollywood landscape" is "the car" (Clark, *Driving Women*, 93). Yet if the car is indeed her "anchor," then it would seem to form her "strongest tie."

74. Erin Hogan, *Spiral Jetta: A Road Trip through the Land Art of the American West* (Chicago: University of Chicago Press, 2008), 2.

75. Ibid., 6.

76. Quoted in Fried, *Art and Objecthood*, 157–58.

77. Ibid., 158–59. On the separation of aesthetic experience from the art object, see Martin Jay, "Drifting into Dangerous Waters," in Pamela R. Matthews and David McWhirter, eds., *Aesthetic Subjects* (Minneapolis: University of Minnesota Press, 2003), 3–28.

78. Fried, *Art and Objecthood*, 160. On "Art and Objecthood" as a work of mourning, see Craig Owens, *Beyond Recognition: Representation, Power, and Culture* (Berkeley: University of California Press, 1992), 110.

79. For an excellent overview of Chamberlain's career, see the lush catalog that accompanied his 2012 retrospective at the Guggenheim: Susan Davidson, ed., *John Chamberlain: Choices* (New York: Solomon R. Guggenheim Foundation, 2012).

80. Fried, *Art and Objecthood*, 280.

81. Ibid.

82. Hogan, *Spiral Jetta*, 162.

83. Donald Judd, *Complete Writings, 1959–1975* (Nova Scotia, Canada: Press of the Nova Scotia College of Art and Design, 2005), 10.

84. "I gave up on Michael Fried," Judd wrote in 1969, "when I heard him say during a symposium that he couldn't see how anyone who liked Noland and Olitski or Stella could also like Oldenburg and Rauschenberg or Lichtenstein, whichever" (198).

85. Diane Waldman, ed., *John Chamberlain* (New York: Solomon R. Guggenheim Foundation, 1971), 15.

86. Fried, *Art and Objecthood*, 280.

87. Ibid., 156.

88. Latour, *Aramis*, 59; italics in the original.

89. Ibid., 58.

90. Daniel Miller, *Car Cultures* (London: Berg, 2001), 2.

91. Bruno Latour, *Reassembling the Social: An Introduction to Actor-Network-Theory* (Oxford: Oxford University Press, 2005), 132.

4: RUINS (THOMAS PYNCHON, ROBERT SMITHSON)

1. Tom Lewis, *Divided Highways: Building the Interstate Highways, Transforming American Life* (New York: Penguin, 1997), 145–47.

2. Jane Jacobs, *The Death and Life of Great American Cities* (New York: Modern Library, 1993), 440.

3. Robert Smithson, *Collected Writings*, ed. Jack Flam (Berkeley: University of California Press, 1996), 72; hereafter cited parenthetically in the text as *CW*.

4. An important precedent for the comparative work of this chapter was set by Jeremy Gilbert-Rolfe and John Johnston in an essay whose three parts appeared in the first three issues of *October*. See Jeremy Gilbert-Rolfe and John Johnston, "Gravity's Rainbow and the Spiral Jetty," *October* 1 (Summer 1976): 65–85; *October* 2 (Summer 1976): 71–90; and *October* 3 (Spring 1977): 90–101.

5. Ann Reynolds, *Robert Smithson: Learning from New Jersey and Elsewhere* (Cambridge, MA: MIT Press, 2003), 314.

6. Smithson's interest in maps, as Walter Benn Michaels has asserted, indicates his concern with the paradox of representation without resemblance: "It is because they are irreducibly representational (whether or not they are mimetic) that maps are critical to Smithson. Even if, in other words, they cannot be understood as looking like the thing they represent, they also cannot be understood except as representations" (Walter Benn Michaels, *The Shape of the Signifier: 1967 to the End of History* [Princeton, NJ: Princeton University Press, 2004], 93–94). I discuss how Pynchon engaged the paradox of representation without resemblance in David J. Alworth, "Pynchon's Malta," *Post45: Peer Reviewed*, October 1, 2012, http://post45.research.yale.edu/2012/10/pynchons-malta/.

7. Thomas Pynchon, *Slow Learner: Early Stories* (New York: Little, Brown, 1984), 22.

8. Richard Poirier, "Cook's Tour," *New York Review of Books*, June 1, 1963, http://www.nybooks.com/articles/archives/1963/jun/01/cooks-tour/.

9. George Plimpton, "Mata Hari with a Clockwork Eye, Alligators in the Sewer," *New York Times*, April 21, 1963, BR3.

10. Thomas Pynchon, *V.* (New York: Harper Perennial Modern Classics, 2005 [1963]), 423; hereafter cited parenthetically in the text as *V.*

11. Thomas Pynchon, "No, damnit," Box 20, Folder 1, Stephen Michael Tomaske Collection of Thomas Pynchon, Huntington Library.

12. Gilbert-Rolfe and Johnston, "Gravity's Rainbow," 71.

13. Robert Venturi, Denise Scott Brown, and Steven Izenour, *Learning from Las Vegas* (Cambridge, MA: MIT Press, 1977), 85–104.

14. For a broader account of how and why temporality became a widespread concern in the art and art criticism of Smithson's era, see Pamela Lee, *Chronophobia: On Time in the Art of the 1960s* (Cambridge, MA: MIT Press, 2004).

15. On Smithson's interest in dinosaurs, see W.J.T. Mitchell, *The Last Dinosaur Book: The Life and Times of a Cultural Icon* (Chicago: University of Chicago Press, 1998), 265–77.

16. Jennifer L. Roberts, *Mirror-Travels: Robert Smithson and History* (New Haven, CT: Yale University Press, 2004), 1, 4.

17. The scholarship on Pynchon's engagement with history and historiography is vast. Timothy Parrish sums up a significant strain of criticism when he writes that "part of Pynchon's achievement has been to translate the narrative techniques of Joyce to the problems of historical inquiry," thus making Pynchon "the preeminent postmodern novelist-as-historian" (Timothy Parrish, *From the Civil War to the Apocalypse: Postmodern History and American Fiction* [Amherst: University of Massachusetts Press, 2008], 33–34).

18. For the history of the Watts riot, see Gerald Horne, *Fire This Time: The Watts Uprising and the 1960s* (Charlottesville: University Press of Virginia, 1995). Also see Mike Davis, *City of Quartz: Excavating the Future in Los Angeles* (London: Verso, 2006), ch. 1.

19. Thomas Pynchon, "A Journey into the Mind of Watts," *New York Times Magazine*, June 12, 1966, 35, 78–84; hereafter cited parenthetically in the text as *J*.

20. I take this point from Thomas Heise, *Urban Underworlds: A Geography of Twentieth-Century American Literature and Culture* (Rutgers, NJ: Rutgers University Press, 2011), 176–77.

21. For broad but detailed accounts of this history, see Carmel Cassar, *A Concise History of Malta* (Msida, Malta: Mireva, 2000); and Brian W. Blouet, *The Story of Malta* (Valletta, Malta: Progress Press, 2004).

22. On Pynchon's time at and research on Malta, see Arnold Cassola, "Pynchon, *V.*, and the Malta Connection," *Journal of Modern Literature* 12.2 (July 1985): 311–31.

23. The term "chronotope" comes from Mikhail Bakhtin, *The Dialogic Imagination*, trans. Caryl Emerson and Michael Holquist (Austin: University of Texas Press, 1981). Bakhtin writes, in a well-known passage, "We will give the name *chronotope* (literally, 'time space') to the intrinsic connectedness of temporal and spatial relationships that are artistically expressed in literature" (84).

24. Quoted in Robert Hobbs, *Robert Smithson: Sculpture* (Ithaca, NY: Cornell University Press, 1981), 108.

25. W.J.T. Mitchell, *What Do Pictures Want? The Lives and Loves of Images* (Chicago: University of Chicago Press, 2005), 261. In this sense, as Caroline A. Jones has argued, Smithson's sites and nonsites were "rejections of the unitary object," as well as ambitious efforts to expand the field of sculpture; see Jones, *Machine in the Studio: Constructing the Postwar American Artist* (Chicago: University of Chicago Press, 1996), 319.

26. Miwon Kwon, *One Place after Another: Site-Specific Art and Locational Identity* (Cambridge, MA: MIT Press, 2002), 11.

27. Georg Simmel, "Two Essays," trans. David Kettler, *Hudson Review* 11.3 (1958): 379, 385; Walter Benjamin, *The Origin of German Tragic Drama*, trans. John Osborne (London: Verso, 1998), 177–78.

28. Siegfried Kracauer, *The Mass Ornament: Weimar Essays*, trans. Thomas Y. Levin (Cambridge, MA: Harvard University Press, 1995), 229, 264.

29. Ernst Bloch, *The Principle of Hope*, vol. 1, trans. Neville Plaice et al. (Cambridge, MA: MIT Press, 1995), 385.

30. Ann Laura Stoler, "Imperial Debris: Reflections on Ruins and Ruination," *Cultural Anthropology* 23.2 (2008): 194, 202.

31. Nick Yablon, *Untimely Ruins: An Archaeology of American Urban Modernity, 1819–1919* (Chicago: University of Chicago Press, 2009), 12.

32. Andreas Huyssen, *Present Pasts: Urban Palimpsests and the Politics of Memory* (Stanford, CA: Stanford University Press, 2003).

33. Ibid., 7; "palimpsest, n. and adj.," *OED Online*, March 2013, Oxford University Press, http://www.oed.com.

34. Stoler, "Imperial Debris," 195.

35. Walter Benjamin, "One-Way Street," trans. Edmund Jephcott, in Walter Benjamin, *Selected*

Writings: Volume 1, 1913–1926, ed. Marcus Bullock and Michael W. Jennings (Cambridge, MA: Harvard University Press, 2004), 449.

36. Laurence Mizzi, *Wartime Diary of a Maltese Boy* (Rabat, Malta: Wise Owl, 2006), 35.

37. These statistics come from Cassar, *History of Malta*, 225. For a thorough account of Malta during World War II, see James Holland, *Fortress Malta: An Island under Siege, 1940–1943* (London: Orion, 2003).

38. Cassar, *History of Malta*, 222.

39. Jack Belden, "Malta Wins the Siege," *Time*, February 15, 1943, 86.

40. Pynchon gives rare insight into his "haphazard" research for *V.* in a letter written to David Hirsh in which he explains that he was "looking for a report on Malta" at the New York Public Library when he discovered the text on the Bondelswarts affair that informs chapter 9 of the novel (quoted in David Seed, *The Fictional Labyrinths of Thomas Pynchon* [Iowa City: University of Iowa Press, 1988], 240).

41. Belden, "Malta Wins," 86.

42. Paul Boyer, *By the Bomb's Early Light: American Thought and Culture at the Dawn of the Atomic Age* (Chapel Hill: University of North Carolina Press, 1994), 353.

43. Daniel Grausam, *On Endings: American Postmodern Fiction and the Cold War* (Charlottesville: University of Virginia Press, 2011), 45, 51.

44. Julia Hell and Andreas Schönle, eds., *Ruins of Modernity* (Durham, NC: Duke University Press, 2010), 6.

45. For example, Hell and Schönle ask, "Where does the ruin start, and where does it end? Is a well-preserved but empty building already a ruin because it has lost its practical and social function? And, at the other end of the spectrum, does rubble still qualify as ruin? More broadly, is a ruin an object or a process? Does it signal the loss of the endurance of the past?" (6).

46. While Pynchon's spelling is important, as I suggest below, I prefer "Ḥaġar Qim," the proper (i.e., non-Anglicized) Maltese spelling of the name.

47. See Robert Smithson, "The Crystal Land," in *Robert Smithson: The Collected Writings*.

48. "Not only did I complicate this Long Island space," Pynchon writes, referring to one of his early stories, "but I also drew a line around the whole neighborhood, picked it up and shifted it all to the Berkshires, where I still have never been. The old Baedeker trick again. This time I found the details I needed in the regional guide to the Berkshires put out in the 1930s by the Federal Writers Project of the WPA" (Pynchon, *Slow Learner*, 21).

49. Themistocles Zammit, *Malta: The Islands and Their History* (Valletta, Malta: Malta Herald Office, 1926), 44.

50. Ibid., 45.

51. Christopher Tilley, *The Materiality of Stone: Explorations in Landscape Phenomenology* (Oxford, UK: Berg, 2004), 128, 131.

52. David Trump, *Malta: An Archaeological Guide* (London: Faber and Faber, 1972), 95, 93.

53. Zammit, *Malta*, 34.

54. Ibid., 45.

55. On Pynchon's treatment of the Herero genocide, see Cyrus R. K. Patell, *Negative Liberties: Morrison, Pynchon, and the Problem of Liberal Ideology* (Durham, NC: Duke University Press, 2001), ch. 3.

56. Quoted in Seed, *Fictional Labyrinths*, 240.

57. On the planning and construction of Valletta, see Quentin Hughes, "Give Me Time and I Will Give You Life: Laparelli and the Building of Valletta, Malta, 1565–1569," *Town Planning Review* 49.1 (January 1978): 61–74. Valletta, as Hughes notes, was planned by Francesco Laparelli, onetime assistant to Michelangelo, under the auspices of the Knights of St. John.

58. Quoted in Seed, *Fictional Labyrinths*, 241.

59. Bruno Latour, *Reassembling the Social: An Introduction to Actor-Network-Theory* (Oxford: Oxford University Press, 2005), 166; italics in the original.

60. Ibid., 195; italics in the original.

61. Michel Serres, *The Parasite* (Minneapolis: University of Minnesota Press, 2007), 225, 227. By conceptualizing the quasi-object in this manner, Serres echoed his doctoral supervisor, Gaston Bachelard, who had suggested in 1958 that certain physical entities (drawers, desks, and chests) are "hybrid objects" or "subject objects" that "[l]ike us, through us and for us . . . have a quality of intimacy" (Gaston Bachelard, *The Poetics of Space*, trans. Maria Jolas [Boston: Beacon Press, 1969], 78).

62. Latour, *Reassembling the Social*, 238.

63. Serres, "Theory of the Quasi-Object," in *The Parasite*, 225; Latour, *Reassembling the Social*, 5; italics in the original.

64. Latour, *Reassembling the Social*, 61, 25.

65. Quoted in Seed, *Fictional Labyrinths*, 241; Pynchon, *Slow Learner*, 6.

66. Stoler, "Imperial Debris," 203, 195.

5: ASYLUMS (RALPH ELLISON, GORDON PARKS, JEFF WALL)

1. Ann Laura Stoler, "Imperial Debris: Reflections on Ruins and Ruination," *Cultural Anthropology* 23.2 (2008): 195.

2. All the Ellison quotes in this paragraph come from Ralph Ellison, *The Collected Essays of Ralph Ellison* (New York: Modern Library, 2003), 320–22; hereafter cited parenthetically in the text as *CE*.

3. See "asylum, n.," *OED Online*, June 2013, Oxford University Press. As the *OED* reminds us, the term "asylum" designates any "secure place of refuge, shelter, or retreat," although it is often "popularly restricted" to institutions of psychiatric care.

4. Richard Wright, "Psychiatry Comes to Harlem," *Free World* 12 (September 1946): 49.

5. Ibid.

6. Dorothy Norman, "A World to Live In," *New York Post*, March 18, 1946. For a more detailed history of LaFargue, see Dennis Doyle, "'A Fine New Child': The LaFargue Mental Hygiene Clinic and Harlem's African American Communities, 1946–1958," *Journal of the History of Medicine and Allied Sciences* 64.2 (2008): 173–212. On Ellison's involvement with the clinic in particular, see Lawrence Jackson, *Ralph Ellison: Emergence of Genius* (New York: John Wiley & Sons, 2002), ch. 12; and Arnold Rampersad, *Ralph Ellison: A Biography* (New York: Alfred A. Knopf, 2007), ch. 8.

7. Ralph Ellison, "Dear Dick," Box I: 203, Folder 4, "LaFargue Clinic, New York, N.Y., 1946–1953," Ralph Ellison Papers, Manuscript Division, Library of Congress.

8. The first quote in this sentence is from Ralph Ellison, "Dear Dick," Ralph Ellison Papers; the second is from Ralph Ellison, *Collected Essays*, 321.

9. Trained in sociology, Du Bois was highly critical of the discipline, imagining "white sociologists gleefully count[ing]" black "prostitutes" and "bastards" (W.E.B. Du Bois, *The Souls of Black Folk*, in *Writings* [New York: Library of America, 1986], 368). Alain Locke wrote that the sociologist was "at a loss to account for" the New Negro (Alain Locke, ed., *The New Negro: Voices of the Harlem Renaissance* [New York: Touchstone, 1997], 40). James Baldwin, arguing that "literature and sociology are not one in the same," suggested that the latter satisfies "[o]ur passion for categorization" and thus leads to "a breakdown of meaning" (James Baldwin, "Everybody's Protest Novel," in *Collected Essays* [New York: Library of America, 1998], 15). There are several good accounts of Ellison's relationship to sociology: Kenneth W. Warren, *So Black and Blue: Ralph Ellison and the Occasion of Criticism* (Chicago: University of Chicago Press, 2003), ch. 3; Andrew Hoberek, *The Twilight of the Middle Class:*

Post–World War II American Fiction and White-Collar Work (Princeton, NJ: Princeton University Press, 2005), ch. 2; Roderick A. Ferguson, *Aberrations in Black: Toward a Queer of Color Critique* (Minneapolis: University of Minnesota Press, 2004), ch. 2; and Stephen Schryer, *Fantasies of the New Class: Ideologies of Professionalism in Post–World War II American Fiction* (New York: Columbia University Press, 2011), ch. 2.

10. Warren, *So Black and Blue*, 61, 94. On the link between *Invisible Man* and the white-collar sociologies of Riesman, Mills, and White, see Hoberek, *Twilight of the Middle Class*.

11. Heather Love, "Close but not Deep: Literary Ethics and the Descriptive Turn," *New Literary History* 41.2 (Spring 2010): 371–91. Love argues that both sociologists, partly through an interaction with literature and literary theory, employ practices of analytical description that suggest a model for literary criticism, which she dubs "close but not deep" reading.

12. Bruno Latour, *Reassembling the Social: An Introduction to Actor-Network-Theory* (Oxford: Oxford University Press, 2005), 46.

13. Ralph Ellison, *Invisible Man* (New York: Vintage, 1995), 3; hereafter cited parenthetically in the text as *IM*.

14. Ralph Martin, "Doctor's Dream in Harlem," *New Republic*, June 3, 1946, 798.

15. Fredric Wertham, "Psychological Effects of School Segregation," *American Journal of Psychotherapy* 6.1 (January 1952), Ralph Ellison Papers, Manuscript Division, Library of Congress. The year 1952 was also when many of the most prominent social scientists in the United States issued a report, titled "The Effects of Segregation and the Consequences of Desegregation: A Social Science Statement," that was ultimately included in the appendix to the appellant's briefs in the *Brown* decision. See Kenneth B. Clark, *Prejudice and Your Child*, 2nd ed. (Boston: Beacon Press, 1962).

16. Ellison, "Dear Dick."

17. Ralph Ellison, "Two years ago," Ralph Ellison Papers, Manuscript Division, Library of Congress.

18. Ibid.

19. Ralph Ellison, "Like that type of camera," Ralph Ellison Papers, Manuscript Division, Library of Congress.

20. Sara Blair, *Harlem Crossroads: Black Writers and the Photograph in the Twentieth Century* (Princeton, NJ: Princeton University Press, 2007), 115.

21. Ellison, "Two years ago."

22. See "microcosm, n.," *OED Online*, June 2013, Oxford University Press.

23. Ligon makes this observation in his curatorial statement for *Contact: Gordon Parks, Ralph Ellison, and "Invisible Man,"* an exhibition that was held at the Howard Greenberg Gallery in 2012.

24. Goffman defines the "total institution" as "a place of residence and work where a large number of like-situated individuals, cut off from the wider society for an appreciable period of time, together lead an enclosed, formally administered round of life" (Erving Goffman, *Asylums: Essays on the Social Situation of Mental Patients and Other Inmates* [New York: Anchor, 1961], xiii); hereafter cited parenthetically in the text as *A*. On Goffman's "method of analytic induction," see Greg Smith, *Erving Goffman* (New York: Routledge, 2006), 117–18.

25. Goffman, *Asylums*, 360. Many readers have sensed links between Goffman's writings on asylums and Michel Foucault's contemporaneous treatment of such sites, which, Foucault argues, brought into being a system of "social segregation that would guarantee bourgeois morality a universality of fact" (Michel Foucault, *Madness and Civilization: A History of Insanity in the Age of Reason*, trans. Richard Howard [New York: Random House, 1965], 259). Their respective methods, however, were quite different, if also complementary, as Ian Hacking explains in "Between Michel Foucault and Erving Goffman: Between Discourse in the Abstract and Face-to-Face Interaction," *Economy and Society* 33.3 (2004): 277–302.

26. As I discuss below, however, Goffman does address race in *Asylums* and especially in *Stigma*.

27. Michael E. Staub reports that between 1955 and 1985, the number of patients in state mental hospitals dropped from 550,000 to less than 100,000 (*Madness Is Civilization: When the Diagnosis Was Social* [Chicago: University of Chicago Press, 2011], 183). On deinstitutionalization, see Gerald N. Grob, *The Mad Among Us: A History of the Care of America's Mentally Ill* (New York: Free Press, 1994), ch. 10.

28. See Doyle for a full explication of Wertham's "social psychiatry."

29. Erving Goffman, *The Presentation of Self in Everyday Life* (New York: Anchor, 1959), 112, 208.

30. Ellison's relationship to Burke is well documented. For an incisive analysis, see Donald E. Pease, "Ralph Ellison and Kenneth Burke: The Nonsymbolizable (Trans)Action," *boundary 2* 30.2 (2003): 65–96. Also see Bryan Crable, *Ralph Ellison and Kenneth Burke: At the Roots of the Racial Divide* (Charlottesville: University of Virginia Press, 2012).

31. Quoted in Goffman, *Presentation of Self*, 136.

32. On Goffman's debt to Chicago school sociology, see Tom Burns, *Erving Goffman* (New York: Routledge, 1992), ch. 1; Smith, *Erving Goffman*, ch. 2; and Louis Menand, "Some Frames for Goffman," *Social Psychology Quarterly* 72.4 (2009): 296–99.

33. "My reading in sociology," Wright explains, "had enabled me to discern many strange types of Negro characters, to identify many modes of Negro behavior, and what moved me above all was the frequency of mental illness, that tragic toll that the urban environment exacted of the black peasant" (Richard Wright, *Black Boy* [New York: Harper Perennial Modern Classics, 2007], 284). Ellison underscores this last point in his essay on LaFargue. On Wright's links to the Chicago school, see Carla Cappetti, *Writing Chicago: Modernism, Ethnography, and the Novel* (New York: Columbia University Press, 1993), ch. 8 and ch. 9.

34. Robert E. Park and Ernest W. Burgess, *Introduction to the Science of Sociology*, 3rd ed. (Chicago: University of Chicago Press, 1969). The first edition was published in 1921.

35. Robert O'Meally, *The Craft of Ralph Ellison* (Cambridge, MA: Harvard University Press, 1980), 24.

36. Pierre Bourdieu, "Erving Goffman, Discoverer of the Infinitely Small," *Theory, Culture & Society* 2.1 (1983): 112.

37. As Staub puts it, "[T]he case study of the insane asylum in *Asylums* became an occasion for *theorizing more generally* about interhuman relations, the peculiarities of contained settings, and the structure of the human self (and the relationship among the three)" (*Madness Is Civilization*, 81; his emphasis).

38. Susan Stewart, *On Longing: Narratives of the Miniature, the Gigantic, the Souvenir, the Collection* (Durham, NC: Duke University Press, 1993), 162.

39. Adapting Marx, Bill Brown argues that practices like these disclose the "misuse value" of mass-produced objects; see *A Sense of Things: The Object Matter of American Literature* (Chicago: University of Chicago Press, 2003), 74–80.

40. Rampersad, *Ralph Ellison*, 219–20.

41. Erving Goffman, *Stigma: Notes on the Management of Spoiled Identity* (New York: Simon and Schuster, 1963), 3, 43–45.

42. These figures come from Christopher Payne, *Asylum: Inside the Closed World of State Mental Hospitals* (Cambridge: MIT Press, 2009), 7.

43. There is a vast amount of scholarship on moral treatment and the rise of the asylum in nineteenth-century United States. On architectural design specifically, see Carla Yanni, *The Architecture of Madness: Insane Asylums in the United States* (Minneapolis: University of Minnesota Press, 2007). On the history of asylum medicine, see David J. Rothman's pioneering study, *The Discovery of the Asylum: Social Order and Disorder in the New Republic* (Boston: Little, Brown, 1971). For an account of the asylum as a site of cultural production, see

Benjamin Reiss, *Theaters of Madness: Insane Asylums and Nineteenth-Century American Culture* (Chicago: University of Chicago Press, 2008). On the transformation of asylum care into modern psychiatric medicine, see Elizabeth Lunbeck, *The Psychiatric Persuasion: Knowledge, Gender, and Power in Modern America* (Princeton, NJ: Princeton University Press, 1994). Longer histories of mental health care and psychiatric thought in the United States can be found in Gerald N. Grob, *The Mad Among Us*; Robert Castel et al., *The Psychiatric Society* (New York: Columbia University Press, 1982); Andrew Scull, *Social Order/Mental Disorder: Anglo-American Psychiatry in Historical Perspective* (Berkeley: University of California Press, 1989); and Edward Shorter, *A History of Psychiatry from the Era of the Asylum to the Age of Prozac* (New York: John Wiley Sons, 1997).

44. William Dean Fairless, *Suggestions Concerning the Construction of Asylums for the Insane* (Edinburgh: Sutherland and Knox, 1861), 7.

45. For a thorough account of Kirkbride's life and thought, see Nancy Tomes, *The Art of Asylum-Keeping: Thomas Story Kirkbride and the Origins of American Psychiatry* (Philadelphia: University of Pennsylvania Press, 1994).

46. See Christopher Payne's stunning photographs of these ruins in *Asylum*.

47. Thomas Story Kirkbride, *On the Construction, Organization, and General Arrangements of Hospitals for the Insane* (Philadelphia, PA: Lindsay & Blakiston, 1854), 7, 11–12.

48. Kirkbride's environmental determinism was fervent but not unique. As Yanni notes, other examples can be found in the nineteenth-century discourses on prisons, universities, medical hospitals, gardens, and public parks (*Architecture of Madness*, 8–9).

49. Mary Jane Ward, *The Snake Pit* (New York: Random House, 1946), 115.

50. The social impact of the film version of *The Snake Pit* is well documented by Nick Clooney in *The Movies that Changed Us: Reflections on the Screen* (New York: Simon and Schuster, 2002), ch. 9.

51. Albert Q. Maisel, "Bedlam 1946: Most U.S. Mental Hospitals Are a Shame and a Disgrace," *Life*, May 6, 1946, 102.

52. Albert Deutsch, *The Shame of the States* (New York: Harcourt, Brace, 1948), 66, 98.

53. Created by a group of men who had been released from a state hospital, Fountain House (www.fountainhouse.org) initiated the "clubhouse" model of mental health care, which has been highly influential in the United States and around the world. See Yanni, *Architecture of Madness*, 153–58.

54. Fredric Wertham, *The Circle of Guilt* (Oxford: University of Mississippi Press, 2007), 191.

55. Sidney M. Katz, "Jim Crow Is Barred from Wertham's Clinic," *Magazine Digest*, September 1946.

56. Georg Simmel, *Simmel on Culture*, ed. David Frisby and Mike Featherstone (London: Sage, 1997), 175.

57. Quoted in Smith, *Erving Goffman*, 31.

58. Goffman, *Presentation of Self*, xii.

59. John Clark Pratt highlights the intertextual link by including the EST scene from *Invisible Man* in the "Analogies and Perspectives" section of the Viking Critical Library edition of Kesey's novel; see Ken Kesey, *One Flew Over the Cuckoo's Nest*, ed. John Clark Pratt (New York: Penguin, 1996).

60. Kesey, *One Flew Over the Cuckoo's Nest*, 66–67.

61. Robert Penn Warren, *All the King's Men* (New York: Harcourt, Brace, 1946), 335–39.

62. Sylvia Plath, *The Bell Jar* (New York: Harper Perennial Modern Classics, 2013), 226, 140.

63. E. L. Doctorow, *The Book of Daniel* (New York: Random House, 1971), 7.

64. Charles Olson, *Charles Olson and Ezra Pound: An Encounter at St. Elizabeths*, ed. Catherine Seelye (New York: Grossman, 1975), 36–37.

65. Allen Ginsberg, *Howl and Other Poems* (San Francisco: City Lights, 2001), 22, 19.

66. Here I am thinking of Marge Piercy's *Woman on the Edge of Time* (1976) and Walker Percy's

Lancelot (1977). The asylum was also powerfully represented in both narrative and documentary cinema—in films such as Samuel Fuller's *Shock Corridor* (1963), Frederick Wiseman's *Titicut Follies* (1967), and Miloš Forman's 1975 adaptation of *One Flew Over the Cuckoo's Nest*. In addition, Richard Avedon and James Baldwin's photo-text, *Nothing Personal* (1964), contains a section devoted to institutionalized mental patients.

67. Ralph Ellison, "Cadillac Flambé," *Callaloo* 18.2 (Spring 1995): 260.
68. Ralph Ellison, "Pictorial problem," Ralph Ellison Papers, Manuscript Division, Library of Congress.
69. "A Man Becomes Invisible," *Life*, August 25, 1952, 10.
70. Wall has not created a work of installation art in the technical sense of "a situation into which the viewer physically enters" (Claire Bishop, *Installation Art: A Critical History* [London: Tate, 2005], 6). Nonetheless, as Michael Fried and other critics have pointed out, "After 'Invisible Man'" (like most of Wall's photographs) explicitly acknowledges its *stagedness*, and therefore refers back to the site and the labor that made it possible. It invites us, in other words, to marvel at Wall's feat of interior design in addition to his photographic art.
71. Thierry de Duve, ed., *Jeff Wall: The Complete Edition* (London: Phaidon, 2009), 252.
72. Michael Fried, *Why Photography Matters as Art as Never Before* (New Haven, CT: Yale University Press, 2008), 47.
73. Bruno Latour, *Reassembling the Social*; Park and Burgess, *Introduction*, 226.

AFTERWORD: SITE UNSEEN

1. Cormac McCarthy, *The Road* (New York: Vintage, 2006), 146, 130, 14, 6; hereafter cited parenthetically in the text as *TR*.
2. Susan Stewart, *On Longing: Narratives of the Miniature, the Gigantic, the Souvenir, the Collection* (Durham, NC: Duke University Press, 1993), 139.
3. Jennifer Egan, "Men at Work: The Literary Masculinity of Cormac McCarthy," *Slate*, October 10, 2006, http://www.slate.com/articles/news_and_politics/book_blitz/2006/10/men_at_work.html.
4. Susan Mizruchi, "Risk Theory and the Contemporary American Novel," *American Literary History* 22.1 (2010): 124.
5. "McCarthy's remarkable style," asserts Jay Ellis, "appears more often than not, and most powerfully, in his descriptions of setting" (Ellis, *No Place for Home: Spatial Constraint and Character Flight in the Novels of Cormac McCarthy* [New York: Routledge, 2006], 1).
6. Richard Ross, *Waiting for the End of the World* (Princeton, NJ: Princeton Architectural Press, 2004), 11.
7. Paul Virilio, *Bunker Archaeology* (Princeton, NJ: Princeton Architectural Press, 1994), 46.
8. Ross, *Waiting for the End of the World*, 17.
9. Ibid., 22.
10. For an account of this artifact, see http://www.smithsonianmag.com.
11. John F. Kennedy, "Radio and Television Address to the Nation on the Berlin Crisis," July 25, 1961, John F. Kennedy Presidential Library and Museum website, http://www.jfklibrary.org/Asset-Viewer/Archives/JFKWHP-AR6712-C.aspx.
12. "A New Urgency, Big Things to Do—and What You Must Learn," *Life* 51.11 (September 15, 1961); "Civil Defense: The Sheltered Life," *Time*, October 20, 1961, 20; "Use and Limit of Shelters," *Life*, January 12, 1962, 4. For a detailed history of this cultural phenomenon, see Kenneth D. Rose, *One Nation Underground: The Fallout Shelter in American Culture* (New York: NYU Press, 2001).
13. Andrew Hoberek, "Cormac McCarthy and the Aesthetics of Exhaustion," *American Literary History* 23.3 (2011): 486.

14. John Jurgensen, "Hollywood's Favorite Cowboy," *Wall Street Journal*, November 20, 2009, http://online.wsj.com/articles/SB10001424052748704576204574529703577274572.

15. On the climate crisis, the petroleum industry, and American literature, see Stephanie Le-Menager, *Living Oil: Petroleum Culture in the American Century* (Oxford: Oxford University Press, 2014). On the ethics and politics of nuclear weapons, see Elaine Scarry, *Thermonuclear Monarchy: Choosing Between Democracy and Doom* (New York: W. W. Norton, 2014).

16. *The Road* incorporates elements from a wide range of genres, including science fiction, horror, travel narrative, and the western; on the novel of purpose, specifically, see Amanda Claybaugh, *The Novel of Purpose: Literature and Social Reform in the Anglo-American World* (Ithaca, NY: Cornell University Press, 2007). The term "matter of concern" is fully explicated in Bruno Latour, *Reassembling the Social: An Introduction to Actor-Network-Theory* (Oxford: Oxford University Press, 2005), 87–121.

17. Latour, *Reassembling the Social*, 82. For Latour's own take on the climate crisis, see Bruno Latour, "An Attempt at a 'Compositionist Manifesto,'" *New Literary History* 41.3 (2010): 471–90.

BIBLIOGRAPHY

Adams, Rachel. *Continental Divides: Remapping the Cultures of North America*. Chicago: University of Chicago Press, 2009.

———. "Hipsters and *jipitecas*: Literary Countercultures on Both Sides of the Border." *American Literary History* 16.1 (2004): 58–84.

Alworth, David J. "Melville in the Asylum: Literature, Sociology, Reading." *American Literary History* 26.2 (2014): 234–61.

———. "Pynchon's Malta." *Post45: Peer Reviewed*. October 1, 2013. http://post45.research.yale.edu/2012/10/pynchons-malta/.

———. "Supermarket Sociology." *New Literary History* 41.2 (2010): 301–27.

Ammons, A. R. *Garbage*. New York: Norton, 1993.

Auster, Paul. *The New York Trilogy*. New York: Penguin, 2006.

Bachelard, Gaston. *The Poetics of Space*. Translated by Maria Jolas. Boston: Beacon Press, 1969.

Bakhtin, Mikhail. *The Dialogic Imagination: Four Essays*. Translated by Caryl Emerson and Michael Holquist. Austin: University of Texas Press, 1981.

Baldwin, James. "Everybody's Protest Novel." In *James Baldwin: Collected Essays*, 11–18. New York: Library of America, 1998.

Balsley, Gene. "The Hot-Rod Culture." *American Quarterly* 2.4 (1950): 353–58.

Balzac, Honoré de. *The Wild Ass's Skin*. Translated by Herbert J. Hunt. New York: Penguin, 1977.

Barthes, Roland. "The Reality Effect" (1968). In *The Rustle of Language*, translated by Richard Howard, 141–48. Berkeley: University of California Press, 1989.

Bataille, Georges. *Visions of Excess: Selected Writings, 1927–1939*. Translated by Alan Stoekl with Carl R. Lovitt and Donald M. Leslie Jr. Minneapolis: University of Minnesota Press, 1985.

Baudrillard, Jean. *Simulacra and Simulation*. Translated by Sheila Faria Glaser. Ann Arbor: University of Michigan Press, 1994.

Beckett, Samuel. *Stories and Texts for Nothing*. New York: Grove Press, 1967.

Benjamin, Walter. "Dream Kitsch." Translated by Howard Eiland. In *Walter Benjamin: Selected Writings, Volume 2, Part 1: 1927–1930*, edited by Michael W. Jennings, Howard Eiland, and Gary Smith, 3–5. Cambridge, MA: Belknap Press of Harvard University Press, 1999.

———. "One-Way Street." Translated by Edmund Jephcott. In *Walter Benjamin: Selected Writings: Volume 1, 1913–1926*, edited by Marcus Bollock and Michael W. Jennings, 444–89. Cambridge, MA: Belknap Press of Harvard University Press, 2004.

———. *The Origin of German Tragic Drama*. Translated by John Osborne. London: Verso, 1998.

———. "The Paris of the Second Empire in Baudelaire." Translated by Harry Zohn. In *The*

Writer of Modern Life: Essays on Charles Baudelaire, edited by Michael W. Jennings, 46–133. Cambridge, MA: Belknap Press of Harvard University Press, 2006.

Bennett, Jane. "The Agency of Assemblages and the North American Blackout." *Public Culture* 17.3 (2005): 445–65.

———. *Vibrant Matter: A Political Ecology of Things*. Durham, NC: Duke University Press, 2010.

Bennett, Tony. "Sociology, Aesthetics, Expertise." *New Literary History* 41.2 (2010): 253–76.

Best, Stephen, and Sharon Marcus. "Surface Reading: An Introduction." *Representations* 108.1 (2009): 1–21.

Bishop, Claire. *Installation Art: A Critical History*. London: Tate, 2005.

Blair, Sara. *Harlem Crossroads: Black Writers and the Photograph in the Twentieth Century*. Princeton, NJ: Princeton University Press, 2007.

Bloch, Ernst. *The Principle of Hope*. Vol. 1. Translated by Neville Plaice, Stephen Plaice, and Paul Knight. Cambridge, MA: MIT Press, 1995.

Blouet, Brian W. *The Story of Malta*. Valletta, Malta: Progress Press, 2004.

Bockris, Victor. *With William Burroughs: A Report from the Bunker*. New York: St. Martin's Press, 1996.

Bogost, Ian. *Alien Phenomenology, or, What It's Like to Be a Thing*. Minneapolis: University of Minnesota Press, 2012.

Bois, Yve-Alain, and Rosalind E. Krauss. *Formless: A User's Guide*. New York: Zone Books, 1997.

Bourdieu, Pierre. "Erving Goffman, Discoverer of the Infinitely Small." *Theory, Culture & Society* 2.1 (1983): 112–13.

———. *The Field of Cultural Production*. New York: Columbia University Press, 1993.

Bourriaud, Nicolas. *Relational Aesthetics*. Translated by Simon Pleasance and Fronza Woods with the participation of Mathieu Copeland. Paris: Les presses du reel, 2002.

Bowlby, Rachel. *Carried Away: The Invention of Modern Shopping*. New York: Columbia University Press, 2001.

Boxall, Peter. *Don DeLillo: The Possibility of Fiction*. New York: Routledge, 2006.

Boyer, Paul. *By the Bomb's Early Light: American Thought and Culture at the Dawn of the Atomic Age*. Chapel Hill: University of North Carolina Press, 1994.

Breton, André. *Mad Love*. Translated by Mary Ann Caws. Lincoln: University of Nebraska Press, 1987.

———. *Manifestoes of Surrealism*. Translated by Richard Seaver and Helen R. Lane. Ann Arbor: University of Michigan Press, 1969.

———. *Nadja*. Translated by Richard Howard. New York: Grove Press, 1960.

Brinkley, Douglas, ed. *Windblown World: The Journals of Jack Kerouac, 1947–1954*. New York: Viking Press, 2004.

Brown, Bill. "Introduction: Textual Materialism." *PMLA* 125.1 (2010): 24–28.

———. *A Sense of Things: The Object Matter of American Literature*. Chicago: University of Chicago Press, 2003.

———, ed. *Things*. Chicago: University of Chicago Press, 2004.

———. "Thing Theory." *Critical Inquiry* 28.1 (2001): 1–22.

Buell, Lawrence. *The Dream of the Great American Novel*. Cambridge, MA: Harvard University Press, 2014.

———. *The Future of Environmental Criticism*. Malden, MA: Blackwell, 2005.

Burke, Kenneth. *A Grammar of Motives*. Berkeley: University of California Press, 1945.

Burns, Tom. *Erving Goffman*. New York: Routledge, 1992.

Burroughs, William S. *Letters to Allen Ginsberg, 1953–1957*. New York: Full Court Press, 1982.

———. *Naked Lunch: The Restored Text*. New York: Grove Press, 2001.

Buskirk, Martha. *The Contingent Object of Contemporary Art*. Cambridge, MA: MIT Press, 2003.

Butler, Judith. "Merleau-Ponty and the Touch of Malebranche." In *The Cambridge Companion to*

Maurice Merleau-Ponty, edited by Taylor Carman and Mark B. N. Hansen, 181–205. Cambridge: Cambridge University Press, 2005.

Cappetti, Carla. *Writing Chicago: Modernism, Ethnography, and the Novel*. New York: Columbia University Press, 1993.

Carman, Taylor, and Mark B. N. Hansen, eds. *The Cambridge Companion to Maurice Merleau-Ponty*. Cambridge: Cambridge University Press, 2005.

———. *Merleau-Ponty*. London: Routledge, 2008.

Carson, Rachel. *Silent Spring*. New York: Mariner / Houghton Mifflin, 2002.

Cassar, Carmel. *A Concise History of Malta*. Msida, Malta: Mireva, 2000.

Cassola, Arnold. "Pynchon, *V.*, and the Malta Connection." *Journal of Modern Literature* 12.2 (1985): 311–31.

Chandler, James K. *England in 1819: The Politics of Literary Culture and the Case of Romantic Historicism*. Chicago: University of Chicago Press, 1998.

Charters, Ann, ed. *The Portable Jack Kerouac*. New York: Penguin, 1996.

Chatman, Seymour. *Story and Discourse: Narrative Structure in Fiction and Film*. Ithaca, NY: Cornell University Press, 1978.

Clark, Andy. *Natural-Born Cyborgs: Minds, Technologies, and the Future of Human Intelligence*. Oxford: Oxford University Press, 2004.

Clarke, Deborah. *Driving Women: Fiction and Automobile Culture in Twentieth-Century America*. Baltimore, MD: Johns Hopkins University Press, 2007.

Claybaugh, Amanda. *The Novel of Purpose: Literature and Social Reform in the Anglo-American World*. Ithaca, NY: Cornell University Press, 2007.

Clifford, James. *The Predicament of Culture: Twentieth-Century Ethnography, Literature, and Art*. Cambridge, MA: Harvard University Press, 1988.

Clooney, Nick. *The Movies that Changed Us: Reflections on the Screen*. New York: Simon and Schuster, 2002.

Cohan, Steven, and Ina Rae Hark, eds. *The Road Movie Book*. New York: Routledge, 1997.

Cohen, Lizabeth. *A Consumers' Republic: The Politics of Mass Consumption in Postwar America*. New York: Knopf, 2003.

Cowart, David. *Don DeLillo: The Physics of Language*. Athens: University of Georgia Press, 2002.

Crable, Bryan. *Ralph Ellison and Kenneth Burke: At the Roots of the Racial Divide*. Charlottesville: University of Virginia Press, 2012.

Creeley, Robert. *The Collected Essays of Robert Creeley*. Berkeley: University of California Press, 1989.

———. *For Love: Poems, 1950–1960*. New York: Charles Scribner's Sons, 1962.

Crow, Thomas. *Modern Art in the Common Culture*. New Haven, CT: Yale University Press, 1996.

Cunnell, Howard, ed. *On the Road: The Original Scroll*. New York: Viking Penguin, 2007.

Dant, Tim. "The Driver-Car." *Theory, Culture & Society* 21.4–5 (2004): 61–79.

Danto, Arthur. "The Artworld." *Journal of Philosophy* 61.19 (1964): 571–84.

Daston, Lorraine, ed. *Biographies of Scientific Objects*. Chicago: University of Chicago Press, 2000.

Davidson, Michael. *Guys Like Us: Citing Masculinity in Cold War Poetics*. Chicago: University of Chicago Press, 2004.

Davidson, Susan, ed. *John Chamberlain: Choices*. New York: Solomon R. Guggenheim Foundation, 2012.

Davis, Mike. *City of Quartz: Excavating the Future in Los Angeles*. London: Verso, 2006.

Deleuze, Gilles, and Félix Guattari. *What Is Philosophy?* Translated by Hugh Tomlinson and Graham Burchell. New York: Columbia University Press, 1994.

DeLillo, Don. *Underworld*. New York: Scribner, 1997.

———. *White Noise*. New York: Penguin, 1985.

Defoe, Daniel. *Robinson Crusoe*. New York: Penguin, 2001.

DeKoven, Marianne. *Utopia Limited: The Sixties and the Emergence of the Postmodern*. Durham, NC: Duke University Press, 2004.

DePietro, Thomas, ed. *Conversations with Don DeLillo*. Jackson: University Press of Mississippi, 2005.

Deutsch, Albert. *The Shame of the States*. New York: Harcourt, Brace, 1948.

Deutsch, Tracey. *Building a Housewife's Paradise: Gender, Politics, and American Grocery Stores in the Twentieth Century*. Chapel Hill: University of North Carolina Press, 2010.

Dewey, Joseph. *Beyond Grief and Nothing: A Reading of Don DeLillo*. Columbia: University of South Carolina Press, 2006.

Dick, Philip K. *Time Out of Joint*. New York: Vintage, 2002.

Dickens, Charles. *A Christmas Carol and Other Writings*. New York: Penguin Classics, 2003.

Dickstein, Morris. *Leopards in the Temple: The Transformation of American Fiction, 1950–1970*. Cambridge, MA: Harvard University Press, 2002.

Didion, Joan. *Play It as It Lays*. New York: Farrar, Straus and Giroux, 1970.

———. *We Tell Ourselves Stories in Order to Live: Collected Nonfiction*. New York: Everyman's Library / Alfred A. Knopf, 2006.

Dimendberg, Edward. *Film Noir and the Spaces of Modernity*. Cambridge, MA: Harvard University Press, 2004.

Doctorow, E. L. *The Book of Daniel*. New York: Random House, 1971.

Donoghue, Emma. *Room*. New York: Little, Brown, 2010.

Dos Passos, John. *The Garbage Man: A Parade with Shouting*. New York: Harper and Brothers, 1926.

Douglas, Mary. *Purity and Danger*. London: Routledge, 2003.

Doyle, Dennis. "'A Fine New Child': The LaFargue Mental Hygiene Clinic and Harlem's African American Communities, 1946–1958." *Journal of the History of Medicine and Allied Sciences* 64.2 (2008): 173–212.

Dreiser, Theodore. *Sister Carrie*. Edited by Donald Pizer. New York: W. W. Norton, 2006.

Dubey, Madhu. *Signs and Cities: Black Literary Postmodernism*. Chicago: University of Chicago Press, 2003.

Du Bois, W.E.B. *The Souls of Black Folk*. In *W.E.B. Du Bois: Writings*, 357–547. New York: Library of America, 1986.

Durkheim, Émile. *The Elementary Forms of Religious Life*. Translated by Karen E. Fields. New York: Free Press, 1995.

———. *Sociology and Philosophy*. Translated by D. F. Pocock. New York: Free Press, 1974.

Duvall, John N. "The (Super)Marketplace of Images: Television as Unmediated Mediation in DeLillo's White Noise." In *White Noise: Text and Criticism*, edited by Mark Osteen, 432–55. New York: Penguin, 1998.

Duve, Thierry de, ed. *Jeff Wall: The Complete Edition*. London: Phaidon, 2009.

Eagleton, Terry. *Against the Grain: Essays, 1975–1985*. London: Verso, 1986.

Edwards, Brian T. *Morocco Bound: Disorienting America's Maghreb, from Casablanca to the Marrakech Express*. Durham, NC: Duke University Press, 2005.

Eliot, T. S. *The Waste Land: Authoritative Texts, Contexts, Criticism*. Edited by Michael North. New York: Norton, 2001.

Ellison, Ralph. "Cadillac Flambé." *Callaloo* 18.2 (1995): 249–69.

———. *The Collected Essays of Ralph Ellison*. New York: Modern Library, 2003.

———. "Dear Dick." Box I: 203, Folder 4, "LaFargue Clinic, New York, N.Y., 1946–1953." Ralph Ellison Papers, Manuscript Division, Library of Congress.

———. *Invisible Man*. New York: Vintage, 1995.

———. Ralph Ellison Papers. Manuscript Division. Library of Congress, Washington, DC.

———. *Three Days Before the Shooting*. Edited by John Callahan. New York: Modern Library, 2010.

Ellis, Jay. *No Place for Home: Spatial Constraint and Character Flight in the Novels of Cormac McCarthy.* New York: Routledge, 2006.

Ellmann, Maud. *The Poetics of Impersonality: Eliot and Pound.* Brighton: Harvester, 1987.

Engler, Mira. *Designing America's Waste Landscapes.* Baltimore, MD: Johns Hopkins University Press, 2004.

English, James F. "Everywhere and Nowhere: The Sociology of Literature after 'The Sociology of Literature.'" *New Literary History* 41.2 (2010): v–xxiii.

Epstein, Joseph. *Plausible Prejudices: Essays on American Writing.* New York: W. W. Norton, 1985.

Fairless, William Deane. *Suggestions Concerning the Construction of Asylums for the Insane.* Edinburgh: Sutherland and Knox, 1861.

Felski, Rita. "Context Stinks!" *New Literary History* 42.4 (2011): 573–91.

Felton, Sharon, ed. *The Critical Response to Joan Didion.* Westport, CT: Greenwood Press, 1994.

Ferguson, Roderick A. *Aberrations in Black: Toward a Queer of Color Critique.* Minneapolis: University of Minnesota Press, 2004.

Fiedler, Leslie. *A New Leslie Fiedler Reader.* Amherst, NY: Prometheus Books, 1999.

———. *Waiting for the End.* New York: Stein and Day, 1964.

Finlayson, Iain. *Tangier: City of the Dream.* New York: HarperCollins, 1992.

Fisher, Philip. *Hard Facts: Setting and Form in the American Novel.* Oxford: Oxford University Press, 1985.

Flaubert, Gustave. *Madame Bovary.* New York: W. W. Norton, 2005.

Foster, Hal. *The Return of the Real: The Avant-Garde at the End of the Century.* Cambridge, MA: MIT Press, 1996.

Foucault, Michel. *Madness and Civilization: A History of Insanity in the Age of Reason.* Translated by Richard Howard. New York: Random House, 1965.

———. "Of Other Spaces." Translated by Jay Miskowiec. *Diacritics* 16.1 (1986): 22–27.

Frank, Joseph. "Spatial Form in Modern Literature." *Sewanee Review* 53.2 (1945): 221–40.

Freedgood, Elaine. *The Ideas in Things: Fugitive Meaning in the Victorian Novel.* Chicago: University of Chicago Press, 2006.

Fried, Michael. *Art and Objecthood: Essays and Reviews.* Chicago: University of Chicago Press, 1998.

———. *Why Photography Matters as Art as Never Before.* New Haven, CT: Yale University Press, 2008.

Friedman, Ellen G., ed. *Joan Didion: Essays and Conversations.* Ontario, Canada: Ontario Review Press, 1984.

Fuss, Diana. *The Sense of an Interior: Four Writers and the Rooms that Shaped Them.* New York: Routledge, 2004.

Galloway, Alexander R. "The Poverty of Philosophy: Realism and Post-Fordism." *Critical Inquiry* 39.2 (2013): 347–66.

Gell, Alfred. *Art and Agency: An Anthropological Theory.* Oxford: Oxford University Press, 1998.

Genette, Gérard. *Narrative Discourse: An Essay in Method.* Translated by Jane E. Lewin. Ithaca, NY: Cornell University Press, 1980.

Gifford, Don, and Robert J. Seidman, eds. *Ulysses Annotated: Notes for James Joyce's Ulysses.* Berkeley: University of California Press, 1988.

Gilbert-Rolfe, Jeremy, and John Johnston. "Gravity's Rainbow and the Spiral Jetty." *October* 1 (Summer 1976): 65–85; *October* 2 (Summer 1976): 71–90; and *October* 3 (Spring 1977): 90–101.

Gillmor, Alan. "Interview with John Cage." *Contact* 14 (1976): 21.

Gilroy, Paul. *Darker than Blue: On the Moral Economies of Black Atlantic Culture.* Cambridge, MA: Belknap Presss of Harvard University Press, 2010.

Ginsberg Allen. *Howl and Other Poems.* San Francisco: City Lights, 1956.

Girard, René. *Deceit, Desire, and the Novel: Self and Other in Literary Structure*. Translated by Yvonne Freccero. Baltimore, MD: Johns Hopkins University Press, 1996.

Goffman, Erving. *Asylums: Essays on the Social Situation of Mental Patients and Other Inmates*. New York: Anchor Books, 1961.

———. "The Interaction Order." *American Sociological Review* 48 (1983): 1–17.

———. *The Presentation of Self in Everyday Life*. New York: Anchor, 1959.

———. *Stigma: Notes on the Management of Spoiled Identity*. New York: Simon and Schuster, 1963.

Goodman, Michael Barry. *Contemporary Literary Censorship: The Case History of Burroughs' Naked Lunch*. Metuchen, NJ: Scarecrow Press, 1981.

Gordon, Avery. *Ghostly Matters: Haunting and the Sociological Imagination*. Minneapolis: University of Minnesota Press, 2008.

Grausam, Daniel. *On Endings: American Postmodern Fiction and the Cold War*. Charlottesville: University of Virginia Press, 2011.

Gray, Spalding. *Swimming to Cambodia*. New York: Theatre Communications Group, 1985.

Grazia, Victoria de. *Irresistible Empire: America's Advance through Twentieth-Century Europe*. Cambridge, MA: Belknap Presss of Harvard University Press, 2005.

Greimas, A. J., and J. Courtés. *Semiotics and Language: An Analytical Dictionary*. Bloomington: Indiana University Press, 1982.

Grob, Gerald N. *The Mad Among Us: A History of the Care of America's Mentally Ill*. New York: Free Press, 1994.

Guillory, John. "Bourdieu's Refusal." *Modern Language Quarterly* 58.4 (December 1997): 367–98.

———. "The Sokal Affair and the History of Criticism." *Critical Inquiry* 28.2 (2002): 470–508.

Hacking, Ian. "Between Michel Foucault and Erving Goffman: Between Discourse in the Abstract and Face-to-Face Interaction." *Economy and Society* 33.3 (2004): 277–302.

———. *The Social Construction of What?* Cambridge, MA: Harvard University Press, 1999.

Hansen, Mark B. N. "Engineering Pre-individual Potentiality: Technics, Transindividuation, and 21st-Century Media." *SubStance* 129.41.3 (2012): 32–59.

Haraway, Donna L. *Simians, Cyborgs, and Women: The Reinvention of Nature*. New York: Routledge, 1991.

Harman, Graham. *Prince of Networks: Bruno Latour and Metaphysics*. Melbourne: re.press, 2009.

———. *Tool-Being: Heidegger and the Metaphysics of Objects*. Peru, IL: Open Court, 2002.

———. *Towards a Speculative Realism: Essays and Lectures*. Ropley, UK: Zero Books, 2010.

Harris, Oliver, and Ian MacFadyen, eds. *Naked Lunch @ 50: Anniversary Essays*. Carbondale: Southern Illinois University Press, 2009.

———. *William Burroughs and the Secret Fascination*. Carbondale: Southern Illinois University Press, 2003.

Haug, Wolfgang Fritz. *Critique of Commodity Aesthetics: Appearance, Sexuality, and Advertising in Capitalist Society*. Minneapolis: University of Minnesota Press, 1986.

Hawkins, Gay. *The Ethics of Waste: How We Relate to Rubbish*. Lanham, MD: Rowman & Littlefield, 2006.

Hayes, Kevin J., ed. *Conversations with Jack Kerouac*. Jackson: University Press of Mississippi, 2005.

Hayles, N. Katherine. *How We Became Posthuman: Virtual Bodies in Cybernetics, Literature, and Informatics*. Chicago: University of Chicago Press, 1999.

Heidegger, Martin. *Poetry, Language, Thought*. Translated by Albert Hofstadter. New York: Harper Perennial Modern Classics, 2001.

Heinrich, Thomas, and Bob Batchelor. *Kotex, Kleenex, Huggies: Kimberly-Clark and the Consumer Revolution in American Business*. Columbus: Ohio State University Press, 2004.

Heise, Thomas. *Urban Underworlds: A Geography of Twentieth-Century American Literature and Culture*. Rutgers, NJ: Rutgers University Press, 2011.

Heise, Ursula. "Comparative Literature and the Environmental Humanities." 2014–15 *State of the Discipline Report*. American Comparative Literature Association. March 9, 2014. http://stateofthediscipline.acla.org/entry/comparative-literature-and-environmental-humanities.

———. *Sense of Place and Sense of Planet: The Environmental Imagination of the Global*. Oxford: Oxford University Press, 2008.

Hell, Julia, and Andreas Schönle, eds. *Ruins of Modernity*. Durham, NC: Duke University Press, 2010.

Henderson, Katherine. *Joan Didion*. New York: Ungar, 1981.

Herman, David. "Existentialist Roots of Narrative Actants." *Studies in Twentieth Century Literature* 24.2 (2000): 257–70.

Hobbs, Robert. *Robert Smithson: Sculpture*. Ithaca, NY: Cornell University Press, 1981.

Hoberek, Andrew. "Cormac McCarthy and the Aesthetics of Exhaustion." *American Literary History* 23.3 (2011): 483–99.

———. *The Twilight of the Middle Class: Post–World War II American Fiction and White-Collar Work*. Princeton, NJ: Princeton University Press, 2005.

Hogan, Erin. *Spiral Jetta: A Road Trip through the Land Art of the American West*. Chicago: University of Chicago Press, 2008.

Holland, James. *Fortress Malta: An Island under Siege, 1940–1943*. London: Orion, 2003.

Horne, Gerald. *Fire This Time: The Watts Uprising and the 1960s*. Charlottesville: University Press of Virginia, 1995.

Hoy, Suellen. *Chasing Dirt: The American Pursuit of Cleanliness*. Oxford: Oxford University Press, 1955.

Hughes, Quentin. "Give Me Time and I Will Give You Life: Laparelli and the Building of Valletta, Malta, 1565–1569." *Town Planning Review* 49.1 (January 1978): 61–74.

Hungerford, Amy. *Postmodern Belief: American Literature and Religion since 1960*. Princeton, NJ: Princeton University Press, 2010.

Hutchins, Edwin. *Cognition in the Wild*. Cambridge, MA: MIT Press, 1995.

Huyssen, Andreas. *Present Pasts: Urban Palimpsests and the Politics of Memory*. Stanford, CA: Stanford University Press, 2003.

Jackson, Lawrence. *Ralph Ellison: Emergence of Genius*. New York: John Wiley & Sons, 2002.

Jackson, Shannon. *Social Works: Performing Art, Supporting Publics*. London: Routledge, 2011.

Jacobs, Jane. *The Death and Life of Great American Cities*. New York: Modern Library, 1993.

Jameson, Fredric. *The Political Unconscious: Narrative as a Socially Symbolic Act*. Ithaca, NY: Cornell University Press, 1981.

———. *Postmodernism, or The Cultural Logic of Late Capitalism*. Durham, NC: Duke University Press, 1991.

Jarrell, Randall. *A Sad Heart at the Supermarket*. London: Eyre and Spottiswoode, 1965.

Jay, Martin. "Drifting into Dangerous Waters." In *Aesthetic Subjects*, edited by Pamela R. Matthews and David McWhirter, 3–27. Minneapolis: University of Minnesota Press, 2003.

Jerome, John. *The Death of the Automobile*. New York: W. W. Norton, 1972.

Johnson, Joyce. *Minor Characters: A Beat Memoir*. New York: Penguin, 1999.

Jones, Caroline A. *Machine in the Studio: Constructing the Postwar American Artist*. Chicago: University of Chicago Press, 1996.

Joyce, James. *Dubliners*. Edited by Margot Norris. New York: W. W. Norton, 2006.

———. *Ulysses*. New York: Vintage, 1986.

Judd, Donald. *Complete Writings, 1959–1975*. Nova Scotia, Canada: Press of the Nova Scotia College of Art and Design, 2005.

Jurca, Catherine. *White Diaspora: The Suburb and the Twentieth-Century American Novel*. Princeton, NJ: Princeton University Press, 2001.

Katz, Jack. *How Emotions Work*. Chicago: University of Chicago Press, 1999.

Keenleyside, Heather. "Animals and Other People in Eighteenth-Century Literature." PhD diss., University of Chicago, 2008.

Kenner, Hugh. *The Pound Era*. Berkeley: University of California Press, 1971.

Kerouac, Jack. *On the Road*. New York: Penguin, 1976.

———. *On the Road: The Original Scroll*. Edited by Howard Cunnell. New York: Viking Press, 2007.

———. *Selected Letters, Volume 1: 1940–1956*. New York: Viking Press, 1995.

Kesey, Ken. *One Flew Over the Cuckoo's Nest*. Edited by John Clark Pratt. New York: Penguin, 1996.

Kirkbride, Thomas Story. *On the Construction, Organization, and General Arrangements of Hospitals for the Insane*. Philadelphia, PA: Lindsay & Blakiston, 1854.

Kouwenhoven, John A. "Waste Not, Have Not: A Clue to American Prosperity." *Harper's Magazine*, March 1959, 72–81.

Kracauer, Siegfried. *The Mass Ornament: Weimar Essays*. Translated by Thomas Y. Levin. Cambridge, MA: Harvard University Press, 1995.

Kristeva, Julia. *Powers of Horror: An Essay on Abjection*. New York: Columbia University Press, 1981.

Kwon, Miwon. *One Place after Another: Site-Specific Art and Locational Identity*. Cambridge, MA: MIT Press, 2002.

Lackey, Kris. *Road Frames: The American Highway Narrative*. Lincoln: University of Nebraska Press, 1999.

Ladd, Brian. *Autophobia: Love and Hate in the Automotive Age*. Chicago: University of Chicago Press, 2008.

Ladenson, Elisabeth. *Dirt for Art's Sake: Books on Trial from Madame Bovary to Lolita*. Ithaca, NY: Cornell University Press, 2007.

Laderman, David. *Driving Visions: Exploring the Road Movie*. Austin: University of Texas Press, 2002.

Latour, Bruno. *Aramis, or The Love of Technology*. Translated by Catherine Porter. Cambridge, MA: Harvard University Press, 1996.

———. "An Attempt at a 'Compositionist Manifesto.'" *New Literary History* 41.3 (2010): 471–90.

———. "From Realpolitik to Dingpolitik, or How to Make Things Public." In *Making Things Public: Atmospheres of Democracy*, edited by Bruno Latour and Peter Weibel, 4–31. Cambridge, MA: MIT Press, 2005.

———. "Gabriel Tarde and the End of the Social." In *The Social in Question: New Bearings in History and the Social Sciences*, edited by Patrick Joyce, 117–33. New York: Routledge, 2002.

———. *An Inquiry into Modes of Existence: An Anthropology of the Moderns*. Translated by Catherine Porter. Cambridge, MA: Harvard University Press, 2013.

———. *Pandora's Hope: Essays on the Reality of Science Studies*. Cambridge, MA: Harvard University Press, 1999.

———. *Politics of Nature: How to Bring the Sciences into Democracy*. Cambridge, MA: Harvard University Press, 2004.

———. *Reassembling the Social: An Introduction to Actor-Network-Theory*. Oxford: Oxford University Press, 2005.

———. *Science in Action: How to Follow Scientists and Engineers through Society*. Cambridge, MA: Harvard University Press, 1987.

———. *We Have Never Been Modern*. Translated by Catherine Porter. Cambridge, MA: Harvard University Press, 1993.

———. "Why Has Critique Run Out of Steam? From Matters of Fact to Matters of Concern." *Critical Inquiry* 30 (2004): 225–48.

Latour, Bruno, and Steve Woolgar. *Laboratory Life: The Construction of Scientific Facts*. Princeton, NJ: Princeton University Press, 1986.

Laure-Ryan, Marie. "Space." In Peter Hühn et al., eds., *The Living Handbook of Narratology*. Hamburg: Hamburg University Press, 2012. http://wikis.sub.uni-hamburg.de/lhn/index.php/Space.

Law, John. "Notes on the Theory of the Actor-Network: Ordering, Strategy, and Heterogeneity." *Systems Practice* 5 (1992): 379–93.

Leavitt, Helen. *Superhighway—Superhoax*. New York: Doubleday, 1971.

LeClair, Tom. *In the Loop: Don DeLillo and the Systems Novel*. Urbana: University of Illinois Press, 1987.

Lee, Pamela. *Chronophobia: On Time in the Art of the 1960s*. Cambridge, MA: MIT Press, 2004.

Lefebvre, Henri. *The Production of Space*. Translated by Donald Nicholson-Smith. Malden, MA: Blackwell, 1991.

Leland, John. *Why Kerouac Matters: The Lessons of "On the Road" (They're Not What You Think)*. New York: Viking Penguin, 2007.

LeMenager, Stephanie. *Living Oil: Petroleum Culture in the American Century*. Oxford: Oxford University Press, 2014.

Lentricchia, Frank. *Introducing Don DeLillo*. Durham, NC: Duke University Press, 1991.

———. "Tales of the Electronic Tribe." In *New Essays on White Noise*, edited by Frank Lentricchia, 87–113. Cambridge: Cambridge University Press, 1991.

Lepenies, Wolf. *Between Literature and Science: The Rise of Sociology*. Translated by R. J. Hollingdale. Cambridge: Cambridge University Press, 1988.

Levin, Ira. *The Stepford Wives*. New York: HarperCollins Perennial, 2002.

Lewis, Tom. *Divided Highways: Building the Interstate Highways, Transforming American Life*. New York: Penguin, 1997.

Locke, Alain, ed. *The New Negro: Voices of the Harlem Renaissance*. New York: Touchstone, 1997.

Loranger, Carol. "'This Book Spill Off the Page in All Directions': What Is the Text of *Naked Lunch*?" *Postmodern Culture* 10.1 (1999). http://pmc.iath.virginia.edu/text-only/issue.999/10.1loranger.txt.

Lotringer, Sylvère, ed. *Burroughs Live: The Collected Interviews of William S. Burroughs, 1960–1997*. Los Angeles, CA: Semiotext(e), 2001.

Love, Heather. "Close but not Deep: Literary Ethics and the Descriptive Turn." *New Literary History* 41.2 (2010): 371–91.

Lucsko, David N. *The Business of Speed: The Hot Rod Industry in America, 1915–1990*. Baltimore, MD: Johns Hopkins University Press, 2008.

Lukács, Georg. *History and Class Consciousness*. Translated by Rodney Livingstone. Cambridge, MA: Harvard University Press, 1972.

———. "Narrate or Describe? A Preliminary Discussion of Naturalism and Formalism." In *Writer and Critic and Other Essays*, translated by Arthur D. Kahn, 110–48. New York: Merlin Press, 1970.

Lukes, Steven. *Émile Durkheim: His Life and Work*. New York: Penguin, 1973.

Lunbeck, Elizabeth. *The Psychiatric Persuasion: Knowledge, Gender, and Power in Modern America*. Princeton, NJ: Princeton University Press, 1994.

Lutz, Catherine, and Anne Lutz Fernandez. *Carjacked: The Culture of the Automobile and Its Effect on Our Lives*. New York: Palgrave Macmillan, 2010.

Macdonald, Dwight. "Masscult and Midcult." *Partisan Review* 17.2–3 (1960): 203–33, 589–631.

Maher, Paul, Jr. *Jack Kerouac's American Journey: The Real-Life Odyssey of "On the Road."* New York: Thunder's Mouth Press, 2007.

Maisel, Albert Q. "Bedlam 1946: Most U.S. Mental Hospitals Are a Shame and a Disgrace." *Life*, May 6, 1946, 102–18.

May, Elaine Tyler. *Homeward Bound: American Families in the Cold War Era*. New York: Basic Books, 1989.

McCarthy, Cormac. *The Road*. New York: Vintage, 2006.

McCarthy, Mary. *The Writing on the Wall and Other Literary Essays*. Orlando, FL: Harcourt Brace Jovanovich, 1970.

McGurl, Mark. *The Program Era: Postwar Fiction and the Rise of Creative Writing*. Cambridge, MA: Harvard University Press, 2010.

Mead, Margaret. "Cultural Bases for Understanding Literature." *PMLA* 68.2 (1953): 13–23.

Melosi, Martin V. *Garbage in the Cities: Refuse Reform and the Environment*. Pittsburgh, PA: University of Pittsburgh Press, 2004.

Menand, Louis. "Drive, He Wrote: What the Beats Were About." *New Yorker*, October 1, 2007, 88–93.

———. "Some Frames for Goffman." *Social Psychology Quarterly* 72.4 (2009): 296–99.

Merleau-Ponty, Maurice. *The Visible and the Invisible*. Evanston, IL: Northwestern University, 1968.

Michaels, Walter Benn. *The Shape of the Signifier: 1967 to the End of History*. Princeton, NJ: Princeton University Press, 2004.

Miles, Barry. *William Burroughs: El Hombre Invisible*. London: Virgin Books, 2002.

Miller, Daniel. *Car Cultures*. London: Berg, 2001.

Mills, C. Wright. *The Sociological Imagination*. New York: Oxford University Press, 1959.

Mills, Katie. *The Road Story and the Rebel: Moving through Film, Fiction, and Television*. Carbondale: Southern Illinois University Press, 2006.

Mitchell, W.J.T., ed. *Landscape and Power*. 2nd ed. Chicago: University of Chicago Press, 2002.

———. *The Last Dinosaur Book: The Life and Times of a Cultural Icon*. Chicago: University of Chicago Press, 1998.

———. *What Do Pictures Want? The Lives and Loves of Images*. Chicago: University of Chicago Press, 2005.

Mizruchi, Susan. "Risk Theory and the Contemporary American Novel." *American Literary History* 22.1 (2010): 109–35.

———. *The Science of Sacrifice: American Literature and Modern Social Theory*. Princeton, NJ: Princeton University Press, 1998.

Mizzi, Laurence. *Wartime Diary of a Maltese Boy*. Rabat, Malta: Wise Owl, 2006.

Mohl, Raymond A. "Stop the Road: Freeway Revolts in American Cities." *Journal of Urban History* 30.5 (2004): 674–706.

Molesworth, Helen. "House Work and Art Work." *October* 92 (2000): 71–97.

Moretti, Franco. *Atlas of the European Novel, 1800–1900*. New York: Verso, 1999.

———. *Distant Reading*. New York: Verso, 2013.

Morgan, Ted. *Literary Outlaw: The Life and Times of William S. Burroughs*. New York: Henry Holt, 1988.

Morton, Timothy. *Hyperobjects: Philosophy and Ecology after the End of the World*. Minneapolis: University of Minnesota Press, 2013.

Mowbray, A. Q. *Road to Ruin*. Philadelphia, PA: J. B. Lippincott, 1969.

Nader, Ralph. *Unsafe at Any Speed: The Designed-In Dangers of the American Automobile*. New York: Grossman, 1965.

Nixon, Rob. *Slow Violence and the Environmentalism of the Poor*. Cambridge, MA: Harvard University Press, 2011.

Norman, Donald A. *The Design of Future Things*. New York: Basic Books, 2007.

———. *Emotional Design: Why We Love (or Hate) Everyday Things*. New York: Basic Books, 2004.

Olson, Charles. *Charles Olson and Ezra Pound: An Encounter at St. Elizabeths*. Edited by Catherine Seelye. New York: Grossman, 1975.

O'Meally, Robert. *The Craft of Ralph Ellison*. Cambridge, MA: Harvard University Press, 1980.

Orgeron, Devin. *Road Movies: From Muybridge and Méliès to Lynch and Kiarostami*. New York: Palgrave Macmillan, 2008.

Orvell, Miles. *The Real Thing: Imitation and Authenticity in American Culture, 1880–1940*. Chapel Hill: University of North Carolina Press, 1989.

Osteen, Mark, ed. *White Noise: Text and Criticism*. New York: Penguin, 1998.

Owens, Craig. *Beyond Recognition: Representation, Power, and Culture*. Berkeley: University of California Press, 1992.

Packard, Vance. *The Hidden Persuaders*. New York: David McKay, 1957.

———. *The Waste Makers*. Brooklyn, NY: Ig Publishing, 1960.

Park, Robert E., and Ernest W. Burgess. *Introduction to the Science of Sociology*. 3rd ed. Chicago: University of Chicago Press, 1969.

Parrish, Timothy. *From the Civil War to the Apocalypse: Postmodern History and American Fiction*. Amherst: University of Massachusetts Press, 2008.

Patell, Cyrus R. K. *Negative Liberties: Morrison, Pynchon, and the Problem of Liberal Ideology*. Durham, NC: Duke University Press, 2001.

Payne, Christopher. *Asylum: Inside the Closed World of State Mental Hospitals*. Cambridge: MIT Press, 2009.

Pease, Donald E. "Ralph Ellison and Kenneth Burke: The Nonsymbolizable (Trans)Action." *boundary 2* 30.2 (2003): 65–96.

Perry, Paul. *On the Bus: The Complete Guide to the Legendary Trip of Ken Kesey and the Merry Pranksters and the Birth of the Counterculture*. New York: Thunder's Mouth Press, 1997.

Plath, Sylvia. *The Bell Jar*. New York: Harper Perennial Modern Classics, 2013.

Poe, Edgar Allan. *Poetry and Tales*. New York: Library of America, 1984.

Poirier, Richard. "Cook's Tour." *New York Review of Books*, June 1, 1963. http://www.nybooks.com/articles/archives/1963/jun/01/cooks-tour/.

Poovey, Mary. "The Liberal Civil Subject and the Social in Eighteenth-Century British Moral Philosophy." *Public Culture* 14.1 (2002): 125–45.

Posnock, Ross. "'Don't think, but look!': W. G. Sebald, Wittgenstein, and Cosmopolitan Poverty." *Representations* 112.1 (2010): 110–39.

Price, Leah. *How to Do Things with Books in Victorian Britain*. Princeton, NJ: Princeton University Press, 2012.

Primeau, Ronald. *Romance of the Road*. Bowling Green, OH: Bowling Green State University Popular Press, 1996.

Pynchon, Thomas. "A Journey into the Mind of Watts." *New York Times Magazine*, June 12, 1966. http://www.nytimes.com/books/97/05/18/reviews/pynchon-watts.html.

———. "No, damnit," Box 20, Folder 1, Stephen Michael Tomaske Collection of Thomas Pynchon, Huntington Library.

———. *Slow Learner: Early Stories*. New York: Little, Brown, 1984.

———. *V.* New York: Harper Perennial Modern Classics, 2005.

Rampersad, Arnold. *Ralph Ellison: A Biography*. New York: Alfred A. Knopf, 2007.

Rathje, William, and Cullen Murphy. *Rubbish! The Archaeology of Garbage*. New York: Harper-Collins, 1992.

Rathje, William, W. W. Hughes, D. C. Wilson, M. K. Tani, G. H. Archer, R. G. Hunt, and T. W. Jones. "The Archaeology of Contemporary Landfills." *American Antiquity* 57.3 (1992): 437–47.

Reeve, N. H., and Richard Kerridge. "Toxic Events: Postmodernism and Don DeLillo's White Noise." *Cambridge Quarterly* 23 (1994): 303–23.

Reiss, Benjamin. *Theaters of Madness: Insane Asylums and Nineteenth-Century American Culture*. Chicago: University of Chicago Press, 2008.

Rembar, Charles. *The End of Obscenity: The Trials of "Lady Chatterley's Lover," "Tropic of Cancer," and "Fanny Hill."* New York: Harper & Row, 1986.

Reynolds, Ann. *Robert Smithson: Learning from New Jersey and Elsewhere*. Cambridge, MA: MIT Press, 2003.

Rhodes, Chip. *Politics, Desire, and the Hollywood Novel*. Iowa City: University of Iowa Press, 2008.

Rich, Adrienne. "Compulsory Heterosexuality and Lesbian Existence." In *Adrienne Rich's Poetry and Prose*, edited by Barbara Charlesworth Gelpi and Albert Gelpi, 203–24. New York: Norton, 1993.

Robbe-Grillet, Alain. *For a New Novel*. Evanston, IL: Northwestern University Press, 1989.

Roberts, Jennifer L. *Mirror-Travels: Robert Smithson and History*. New Haven, CT: Yale University Press, 2004.

Rose, Kenneth D. *One Nation Underground: The Fallout Shelter in American Culture*. New York: NYU Press, 2001.

Rose, Mark H. *Interstate: Express Highway Politics, 1939–1989*. Knoxville: University of Tennessee Press, 1990.

Ross, Kristin. *Fast Cars, Clean Bodies: Decolonization and the Reordering of French Culture*. Cambridge, MA: MIT Press, 1995.

Ross, Richard. *Waiting for the End of the World*. New York: Princeton Architectural Press, 2004.

Rothman, David J. *The Discovery of the Asylum: Social Order and Disorder in the New Republic*. Boston: Little, Brown, 1971.

Scandura, Jani. *Down in the Dumps: Place, Modernity, American Depression*. Durham, NC: Duke University Press, 2008.

Scanlan, John. *On Garbage*. London: Reaktion, 2005.

Scarry, Elaine. *Thermonuclear Monarchy: Choosing Between Democracy and Doom*. New York: W. W. Norton, 2014.

Schneider, Kenneth R. *Autokind vs. Mankind: An Analysis of Tyranny; A Proposal for Rebellion; A Plan for Reconstruction*. New York: W. W. Norton, 1971.

Schryer, Stephen. *Fantasies of the New Class: Ideologies of Professionalism in Post–World War II American Fiction*. New York: Columbia University Press, 2011.

Scull, Andrew. *Social Order/Mental Disorder: Anglo-American Psychiatry in Historical Perspective*. Berkeley: University of California Press, 1989.

Sedgwick, Eve Kosofsky. *Between Men: English Literature and Male Homosocial Desire*. New York: Columbia University Press, 1985.

Seed, David. *The Fictional Labyrinths of Thomas Pynchon*. Iowa City: University of Iowa Press, 1988.

Seiler, Cotten. *Republic of Drivers: A Cultural History of Automobility in America*. Chicago: University of Chicago Press, 2008.

Seltzer, Mark. "The Official World." *Critical Inquiry* 37.4 (2011): 724–53.

———. *Serial Killers: Death and Life in America's Wound Culture*. New York: Routledge, 1998.

Serres, Michel. "The Theory of the Quasi-Object." In *The Parasite*, translated by Lawrence R. Schehr, 224–34. Minneapolis: University of Minnesota Press, 2007.

Shanks, Michael, David Platt, and William L. Rathje. "The Perfume of Garbage: Modernity and the Archaeological." *Modernism/modernity* 11.1 (2004): 61–83.

Shaw, Lytle. *Fieldworks: From Place to Site in Postwar Poetics*. Tuscaloosa: University of Alabama Press, 2013.

Shorter, Edward. *A History of Psychiatry from the Era of the Asylum to the Age of Prozac*. New York: John Wiley Sons, 1997.

Simmel, Georg. "The Metropolis and Mental Life." In *On Individuality and Social Forms*, edited by Donald L. Levine, 324–39. Chicago: University of Chicago Press, 1971.

———. *Simmel on Culture*. Edited by David Frisby and Mike Featherstone. London: Sage, 1997.

———. "Two Essays." Translated by David Kettler. *Hudson Review* 11.3 (1958): 371–85.

Sinclair, Upton. *The Jungle*. New York: Oxford University Press, 2010.

Skerl, Jennie, and Robin Lydenberg. *William S. Burroughs at the Front: Critical Reception, 1959–1989*. Carbondale: Southern Illinois University Press, 1991.

Smith, Greg. *Erving Goffman*. New York: Routledge, 2006.

Smith, Sidonie. *Moving Lives: Twentieth-Century Women's Travel Writing*. Minneapolis: University of Minnesota Press, 2001.

Smithson, Robert. *Collected Writings*. Edited by Jack Flam. Berkeley: University of California Press, 1996.

Staub, Michael E. *Madness Is Civilization: When the Diagnosis Was Social*. Chicago: University of Chicago Press, 2011.

Stevens, Wallace. *The Collected Poems*. New York: Vintage, 1990.

Stewart, Susan. *On Longing: Narratives of the Miniature, the Gigantic, the Souvenir, the Collection*. Durham, NC: Duke University Press, 1993.

Stoler, Ann Laura. "Imperial Debris: Reflections on Ruins and Ruination." *Cultural Anthropology* 23.2 (2008): 191–219.

Strasser, Susan. *Waste and Want: A Social History of Trash*. New York: Henry Holt, 1999.

Sturken, Marita. *Tourists of History: Memory, Kitsch, and Consumerism from Oklahoma City to Ground Zero*. Durham, NC: Duke University Press, 2007.

Suárez, Juan. *Pop Modernism: Noise and the Reinvention of the Everyday*. Urbana: University of Illinois Press, 2007.

Tate, Allen. "Techniques of Fiction." In *Essays of Four Decades*, 124–41. Chicago: Swallow Press, 1968.

Theweleit, Klaus. *Male Fantasies*. Vol. 1, *Women, Floods, Bodies, History*. Minneapolis: University of Minnesota Press, 1987.

Tilley, Christopher. *The Materiality of Stones: Explorations in Landscape Phenomenology*. New York: Berg, 2004.

Tomaske, Stephen. *Stephen Michael Tomaske Memorial Collection of Thomas Pynchon*. Huntington Library, San Marino, CA.

Tomes, Nancy. *The Art of Asylum-Keeping: Thomas Story Kirkbride and the Origins of American Psychiatry*. Philadelphia: University of Pennsylvania Press, 1994.

Trump, David. *Malta: An Archaeological Guide*. London: Faber and Faber, 1972.

Ukeles, Mierle Laderman. "Manifesto for Maintenance Art, 1969! Proposal for an Exhibition 'Care.'" Ronald Feldman Fine Arts. http://www.feldmangallery.com/pages/home_frame.html.

Updike, John. *Pigeon Feathers and Other Stories*. New York: Alfred A. Knopf, 1962.

Vanderbilt, Tom. *Traffic: Why We Drive the Way We Do (and What It Says About Us)*. New York: Knopf, 2008.

Venturi, Robert, Denise Scott Brown, and Steven Izenour. *Learning from Las Vegas*. Cambridge, MA: MIT Press, 1972.

Virilio, Paul. *Bunker Archaeology*. Princeton, NJ: Princeton Architectural Press, 1994.

Wagner, Aleksandra, and Carin Kuoni, eds. *Considering Forgiveness*. New York: Vera List Center for Art and Politics, New School, 2009.

Wagner, Peter. "'An Entirely New Object of Consciousness, of Volition, of Thought': The Coming into Being and (Almost) Passing Away of 'Society' as a Scientific Object." In *Of Scientific Objects*, edited by Lorraine Daston. Chicago: University of Chicago Press, 2000.

Waldman, Diane, ed. *John Chamberlain*. New York: Solomon R. Guggenheim Foundation, 1971.

Wall, Cynthia Sundberg. *The Prose of Things: Transformations of Description in the Eighteenth Century*. Chicago: University of Chicago Press, 2006.

Ward, Mary Jane. *The Snake Pit*. New York: Random House, 1946.

Warhol, Andy, and Pat Hackett. *The Andy Warhol Diaries*. New York: Hatchett, 2009.

———. *The Philosophy of Andy Warhol: From A to B and Back Again*. New York: Harcourt, 1975.

Warren, Kenneth W. *So Black and Blue: Ralph Ellison and the Occasion of Criticism*. Chicago: University of Chicago Press, 2003.

Warren, Robert Penn. *All the King's Men*. New York: Harcourt, Brace, 1946.

Watt, Ian. *The Rise of the Novel: Studies in Defoe, Richardson, and Fielding*. Berkeley: University of California Press, 1957.

Weingarten, Marc. *The Gang that Wouldn't Write Straight: Wolfe, Thompson, Didion, Capote, and the New Journalism Revolution*. New York: Three Rivers Press, 2005.

Welty, Eudora. *Stories, Essays & Memoir*. New York: Library of America, 1998.

Wertham, Fredric. *The Circle of Guilt*. Oxford: University Press of Mississippi, 2007.

———. "Psychological Effects of School Segregation." *American Journal of Psychotherapy* 6.1 (1952): 94–103.

Whiting, Frederick. "Monstrosity on Trial: The Case of *Naked Lunch*." *Twentieth-Century Literature* 52.2 (2006): 145–74.

Williams, Raymond. *Keywords: A Vocabulary of Culture and Society*. London: Flamingo, 1986.

Winchell, Mark. *Joan Didion*. Boston: Twayne, 1980.

Wolfe, Cary. *What Is Posthumanism?* Minneapolis: University of Minnesota Press, 2009.

Wolfe, Tom. *The Electric Kool-Aid Acid Test*. New York: Picador, 2008.

———. *The Kandy-Kolored Tangerine-Flake Streamline Baby*. New York: Bantam Books, 1999.

———, ed. *The New Journalism*. New York: Harper & Row, 1973.

Woloch, Alex. *The One vs. the Many: Minor Characters and the Space of the Protagonist in the Novel*. Princeton, NJ: Princeton University Press, 2003.

Woolf, Virginia. "Modern Fiction." In *The Common Reader*, 184–95. London: L. & V. Woolf at the Hogarth Press, 1929.

Wright, Richard. *Black Boy*. New York: Harper Perennial Modern Classics, 2007.

———. "Psychiatry Comes to Harlem." *Free World* 12 (September 1946): 49–51.

Yablon, Nick. *Untimely Ruins: An Archaeology of American Urban Modernity, 1819–1919*. Chicago: University of Chicago Press, 2009.

Yanni, Carla. *The Architecture of Madness: Insane Asylums in the United States*. Minneapolis: University of Minnesota Press, 2007.

Zammit, Themistocles. *Malta: The Islands and Their History*. Malta: Malta Herald Office, 1926.

Zimmerman, M. M. *The Super Market: A Revolution in Distribution*. New York: McGraw Hill, 1955.

Zola, Émile. *The Ladies' Paradise*. Translated by Brian Nelson. Oxford: Oxford University Press, 2008.

INDEX

Numbers in italic indicate pages where figures appear.

Dick, Philip K., 30
Dickens, Charles, 31–32
Dickstein, Morris, 79
Didion, Joan, 20; on automobility, 87–88; and the hyperreal, 88–89; *Slouching Toward Bethlehem,* 86, 88; *Where I Was From,* 90; *The White Album,* 88. See also Play It as It Lays (Didion)
distributed agency, 29–30, 45
diversity/conformity, 135–36
Doctorow, E. L., 142
Donoghue, Emma. See Room (Donoghue)
Dos Passos, John, 58
Douglas, Mary, 59
"dramatism" (per Burke), 21, 124, 131
Duchamp, Marcel, 43–44
dumps, 20, 48; as site of putrefaction and translation, 52–53; as social sculptures, 51, 69
Durkheim, Émile, 3, 12, 25–28, 85

Earth as site, 149–50, 155–56
Earthworks (Aldiss), 99
Earthworks (exhibition, 1968), 104
Egan, Jennifer, 152
Eisenhower, Dwight D., 96
The Electric Kool-Aid Test (Wolfe), 84–85
The Elementary Forms of Religious Life (Durkheim), 3
Eliot, T. S., 60, 112
Ellison, Ralph: establishment of LaFargue Psychiatric Clinic, 122; influences on, 131–32; and relationship between environment and identity, 136; sociology and, 123–24. See also Invisible Man
embodiment: of "The Bad Priest" figure in Pynchon's *V.,* 110–11; bodily decomposition in Burroughs, 63–65; body as site, 65–66; flesh and subject/object constitution, 66–67; human, 40–41, 65–66
English, James F., 2, 12
Epstein, Joseph, 89
Every Building on the Sunset Strip (Ruscha), 76

false advertising, 44
Family Shelter, Salt Lake City, Utah (Ross), *153,* 153–54, *154*
Felski, Rita, 3
Fiedler, Leslie, 37, 65
Finlayson, Iain, 54

Flaubert, Gustave, 10–11, 17, 27
flesh. *See* embodiment
Foster, Hal, 22
Foucault, Michel, 22, 74
Fountain (Duchamp), 43–44
Frank, Joseph, 17
Frank, Robert, 75–76
Freedgood, Elaine, 10
Fresh Kills Landfill, 51–53, 69–70, 170n2
Fried, Michael, 76, 91–93
Friedlander, Lee, 76
Fuss, Diana, 54–55

garbage. *See* waste
Garbage (Ammons), 60
garbage archaeology, 51–53, 69
The Garbage Man (Dos Passos), 58
Garbage Project, 52
Gell, Alfred, 29
gender: cars as gendered, 81; in Didion's *Play It as It Lays,* 89–90; and nonhuman actants in Donoghue's *Room,* 5; of travel, 88, 89–90
Genette, Gérard, 7
genocides, 116
geology: rock in Pynchon's *V.,* 103, 109, 113–14, 117, 120; Smithson and, 101, 104
Gilbert-Rolfe, Jeremy, 100
Ginsberg, Allen, 20, 33, 143; correspondence with Burroughs, 53, 55, 56; correspondence with Kerouac, 79
Girodias, Maurice, 56
Giroux, Robert, 80
Glue Pour (Smithson), 69
Goffman, Erving, 1, 8, 13, 21, 123–24; and asylums as sites, 129–42, 145–46; influences on, 131–32; on racial segregation, 136–37; on secondary adjustments, 134–35, 146–47
Gordon, Avery, 13
A Grammar of Motives (Burke), 11
Grausman, Daniel, 111
Gray, Spalding, 31
Greimas, A. J., 28–29, 33
Guattari, Felix, 66
guns: and identity, 135

Ḥaġar Qim, *114;* as analogy for narrative of V., 113–15
Hansen, Mark B. N., 29

tialization of time, 97. *See also* automobiles

Robbe-Grillet, Alain, 33

Roberts, Jennifer L., 101

Robinson Crusoe (Defoe), 8–9

rocks. *See* geology

Room (Donoghue), 4–10, 18, 23; nonhuman actants and sociality in, 5–10; as reworking of *Robinson Crusoe*, 8–10

Ross, Kristin, 67

Ross, Richard, 152–54

ruins, 20–21, 48; agency of, 118; and boundaries or limits, 119; construction/destruction dialectic, 96–97; highway projects as ruins in reverse, 96–97; and logic of narrative representation in Pychon's *V.*, 105–7, 117, 119; as nonsites, 105; as palimpsest, 100–101, 117; Pynchon's "A Journey into the Mid of Watts" and urban, 98; ruination as ongoing process (translation), 20–21, 96–97, 102, 106–7, 108, 111, 119, 121; and spatialization, 115; temporality and, 115–19

Ruscha, Ed, 76

A Sad Heart at the Supermarket (Jarrell), 37

St. Elizabeths Psychiatric Hospital, 21, 123, 129–30, 132–34, 137, 140–43

Saunders, Clarence, 35

Schneider, Kenneth R., 87

Schönle, Andreas, 111–12

secondary adjustments per Goffman, 134–35, 146–47

Sedgwick, Eve, 75, 78

segregation: asylums as segregated societies, 130, 134; Goffman on racial, 136–37; and identity formation, 126–30, 134–37; racial, 136–37; as restriction of agency, 135

Seiler, Cotten, 74

self-service supermarkets, 35–36, 61–62

Seltzer, Mark, 21

Semiotics and Language (Greimas and Courtés), 28–29

Serra, Richard, 22, 69

Serres, Michel, 28, 118–19

setting in literature: characters distinguished from, 17–18

sex: cars and sexual activity, 75; and desire in Kerouac's *On the Road*, 75, 78–82; human embodiment and sexuality, 40–41; Kotex as image, 61–62; *Naked Lunch* and, 55,

63–66; posthuman sexuality, 65; and relationship between subject and object, 42

Shadow and Act, 121, 131

Shanks, Michael, 57

shock, 41, 44

Silent Spring (Carson), 62–63

Simmel, Georg, 85–86, 106, 108, 140

Sinclair, Upton, 59–60

sites: as actants, 20; art and exploration of, 22–23; as containers for social connections, 82; and mediation of sociality, 11, 18–19, 81, 130, 140, 150, 153; nonsite/site dialectic, 98, 103–5, 112, 119, 155; as "nowhere," 127–28 (*See also* nonsite/site dialectic *under this heading*); use of term, 18–19

site-specificity, 10–11, 69; as investigation of social form, 22–23

Slouching Toward Bethlehem (Didion), 86, 88

Smith, Corlies, 99

Smithson, Robert: artists and exploration of sites, 22–23; automobility in works of, 76; dumping as art-making, 69, 76, 91; entropy, homogenization, and temporality in, 100; and hyperspecificity, 99–100; influences on, 97–98; and monuments as subjects, 100; and nonsite/site dialectic, 103–5, 112; and palimpsest trope, 100–101, 117; Pynchon and, 97–98, 100, 102, 116–17, 119; site exploration and art, 22–23; "Site Selection Study," 97; *Spiral Jetty* and earthworks, 23, 91; and time as spatialized or materialized, 97, 100–101; "Tour of the Monuments of Passaic," 76, 96–97, 99–102, 116

The Snake Pit (Ward), 138

sociality: and assemblages, 27–28; collective object making and, 85; and decay in Burroughs, 71; novels and theorization of, 4; similes and, 151–52; sites and mediation of, 11, 18–19, 81, 130, 140, 150, 153; the social as dump in Burroughs, 68–69, 71; space and, 11

sociality, theorization in fiction, 2

The Social Mirror (Ukeles), 70–71, *71*

society: Latourian theory of, 12–13

Sontag, Susan, 60

spatiality: as relationship among sites, 22

Spiral Jetta (Hogan), 91

Spiral Jetty (Smithson), 22–23, 91, 100

Stepford Wives (Levin), 30

Stevens, Wallace, 60

Stewart, Susan, 9, 135, 150–51

Stigma (Goffman), 131, 136

Stoler, Ann Laura, 106–7, 108, 119, 121

Suárez, Juan A., 33–34, 42

subject/object relationships: art and reanimation of the degraded object, 70; in Burroughs, 63–67; dichotomy as artificial, 42; as fabricator and fabricated, 136; flesh and constitution of, 66–67; Fried's "Art and Objecthood" and, 91–92; hybridity and, 34–35, 52–53, 65–66, 68; Latour and collective subjects, 75; objects as material entities, 33; psychiatry and, 127; quasi-objects and intersubjectivity, 118–20

"A Supermarket in California" (Ginsberg), 33

supermarkets: *American Supermarket* exhibition, 42–44; commercial sites in literary fiction, 31–32; as cultural nodes, 27; in DeLillo, 20, 30–35; display shelves as networks of nonhuman actants, 39–46; evolution as commercial space, 35–36; human body and interaction with, 40–41; in Latour, 14, 20, 29; "metaphor of the supermarket," 29; middle-brow culture and, 37–38; and nonhuman actants, 61–62; nonhuman sociality and, 47; as postmodern site, 20; as temples, 32

Supermarket Sweep (game show), 38

surrealism, 1, 33–34, 42, 127–28

Swannanoa/Swannanoa II (Chamberlain), 92–94

Swimming to Cambodia (Gray), 31

"symbolic action" (per Burke), 131

symptomatic reading, 2, 3

Tangier, Burroughs's *Naked Lunch* and, 53–54, 57

Tarde, Gabriel, 12

Tate, Allen, 10–11

technograms, 95

texts: as conceptual resource for social theorists, 12–13, 26–30; as nonhuman actants or "matter of concern," 5

The Americans (Frank), 75–76

"Theory of the Quasi-Object" (Serres), 118–19

Thing theory, 1, 26

time: as both simultaneous and successive, 115–18; Pynchon and exploration of, 101; ruins and, 115–19; ruins and simultaneity, 99, 115–18; sites and materialization of, 91, 100–101, 115–16; sites and spatialization of, 97, 115; site-specificity of, 101; souvenirs and, 150–51; temporality in Smithson, 97, 100–101; Watts Towers and, 101–2

Time Out of Joint (Dick), 30

totems and totemism, 85

"Tour of the Monuments of Passaic" (Smithson), 76, 96–97, 99–102, 116; temporality in, 100–101

translation: in Burroughs's *Naked Lunch*, 20, 52–53, 56, 63–66; in Burroughs's *Naked Lunch*, 71–72; dumps and putrefaction as, 52–53; entropy and homogenization in Smithson, 100; garbage trucks and, 70; hybridity and, 34–35, 52–53, 65–66, 71–72; logic of, 20, 35, 52, 71; mosaic reconstitution of waste, 58, 63–66; nonhuman actants and, 19; as process in Latour, 19, 20, 34; and the reanimation of the degraded object, 70; roads as sites of, 95; rumination as ongoing process, 20–21, 96–97, 102, 106–7, 108, 111, 119, 121

Trump, David, 115

Tunafish Disaster (Warhol), 44–45

Twenty-Six Gasoline Stations (Ruscha), 76

Ukeles, Mierle Laderman, 22, 23, 51, 52, 69–71

Ulysses (Joyce), 14–19, 59–60

Underworld (DeLillo), 51–52, 69

"Untitled, Harlem New York, 1952" (Parks), 128–29, *129*

V. (Pynchon), 101,–112; alternative titles proposed for, 99; chronotropes in, 103; critical reception of, 98; Ħaġar Qim and, 112–16; and limits of the social, 98, 116–17; and Malta as site (*See* Malta); non-site/site dialectic in, 98, 103–5, 112, 119; palimpsest trope in, 107–9, 116, 117–18; research and, 98–99, 103, 109, 114; site/nonsite dialectic in, 98–99; social interactions and site in, 119; and threat of nuclear destruction, 111–12; V. as quasi-object in, 118–20

Venturi, Robert, 20, 38–39, 100